D0121788

PRAISE FOR *WEconomy*

"As global citizens, it is important that we all decide how we can help build a better future for everyone who inhabits this planet. A planet we must come to realize we all share. In the *WEconomy,* Holly, Marc and Craig share not only entertaining and insightful stories, but top tips on how, both personally and professionally, we can work together to achieve just that."
—Scooter Braun, entrepreneur and founder of SB Projects

"As people continue to look for meaningful ways they can uniquely contribute personally and professionally to this world, *WEconomy* illustrates ways we can all do good and do well."
—Pete Carroll, head coach of the Seattle Seahawks, NFL champions

"Through fun, inspiring, and revealing stories the authors not only bring the *WEconomy* to life, but bring the reader along for the ride. As the most connected generation in history, never before has there been such an incredible opportunity to make the 'WE' a powerful movement for positive change."
—Ed Sheeran, Grammy Award-winning singer/songwriter

Published by John Wiley & Sons, Inc., Hoboken, New Jersey.
Published simultaneously in Canada.

Edited by Katie Hewitt and Jackie McQuillan.

For general information about our other products and services, please contact our Customer Care Department within the United States at (800) 762-2974, outside the United States at (317) 572-3993 or fax (317) 572-4002.

Wiley publishes in a variety of print and electronic formats and by print-on-demand. Some material included with standard print versions of this book may not be included in e-books or in print-on-demand. If this book refers to media such as a CD or DVD that is not included in the version you purchased, you may download this material at http://booksupport.wiley.com. For more information about Wiley products, visit www.wiley.com.

Library of Congress Cataloging-in-Publication Data:

Names: Kielburger, Craig, author. | Branson, Holly, author. | Kielburger,
   Marc, author.
Title: WEconomy : you can find meaning, make a living and change the world /
   by Craig Kielburger, Holly Branson and Marc Kielburger.
Description: Hoboken, New Jersey : John Wiley & Sons, Inc., [2018] | Includes
   bibliographical references and index. |
Identifiers: LCCN 2017051206 (print) | LCCN 2017056888 (ebook) | ISBN
   9781119447832 (pdf) | ISBN 9781119447818 (epub) | ISBN 9781119447795
   (cloth)
Subjects: LCSH: Social responsibility of business. | Social entrepreneurship.
Classification: LCC HD60 (ebook) | LCC HD60 .K4845 2018 (print) | DDC
   658.4/08--dc23
LC record available at https://lccn.loc.gov/2017051206

Printed in the United States of America

10 9 8 7 6 5 4 3 2 1

WEconomy

You can find meaning,
make a living, and change the world

CRAIG KIELBURGER HOLLY BRANSON MARC KIELBURGER

WILEY

TABLE OF CONTENTS

Dear Reader,

Did you jump out of bed this morning excited to go to work?

At your office, do you feel valued as a human being?

Is your business making money and changing the world?

If yes, congrats. You're at the vanguard of the WEconomy, where companies work for the greater good and individuals can give back through their daily habits, as both workers and consumers.

If no, don't worry. The WEconomy is just emerging. There's still time to carve out your place in the movement that is changing the face of business. You can help the WEconomy make our world better.

Welcome to the WEconomy

Part One
What:

An introduction to the WEconony: What is it? Why now? How is it changing business for good?

Who:

The authors share their personal journeys and lessons on business, charity, and social enterprise—learned the hard way.

Part Two
Why?

Because successful businesses now work for the greater good, and purpose is profitable. The stories that follow are proof that companies are thriving by tackling social issues with business plans. It's "Business with Benefits"—for people, planet, and profit.

You may sit with the investment or marketing department and think that changing the world is the unenviable problem of the Corporate Social Responsibility team. In fact, everyone has the chance to push companies to scale social change, and to find more meaning at work.

Part Three

How:

A step-by-step guide to embedding purpose right at the heart of everything you do, both as an individual and as a business. Find a cause that suits you, build a plan, perfect your pitch, and much more.

This is everything you want to know about getting involved in the WEconomy. This is your roadmap for doing good and getting paid for it.

Endnotes for this book can be found at wiley.com/go/weconomy.

FOREWORD

By Sheryl Sandberg

It was my first day on the ground in India. The year was 1992 and I had graduated from college a few months before. I was working as a research assistant at the World Bank and this was my first chance to leave the air-conditioned Washington, D.C., headquarters and see what development work actually was like in the field.

I remember the heat hitting me as my colleague Dr. Salim Habayeb and I walked out of the airport. We headed toward our cab and before we made it to the door, a small boy came up to us, grabbed my leg, lifted up his shirt to show the burn marks covering his chest, and then held out his hand to beg for money. After freezing for a minute in shock, I started to reach for my purse. Salim, who had worked in public health for many years, kindly put his hand over mine and said a firm "no." He explained that someone had likely burned this boy to enable him to beg more effectively, and if I gave him money, they would do it again. We got into the cab and drove away, tears pouring down my face.

Over the next few weeks as Salim and our colleague Maria Donoso Clark and I traveled throughout India working on a program to treat leprosy, I had many such learning moments. I met patients who had been cast out of their homes and families due to their disease. I saw acts of despair, acts of kindness, and acts of greatness—all in an environment that nothing in my childhood in Miami could have prepared me for. Most importantly, I saw how dedicated people could make a real difference. During the days, I worked harder than I ever had in my life trying to do my small part to help. At night, I cried myself to sleep.

In the decades since my first trip to India, a lot has improved, even though the gap between rich and poor has increased dramatically and deep poverty remains. India's economy has developed. Leprosy has gone from afflicting more than 3 million people to fewer than 100,000. Each time I visit I am amazed at the vibrancy of the Indian people and economy and the improvements to health they have achieved.

I was last in India three years ago. I was there not as a 22-year-old in her first job but on an official visit as the chief operating officer of Facebook. More importantly, I was visiting as a mother—on this trip, Craig Kielburger and my nine-year-old son and six-year-old daughter were with me. I want my children to grow up understanding what I did not learn until I was 22—that the luck of birth determines so much of our lives and that those of us with opportunity also have responsibility. And I want my children to see how even when problems might seem overwhelmingly large, individuals can make a difference.

Our time with Craig in Rajasthan showed all of this so clearly. We visited a one-room village school and helped build a wall for a new school that will provide multiple classrooms so more children will have the opportunity to learn. We helped families who had relied on polluted water sources carry clean water from their new community well to their homes. We attended a Lean In Circle meeting with women who are participating in a financial literacy program that has helped them save money and send their daughters to school for the first time. All of this is happening because WE Charity, a program started by Craig when he was just 12 years old, is working in these communities—and making a huge difference.

This book is about how we can all work to improve the lives of others. The problems in the world can seem overwhelming—5.9 million children under the age of five die each year of preventable or curable diseases,[1] more than 700 million people still lack access to clean water,[2] and 46 million people live in slavery.[3] But even a single person can make a huge difference, as each of the authors of this book shows us every day. There are no simple solutions, but there are solutions that can be created and deployed. Companies, nonprofits, governments, and hybrid social enterprises each have their own role to play—and the authors of this book have been leaders in all these realms. As Holly Branson, Marc Kielburger, and Craig Kielburger share their stories and insights in these pages, the interwoven nature of the "WEconomy" is brought to light for all of us. As you start out on your own journey, ask yourself: What kind of world do you want to live in? Dream big—dream of a world that is just and fair, where all have equal opportunity to live healthy, happy, and productive lives. How much will you do to create that better world? Whatever your path may be—in business, in government, in a nonprofit—how will you contribute to the lives of others? What legacy will you leave for your children and for all children?

At Facebook, we have posters on the walls that inspire us, such as Fortune Favors the Bold or Done Is Better Than Perfect. I have two favorites: Nothing at Facebook Is Someone Else's Problem and What Would You Do If You Weren't Afraid? What would you do if you believed that all of the problems out there could be solved and that it was your responsibility to solve them? What would you do if you weren't afraid?

Please ask yourself those questions and decide what you'd do. And then go do it.

Sheryl Sandberg

PART ONE: INTRODUCTION

WELCOME TO THE WECONOMY

By Craig Kielburger, Holly Branson, and Marc Kielburger

In the WEconomy, you can make money and change the world — you can make money by changing the world. It's that simple.

The WEconomy is an emerging economic system driven by purpose and profit. It reflects the interconnected nature of our economy, environment, and social welfare so that business works in the interest of the greater good.

We live in turbulent times. As antiglobalization forces have so visibly impacted the world, so many are understandably afraid that humanity is moving backwards when it comes to helping the planet's most impoverished and disadvantaged. Problems that should unite us, like climate change and a growing wealth gap, are abandoned to partisan politics. World leaders promise to build walls, exit political unions, and retreat from economic alliances, withdrawing inward. So many of us are divided along racial, religious, and political lines that the rise of the individual and a "me first" mentality seems inevitable. It's enough to make even the most optimistic idealists furrow their brows.

But progress happens in fits and starts; this too shall pass. We're firm believers that the "building walls" sentiment is a blip fostered by fear and

WHEN PURPOSE AND PROFIT UNITE — AND WE WILL SHOW YOU THAT THEY DO — THE ECONOMY, THE INDIVIDUAL, AND THE COMMUNITY THRIVE.

misunderstanding, and that humankind is generally on a march toward a more open, interconnected world. Our global village is smaller than at any other time in human history. Individuals are connected and empowered by more knowledge, more information, and more tools, and can more easily mobilize around a cause. Across the globe, millions of individual volunteers and people in business, government, and nonprofits are committed to making the world a better place.

"I truly believe that if every company in the world adopted this philosophy, all of the world's problems could be solved."

—Richard Branson

So, despite what may seem like doomsday headlines, it's not the end of the world as we know it. Why? Because many of us are focused on moving the world forward, on fostering progress, not just by engaging politically or reaching out to our neighbors, but also by turning business into a force for good. It's now possible to build companies and social enterprises that tackle the planet's most dire problems. Workers can now bring their personal values to the office, giving back on company time.

Most people are driven in varying degrees by the need to do good, balanced against the need to be financially successful. We came together to write this book because we all learned, despite our different paths, that choosing profit or purpose at the expense of the other is a false dichotomy. You can do both. You should do both.

When purpose and profit unite—and we will show you that they do—the economy, the individual, and the community thrive.

Changing the world shouldn't be a task saved for extreme altruists working without pay. The best and brightest from all economic and social sectors can survive and thrive while tackling our planet's biggest challenges.

As three thirty-somethings on the cusp of this new movement, we are in a unique position, each bringing a different voice from the big three players in the WEconomy: business (Holly Branson), charity (Craig Kielburger), and social enterprise (Marc Kielburger). Over the past couple of years, we've pored over countless business books, but never found one that brought together voices from all three sectors. We each have our own experiences to draw from (you will hear a lot about Virgin, WE Charity, and ME to WE). We write about what we know—drawing from our mistakes and learnings. We'll, of course, introduce ourselves properly, but first, we would like to introduce you to our mentors—those who helped us recognize the power of purpose and profit combined.

Our Big Three Inspirations: Oprah, Richard, and Jeff

We are lucky to have picked the brains and learned from three prominent innovators in the worlds of business and social enterprise. These titans were the forerunners of the WEconomy, and as such, we tip our hats to our favorite teachers.

Not many of us would mind being Oprah Winfrey, Richard Branson, or Jeff Skoll—at least for a few days anyway.

Lady O

It's not that you want to read more Nora Roberts novels or make celebrities cry in front of a live studio audience, but you want to *be* Oprah.

While everyone wants to be Oprah to some degree, it might not be for the reasons you expect. It's not about the money, fame, or power. Frankly, there are other influential billionaires who don't provoke the same affection and envy. The Oprahness we all aspire to isn't just about wealth or status—it's about making a successful career out of a purposeful life.

People want to be Oprah because she fosters her passions while giving back—*and* she gets paid to do so. *The Oprah Winfrey Show* was devoted to health and fitness, relationships, and literacy because Oprah commiserates with our family issues and wants to be part of our book club. Like us, Oprah is on the treadmill the first month of the year, fighting the five pounds of chocolate she ate over the holidays. She is a self-made business magnate whose brand is, when you break it down, devoted to living one's best life. She wants to help people be

Oprah Winfrey
Some things you might not know

The Oprah Winfrey Show was the highest-rated television talk show in U.S. history. It drew in 48 million viewers per week.[1]

O, The Oprah Magazine, has the highest women's magazine circulation in North America with 2.4 million copies sold per year.[2]

Oprah invested $40 million to create the Oprah Winfrey Leadership Academy for Girls. The school in South Africa for disadvantaged girls was lauded by Nelson Mandela.

Oprah's Book Club leads to 55 million books sold after promotion on the show.

Fortune magazine named her the world's most charitable celebrity.

better—mentally, emotionally, physically—by sharing her personal struggles. Not only did Oprah make money and do good, she made money by doing good. Then, through donations and her own foundations, Oprah funded other causes. She has built schools, helped abandoned or abused children, worked to combat HIV/AIDS and climate change, committing almost $1 billion to philanthropic causes in her lifetime. Now worth an estimated $3 billion,[3] Oprah is regularly named one of the world's most powerful women, sharing the list with the likes of Melinda Gates and former First Lady Michelle Obama.[4]

Oprah feeds that craving in all of us that tells us we can make a difference in the world *and* make a living. It doesn't have to be Oprah-scale wages either—most of us simply want enough to support our families and occasionally take a vacation. Most of us also want a purpose, a reason to get up in the morning, a way to make a contribution. But we also need the sense of security that comes with a steady paycheck. Oprah built a corporate empire on this fusion of purpose and profit that the whole working world is after. And we're not just saying all of this because she is one of our greatest mentors.

When Marc and Craig met Oprah for the first time, they were teenagers at the helm of a brand new charity they'd launched with . . . well, a bunch of other teenagers. The organization had a naïve mission to help kids get an education by building schools, but had no formal game plan. The novelty of kids helping kids earned Craig a spot on the show, which parlayed into a partnership. Oprah would go on to build over 50 schools and dozens more projects with them, lending her business acumen and guidance. Craig and Marc would sit on her famous couch four more times.

Oprah helped mentor the brothers to transform the fledgling charity into a sustainable development organization, now with over $50 million in annual donations.

Dr. Yes

If jumping off buildings in a tux is more your speed, you probably want to be Sir Richard Branson (or James Bond). Richard built an empire with gut instinct, guerilla marketing, and good intentions. He launched his first venture, *Student* magazine, in 1968 with £300 borrowed from his mother, driven by the belief that young people had something important to say and a desire to take a stand on important issues, like opposing the Vietnam War. He's since formed a global mega-brand. The Virgin Group employs 70,000 people in more than 35 countries. But Virgin had humble

Richard Branson
Some under-the-radar initiatives

In the 1980s he donated £5 million to establish Mates condoms as a competitor to Durex during the AIDS epidemic. All profits went to charity. Because of that, the BBC ran Mates ads for free and helped educate millions of people about the importance of using condoms.

In 1985 Richard took a gamble on a 23-year-old Jane Tewson by agreeing to cover the full overhead of a new charity: the now famous Comic Relief/Red Nose Day. Because of Richard's backing, 100 percent of money raised could be directed to good causes. By 2015 Comic Relief had raised over £1 billion for charity and has helped over 50 million people in the UK and overseas.

In the same way that Richard is a serial entrepreneur in business, he is also a serial philanthropist. He has established dozens of not-for-profit organizations that seek to tackle a range of social and environmental issues:
- The Elders (independent global leaders working for peace and human rights)
- Ocean Unite and the Ocean Elders (ocean conservation)
- the B Team (to rally business leaders to change business for good) and the Carbon War Room (to combat climate change)
- the Help Advisory Centre (counseling for troubled youth, started when he was a student himself)

beginnings in Richard's battle to defend customers from price gouging and robotic sounding customer service reps. This purpose, to protect consumers from untrustworthy and exploitative businesses by offering a fair, friendly alternative, is what Virgin is all about. In fact, the Virgin Group has a policy: don't start a new venture unless it will improve the customer experience. The business plan puts people first.

Richard anticipated viral marketing before the advent of social media. He dressed in drag, drove an army tank through New York's Times Square, and raced in hot air balloons to steal attention away from corporate goliaths. All to build a global brand without forking out for traditional advertising. His mantra was, and remains, "screw business as usual." This also extends to corporate social responsibility (CSR). Rather than tack on a CSR plan with no real resources or support, Virgin uses its core business for social good, in some cases starting companies purely to solve a social problem, and not worrying about the profit potential until much later on. Richard's brilliant feat of launching and growing companies, with purpose at their heart, is transforming business and changing the world.

> *"Aid is just a stop-gap. Commerce, entrepreneurial capitalism takes more people out of poverty than aid."*
>
> —Bono, activist and lead singer for U2

Part of a company's core mission today should involve social purpose, and Richard knew this long before nearly everyone else. Richard's motivation for launching a business has always been driven by two questions: By shaking up this market, are we introducing competition that will benefit the customer? Will we bring customers a more rewarding and fair experience? He's been very successful—because building social impact into business isn't just the right thing to do, it's also profitable.

After Holly had embarked on a career in medicine, the realization of her childhood dream, her father suggested she take a year out to learn about business. It was Richard who helped Holly realize she might help more people in a boardroom than she could in a hospital room. Her dad taught her that business can be the biggest force for social change.

The Protagonist

You may not know that you want to be Jeff Skoll because he's not a first-name-only celebrity. But trust us, you do. Who wouldn't want to be a Hollywood magnate with a conscience? Jeff is a Canadian-born, Stanford-educated tech entrepreneur, the first president of eBay and the founder of Participant Media, a production company that promotes awareness for some of the biggest problems facing the world today. He's also a self-proclaimed sci-fi geek and a bit of a bookworm, hobbies that prepared him to take strange and daunting subject matter and make it accessible.

One of Participant's early films evolved from a slideshow about climate change presented by Al Gore, former Vice President of the United

Jeff Skoll:
The Canadian entrepreneur with a conscience

$1 Billion

Skoll is one of only a few dozen people to donate $1 billion.

His foundation's initiatives include an investment firm dedicated to ethical money management, as well as TakePart.com, an offshoot of Participant Media that works to convert people's concerns about issues into individual and collective action.

His films don't just raise consciousness, they win awards and attract big audiences. *An Inconvenient Truth, Spotlight, The Help, Syriana, Lincoln,* and *Deepwater Horizon* are among the films he's produced. He's worked with top talent in Hollywood: Matt Damon, George Clooney, and Emma Stone, among other stars.

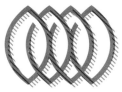

The Skoll Global Threats Fund looks for strategies to prevent or cope with disasters, including nuclear meltdowns, pandemics, water shortages, climate change, and conflict in the Middle East.

States. It's hard to imagine anything less entertaining or marketable. But *An Inconvenient Truth* went on to win an Oscar and become one of the top-grossing documentaries of all time. Jeff uses the money-making machine that is the film industry to raise awareness of social issues. Participant Media brings production value, heavyweight actors, and mainstream publicity to films that would otherwise be seen only by a niche audience of activists.

Jeff leveraged that public interest with action campaigns that complement the movie's themes, giving people a tangible way to respond to their feelings postviewing. To enhance *Lincoln*, a drama about the 16th U.S. president, the film was distributed to middle schools and high schools in the

United States. The educational outreach package came with lesson plans to help teachers introduce students to this iconic figure in American history.

Not all of Participant's films make money, but Jeff finances his passion projects with smart (mostly eco-oriented) investments. He's since made money on everything from renewable energy to his personal favorite investment at the moment—flush-free urinals. Jeff also happens to be one of our greatest mentors (we hope you're picking up on the theme here).

When Marc decided to forgo a handsome salary and a corner office to increase the scale of a charity, he struggled with whether he could start a family on a nonprofit salary. He wondered how a charity could stay sustainable without all the trappings of a business. Jeff's advice?

Don't choose between purpose and profit; it's not an either-or proposition.

Jeff taught Marc that the future of social change lies with social enterprise.

Pioneers of Purpose and Profit

So what do a media mogul from Chicago, a British serial entrepreneur, and a Canadian sci-fi fan have in common? All hit on the combination of purpose and profit early on, achieved massive success, and continued to use the power and resources of corporate engines to create positive change. This combination of purpose and profit is the bedrock of the WEconomy, and it is achievable for everyone, regardless of your sector or the stage of your career. You don't have to be a business owner to reap benefits in the WEconomy.

We look to Oprah, Richard, and Jeff, not because they founded companies, but because they were part of the first cohort to get it right—to achieve both financial success and social impact on a massive scale. Ironically, we also know that each would quibble with being called pioneers of a trend they hadn't predicted. They just wanted to do good. We learned some of our greatest business lessons from these three innovators, which we'll talk about more when we introduce ourselves properly.

From the recent graduate to the CEO, everyone will learn something from this book

 CEOs will learn how to embed purpose into the DNA of their business to inspire their employees and boost the bottom line.

 Marketers will learn how to connect more deeply with customers and engage previously untapped demographics.

 Entrepreneurs will use purpose as a launch pad to develop "the next big thing."

 Team members will learn to write purpose into their job descriptions for a more meaningful career, a move that also benefits their employers.

 HR leaders will learn to inspire their teams, recruit new talent, and build loyalty.

 New starters will get a crash course on purpose that will help them climb the corporate ladder.

Before launching a career as a social entrepreneur, Marc served water in the Canadian House of Commons, worked with AIDS patients in Bangkok, and collected degrees from Harvard and Oxford. Now he counts himself among those who do good and still make a living. Before arriving at Virgin, Holly volunteered at an African orphanage, worked with various charities, completed medical and physiology degrees, and practiced medicine at Chelsea and Westminster Hospital in London. Holly then joined the ranks of a company involved in everything from financial services to spaceships. Craig didn't do much before he launched a children's charity. Of course, he was 12 at the time. But since then, his two decades of work as a social activist have taken him everywhere from urban slums to Mother Teresa's home to the mountains at Davos to Oprah's famous couch. After all this, he discovered that his degree in peace and conflict studies could use a shot in the arm—sheer earnestness is not enough to change the world—and so he earned an MBA to bring more business rigor to the nonprofit world. Now a leader in the nonprofit sector, he dreams of starting his own social accelerator to help others scale.

80 percent of global consumers say business must play a role in addressing societal issues.

—Edelman Trust Barometer

Why Read This Book?

This book will show you how to become Oprah Winfrey.

Okay, not really, but it will show you how to find meaning and self-fulfillment at work, and to live your values while making a living. The WEconomy is about helping you unlock and harness the potential of purpose and profit.

Companies will learn how to find a social mission that fits the business, and then execute it well.

Charities will learn to develop partnerships and use business strategies to achieve greater scale of impact and sustainable growth.

Individuals will learn that tackling the biggest issues of our time shouldn't mean sacrificing a comfortable life.

We'll help you find this tricky pairing of purpose and profit that— we promise you—is going to be one hell of a sea change.

Social purpose is the biggest thing to happen to business since the assembly line. All evidence points to the fact that workers and consumers respond to businesses that do good. Corporate surveys, behavioral economists, and the authors' own experiences prove that

WEconomy companies are rewarded with more talent and better business, making an enticing argument for social purpose, even for profit-making machines. Profit is not only possible for companies that give back, it can be a driving force to solve the world's most intractable problems. Businesses need an incentive to find solutions, putting the power and resources of large companies on our side. Profit becomes growth, which becomes investment in more solutions. Companies can be one of the greatest forces for social good because they have the resources to scale and make change on a massive level. Still, most companies mistake purpose for a passing trend, forfeiting the chance to solve both social issues and business challenges. We can help you do purpose right, and cash in on this new normal.

No matter who you are or where you are on your career path, you can find a place in the WEconomy. We'll take you through our personal journeys to do well and do good. Each of us falls on a different point of the business-charity spectrum, but we share a belief in channeling the power of capitalism to create social impact. We're sharing our stories because we know we're not alone.

Part One will:

- *Follow the authors on their personal journeys through the WEconomy*
- *Introduce the power of companies to drive social change (Virgin)*
- *Follow the evolution of a charity through failure and innovation (WE Charity)*
- *Discover social enterprise as a means to scale impact and help consumers do good (ME to WE)*
- *Inspire you to forge your own path to purpose and profit*

In Part Two, we'll help you make the business case. First, we'll explore the WEconomy's effect on the workforce, a shift in attitude that has young workers and mid-career professionals alike demanding more than just a paycheck. Then, we'll convince you that purpose is like Miracle-Gro for your company: there are few aspects of the business that won't be better off with an injection of smart social responsibility. Core fundamentals still need to be strong—even a cause won't cure a bad business plan. But if you have the building blocks right, purpose will give you an edge.

In Part Two, we'll show you how to use purpose as a catalyst to:

- *Build new products and create "the next big thing".*
- *Differentiate established products to stand out in an age of parity*
- *Inspire brand fanatics, loyal to your social mission and company*
- *Enter new markets at home and abroad*
- *Increase employee engagement, loyalty, and retention*
- *Boost your bottom line*
- *Invest in social change for monetary returns*
- *Move up the ranks in your company*

It's not enough to know that purpose is important; you have to know how to execute it. In Part Three, we'll show you, step by step, how to find, implement, and amplify a cause that aligns with your core business or individual interests. The bad news is that most companies do this poorly. We'll share what we've learned, what to avoid, and the keys to pulling off a successful corporate–charity partnership.

What follows is our recipe for increased earnings, scalability, self-sufficiency, and, ultimately, positive social change.

This book will help you profit from the next big wave in the world of business, whether you're the one calling the shots or a junior employee looking to advance your career.

Get paid to change the world—who wouldn't want to be the person doing that?

You're already changing the world . . .

WE Give Opportunity

The book you're holding comes with a Track Your Impact code and a charitable donation. Proceeds from every book sold will provide women in developing communities with access to small business training, empowering them to earn a sustainable income close to home. This program is proof that enterprise can facilitate social change. Visit WE.org/trackyourimpact and enter your Track Your Impact code to find out more about your donation and see photos of families and maps of the regions you have helped by buying this book.

"I wanted to write this book, in part, to show from my experiences at Virgin that business can facilitate unlikely partnerships between governments, commerce, and the social sector, using the market as a lever for social change."

GROWING UP BRANSON

By Holly Branson

Dear Holly and Sam,

Life can seem rather unreal at times. Alive and well and loving one day. No longer there the next.

As you both know I always had an urge to live life to the full . . . I loved every minute of it and I especially loved every second of my time with both of you and mum.

I know that many people thought us foolish for embarking on this latest adventure. I was convinced they were wrong . . . I thought that the risks were acceptable. Obviously I've been proved wrong.

However, I regret nothing about my life except not being with Joan to finally help you grow up. By the ages of twelve and fifteen your characters have already developed. We're both so proud of you. Joan and I couldn't have two more delightful kids.

You are both kind, considerate, full of life (even witty!). What more could we both want?

Be strong. I know it won't be easy. But we've had a wonderful life together and you'll never forget all the good times we've had.

Live life to its full yourselves. Enjoy every minute of it. Love and look after Mum as if she's both of us.

I love you,
Dad

I attempted to read this for the first time on the day my dad's autobiography *Losing My Virginity* was published—but tears prevented me reading beyond the first paragraph. My dad is known for many things, from businessman to philanthropist and in this case adventurer and he'd written this letter in case he didn't survive his latest round-the-world attempt in a hot-air balloon. He survived. Characteristically, Dad forgot to give me and my brother Sam the heads-up that he would open his first book with what might have been his last written words to us. So it came as a bit of a shock, especially as we hadn't seen it before! Richard Branson may well be a world-famous name, but to me he's just Dad.

It is bizarre writing about yourself, like talking in the third person. You have to ask difficult questions and to some extent bare your soul. In the first of many writing sessions for this book, Craig had already hit a nerve. We'd discussed my childhood, medical school, my experiences at Virgin—then Craig turned to me: "Holly, the most important question of all now. What do you want your legacy to the world to be?"

I looked at him stricken, knowing full well that if I asked him the same thing he'd say something off the top of his head that was succinct and annoyingly brilliant.

My mind was spinning with the things I should be saying, like driving Virgin forward in changing business for good, embedding purpose into the heart of the company, making an impact in the world through our foundations. But all I wanted to say was: I want to be a mum. That my dream is to raise a healthy, happy, kind, well-grounded family with my husband, Freddie.

Craig couldn't have known that Freddie and I had spent more than two difficult and distressing years trying to conceive. After two miscarriages and two failed rounds of IVF, we were starting to wonder if we would ever get to be parents.

I decided to be honest, not about my fertility struggles, but about the fact that I wanted my legacy to be having a family that cares about the world at large. That more than anything, coming from families as close as ours, I wanted Freddie and me to have the opportunity to instill the same value systems and love of life, of people and planet, that our parents had instilled in us. Kids who believe they can make a real difference in the world. We wanted to mentor our kids in the same way we were mentored by our parents.

Mom, Dad, Sam . . . and Dreams of Being a Doctor

I am called Holly because I was supposed to come into the world at Christmas. Family legend has it that my arrival six weeks early found my dad sleeping off the previous night's party. My mum, Joan, by then in contractions, had to manhandle him out of bed and into the car. Luckily, they made it to the hospital in time!

My mum, born Joan Templeman, was raised in the center of Glasgow, Scotland, worked in a pawnbroker's shop, and, later, at a London bric-a-brac store on the Portobello Road. It was there that my dad first fell in love with her and, without putting too fine a point on it, essentially stalked her. He turned up at the shop every day for months, buying stuff he didn't want or need. The rest, as they say, is history.

Sam and I had a normal, loving childhood—thanks in the largest part to our wonderful mum. She was the one who took my younger brother and me to the playground and walked us to and from school every day. A stay-at-home mum who was (and still is) always there with a hug, inspiring words of wisdom, and a beautiful, welcoming smile. She is our anchor, the calm voice that acts as a complementary balance to our very energetic father.

Dad was also ever present, camped out on a sofa at one end of the sitting room, first on the houseboat, then in our Holland Park home, orchestrating the growth of Virgin while we tore about under his feet. I called my parents Joan and Richard until I was 11—as that's what everyone who worked for Virgin called them.

Virgin and home life were never separate for Sam and me. We were used to people coming and going, constant phone calls, the beeps of fax machines, paper everywhere. We ran riot in the offices of the wonderful Virgin staff. They never seemed to mind—which was not really surprising given that my old nursery ended up being the Virgin Press Office. We had no idea that the people coming and going to meetings were the likes of the Rolling Stones, Janet Jackson, the boss of Boeing, or a distraught bank manager (on more than one occasion). It was fun and relaxed and—to us—totally normal.

Dad was (and still is) open, honest, and unafraid to ask questions or seek advice—even from his children. We saw him listen much more than he talked. In a nutshell, he taught us to be independent, which I know at times, like many a parent, he regretted—especially when there were four of us involved in making decisions, rather than just one! Later in the book we look at putting your people first and building your trust bank—much of which I learned from my mum and dad at our kitchen table.

Even growing up in the buzz of the family business, I'd always wanted to be a doctor. Childhood dreams of extensive learning and saving lives seemed best indulged within the medical profession. Mum remembers asking me about my ambitions when I was three. I answered unequivocally: "I'd like to be a doctor." Our next-door neighbor and dear friend Peter Emerson was a doctor and I was struck by his fantastic calm in any crisis, like the time I stuck my finger in a blender as an inquisitive child. The blood and gore didn't phase him one bit—to a child like me that made a doctor the coolest thing on the planet.

Growing up knowing what I wanted to be was brilliant because I knew right away which subjects I'd have to take and what grades I needed to get, so my academic career was already mapped out. In the UK, where at age 15 students must strictly narrow the focus of their studies, this was a huge advantage and a lot less stressful than it was for my friends who had no idea what they wanted to end up doing careerwise. I'd always loved biology, and though chemistry gave me trouble, I could manage it. I loved being around people, especially children, and so I dreamed of being a pediatrician. Having that rigorous structure imposed in order to work toward a goal made me a studious young girl.

Except on Necker Island . . . where Sam and I embraced our inner Pirates of the Caribbean.

Sam is nearly four years younger than me, and was my constant childhood companion. We tobogganed down stairways on mattresses and built a makeshift zip line in our backyard, but we had our best adventures on Necker. My parents bought Necker Island, one of the easternmost Virgin Islands, in 1979 for $180,000, and we spent every summer, Christmas, and Easter there. It was the world's greatest playground. Sam and I built sandcastle cities, stowed castaways, staved off pirates, and pillaged for gold, which to most adults looked like seashells.

During our family holidays on Necker, Sam and I would pester our unmarried parents about their different surnames. Finally, one day, Dad took me aside. "Would it be okay if I asked your mum to marry me?" he asked. "Dad," I worried, "what if she says, 'No'?" He had more confidence in her enthusiasm for the idea than I apparently did. My parents were married on Necker on December 20, 1989.

Twenty-two years later to the day, in the same spot on Necker, I married my high-school sweetheart amidst the ruins of the great house that had burned to the ground after a lightning strike, during a hurricane, a couple of months before.

Our romance all started with a family member's hopeless sense of direction. Our arrival at St. Edward's School in Oxford came about by chance one weekend when our family went to the wrong school for an open day; we intended to visit a neighboring school but took a left turn instead of a right. Immediately, we fell in love with the architecture and the open culture of the students.

Among its other plus points, St. Edward's featured boys; my previous schools had not. Founded in 1863 to educate the sons of Anglican clergy, the school didn't become fully coed until 1997, the year I walked through its doors. So, not only did St. Edward's have boys, it had a lot of them: six for every one of the 20 girls enrolled in my year.

Among them was Freddie Andrewes—a tall, handsome, blond-haired boy I came to know better during geography field trips. We became good friends that first year then got together at a party. Smart, charming, and sporty—little did I know he was the man I would marry many years later on Necker. It's strange when I think of it now, but if not for a wrong turn, Freddie and I may never have met.

St. Edward's also introduced me to the rewards of community service. Our academic program required either volunteer service or cadet training. I chose to volunteer as a teacher's assistant at a school for autistic children. Many of the kids were severely affected by the developmental disorder, which, among other things, can make it difficult to look others in the eye. Some researchers believe that eye contact helps with social interactions, so I taught this through clapping games and working with blocks. My natural inclination is to comfort with a hug, so I struggled at first with how to handle these children, many of whom resist touch and process their emotions much differently from the way I do when they are upset. Although difficult at times, the experience was tremendously rewarding.

Children have the most amazing ability to teach adults the true joy of being alive. They delight in the smallest of things. They look at the world through innocent eyes filled with hope, even when they have experienced great loss and struggles. After I graduated from St. Edward's, I was extremely privileged and excited to work with young children again, this time in Africa.

It was there that I met the most wonderful little boy.

Kelvin was a confident, cheeky, chatty little boy. I met him during my gap year between boarding school and medical school when I was an 18-year-old volunteer at an orphanage in Nairobi, Kenya. Kelvin was one of about 200 children living there. He'd follow me around and seize me by the leg, or grab me by the hand to show me his bed or his best friend or his favorite hiding place. He was seven years old, with a lightning grin and eyes bright with both mischief and intelligence.

His peers were apprehensive about newcomers and shied away from those, like me, who came into their lives for months at a time to teach English or to drill them in math. Kelvin didn't suffer from shyness. He loved nothing more than to stir up trouble and rally fellow students to his cause. My best defense against classroom mayhem turned out to be my digital camera, which in the year 2000 was still something of a novelty. When things got out of hand, I'd offer to photograph the children if they agreed to settle down. Kelvin filled my memory card with frame after frame of breakdance poses, zany smiles, and intense close-ups of his eyes and ears and teeth.

He was a marvel of mirth and resilience. No one knew for certain what had happened to his parents, but given the momentum of the HIV/AIDS epidemic at the time, it was easy to guess. In 1990, fewer than one million children in sub-Saharan Africa had lost one or both parents to HIV/AIDS. By 2010, it was more than 15 million.[1]

I wanted to adopt Kelvin. I wanted to take him home to a supportive family, to "fix" things by evacuating him from his circumstances. At 18 years old, my plan was impractical. My reaction to a global epidemic that had left millions orphaned, my instinct to help, had been to pick up one boy and run.

My dad was keen, but it was my level-headed mother who finally convinced me that, at 18 and about to enter medical school, I was in no position to take on a seven-year-old. We decided that the best way to help was to sponsor Kelvin and his education. I cried all the way back to London—my heart breaking but also bursting with joy at my incredible luck to have met a little boy whose eyes shone with hope and the wonder of life in the face of adversity.

Several years later I had my very own brush with the fear of HIV.

I graduated from medical school at University College London in 2008. During my first week on the job as a qualified doctor, I was drawing a blood sample from a patient in the hospital with a urological issue. I went to cover the needle with a safety catch and then—I'm still not sure what happened—the needle pricked my finger. When I peeled off my glove, blood was oozing up in a neat little dot from where the needle had pierced my skin. I snatched the patient's file: female, early 30s, intravenous drug user, Hepatitis-C carrier, high risk for HIV/AIDS, never been tested.

As a nurse or doctor in a hospital, we all know the risks, which are actually pretty high, but we are trained to know what to do should something like this happen. But for that hour or so, immediately after the needle pierces the skin, you can't help feeling crippled by fear. A tearful call to Freddie calmed me down. Always practical, Freddie reminded me there was very little I could do but take the prescribed course of treatment and just get on with life rather than worry myself sick. He was right of course (but don't ever tell him that!).

I was prescribed a powerful cocktail of antiretroviral drugs known as postexposure prophylaxis (PEP) that lower the risk of contracting the virus. If HIV had entered my bloodstream, it would take between a few hours and a few days before it permanently infected me. The drugs can prevent permanent infection, but left me terribly nauseous. When the patient's test came back negative, I discontinued treatment. Due to the diagnostic procedure, it would be six months before doctors could tell me whether I had been infected with Hepatitis-C. For six months, I both had and didn't have Hep-C. Work at the hospital was all-consuming, so it was possible to keep the anxiety boxed into one corner of my mind. Thankfully, my blood tests came back negative, but the incident taught me firsthand what it felt like to be a patient. To put myself in other people's shoes who have no control over their fate was not only humbling but also inspired me forward on my journey to help others.

Mind the Gap

My life as a 27-year-old was full, rewarding, and exciting: I'd signed on as medic in a race across the Atlantic on a stripped-down sailboat, treated a cardiac patient in-flight at 30,000 feet, and completed arduous rounds at Chelsea and Westminster Hospital with my newly minted medical degree; I'd achieved my life's ambition, or so I thought. . . .

There was never one day, one moment, when I resolved to leave medicine. Rather, it was a step-by-step process—a series of small decisions. My transition really began at Chelsea and Westminster Hospital where I discovered that surgery was not my calling. I preferred drawn-out conversations; I preferred to use my bedside manner while the patient was conscious. So when I found out that year two of my medical rotation would be predominantly surgery—young doctors receive a random allocation of duties in Britain—I knew that this would be my only opportunity to defer my studies for a year in the hope that when I reapplied I would find myself on a different medical specialty.

I spent months asking advice from my tutors, fellow doctors, friends, Freddie, and of course family before I finally made the decision to take a year out of medicine. What's a year, after all?

And that's how I found myself in Dad's office (a.k.a.: the sofa at home), sitting across from him and listening to his "year-long" job offer.

Dad had never put pressure on Sam or me to go into the business, but he also never made it a secret that he'd love nothing more than to share his passion with us. It's impossible not to get swept up by Dad's galloping enthusiasms, and Sam and I grew up with the Virgin team being part of our family.

My dad has always believed that "screwing business as usual" will have to become the new norm if we want to avoid running out of room and resources on this planet. Social issues of great magnitude can only be solved when government, nonprofits, and the private sector work together. Old-school charities don't have the resources to grow their impact on their own. Governments have only so much tax revenue. As the only sector with enough resources for scalability, business should take the lead. Traditionally, the purpose of business has been to maximize shareholder value at any cost, a mandate that often justified crimes against people and the environment. In the past, people and planet were rarely economic measurements in the success or failure of a business. But when, in some instances, companies are more powerful than governments, business cannot see itself as separate from the health of our world and its people but responsible for it.

I wanted to write this book, in part, to show from my experiences at Virgin that business can facilitate unlikely partnerships between governments, commerce, and the social sector, using the market as a lever for social change. Thankfully, as they touch millions of people's lives with products and services, companies across the world are waking up to these possibilities, and to their wider responsibility. As Dad would say, "business should make lives better."

When a company leads by example with more progressive social practices, it can alter consumer expectations and force competitors to adopt new strategies, causing a ripple effect that changes market demands and ultimately changes the world for the better.

I had the chance to work for one of those businesses. To join one of the world's biggest, most progressive companies and work toward change on a much larger scale.

How could I turn down an opportunity to be a part of that?

All of a sudden the year had gone by, and I wasn't ready to reapply for a new medical rotation when the time came. I deferred my hospital return to continue along the learning curve at Virgin. I'd started my new job the way most people do these days—with an internship, rotating through all of our larger companies, including Virgin Atlantic, Virgin Money, Virgin Media, and Virgin Trains. Accounting and balance sheets gave me trouble, so I went back to school to get a better handle on them. After a year I wanted to learn more. After two years I knew I needed to learn even more. After three years I finally admitted to myself that I would not be returning to medicine.

During my first few months at Virgin, I was encouraged, challenged, pushed—alongside a passionate team—to come up with ideas and practices that would ensure that our business was a force for good. We were tasked with driving forward a strategy for Virgin that formalized Dad's gut instinct that business was best placed to answer some of the world's most difficult social problems. For years, my dad and his trusted colleagues had built a business based on people and culture, engaging employees in a social mission that permeated every aspect of the business without sacrificing the bottom line. We were tasked with ensuring that "business as a force for good" would be THE most important part of Virgin's DNA going forward.

By the end of this book, I hope to have taken you along on the ride of my own learning curve—which in the beginning was steep!

We were tasked with ensuring that "business as a force for good" would be THE most important part of Virgin's DNA going forward.

My Legacy at Home

A little over a year after that first writing session with Craig and Marc, I was sitting in a makeup chair having my baby bump painted to look like a sea turtle. The third round of IVF had worked, and I was well into my third trimester; I was over the moon.

Six months' pregnant with twins, I was surrounded by a group of women there to create a book in aid of vulnerable mothers around the world. The brainchild of the inspiring Sara Blakely (of Spanx fame), the Belly Art Project is a creative way to help elevate awareness for the 303,000 women who die every year as a result of complications related to pregnancy or childbirth, most of which are preventable. All proceeds from the book will go to Every Mother Counts to help at-risk mothers. As we sat there chatting about morning sickness, cravings, and swollen ankles, I thought about how lucky Freddie and I were. And I realized I'd done it. This was our first mother-baby project for charity. My twins would be helping the world from the womb!

A few weeks later at 33 weeks, I was diagnosed with preeclampsia, a hypertensive disorder and one of the most common causes of death during pregnancy for those 303,000 women every year. I needed an emergency C-section. For any mother-to-be, it is a terrifying experience. I know that had I been a mother in a developing country, I may not have survived. I am lucky; Etta and Artie were born December 20, 2014, on my and Freddie's third wedding anniversary and my parents' twenty-fifth. That date must have a special significance in the stars for my family.

What Became of Kelvin?

The irrepressible Kelvin is now 22 years old (which makes me feel old!) and resides in Kirichwa, Nairobi. I am proud to say he is loving student life at the Kiambu Institute of Science and Technology. He has already earned a certificate in Hospitality Management and will soon begin his diploma qualification in Food and Beverage Production and Sales.

Kelvin has big dreams and has never lost his unstoppable spirit and drive. In the future, he would like to open his own hotel, so that he can support his siblings. Kelvin's passion, and the passion of the many young men and women just like him, confirms my belief that the future of our world is in safe hands.

Virgin Group by the numbers (2017)

43 Million
43+ million followers on social media

53 Million
Over 60 businesses serving over 53 million customers worldwide

£16.6 Billion
£16.6 billion in annual revenue and growing (as of 2016)

70K Employees
70,000 employees in 35 countries

Brand recognition:

99%

UK

96%

United States

99%

Australia

96%

South Africa

"As kids, Marc and I couldn't find
the support that we needed to give back.
So we set out to help others,
to show them that it doesn't have to be
a struggle to do good. That's our purpose
at WE: to make doing good, doable."

BREAKFAST AND A WAKE-UP CALL

By Craig Kielburger

By any measure, my high-school experience was unusual—on those rare occasions I attended. One year, I logged fewer than 30 days in school. I repeatedly failed Grade 9 gym for not showing up. In my comparative religion course, I was docked marks for not properly footnoting a quote from the Dalai Lama. "But I can't cite a written source," I had to protest. "That's what he told me!"

There has always been a negative correlation between WE's success and my life's sense of normalcy. As a teen, I could quote conversations I'd had with world leaders at global forums or development seminars, but I couldn't name a popular song or an Oscar-nominated movie. My classmates went on about a show called *Dawson's Creek*, which was "exactly like our lives!" I watched one episode: it wasn't. I was oblivious to conventional teen angst, being so busy with WE Charity (formerly Free The Children). Balancing a financial statement was more familiar to me than my math textbook. I fired my first employee before I ever broke up with a girl. Looking back, it was like living in a made-for-TV coming-of-age movie. A childhood adventure story about traveling to 50 countries before reaching adulthood, following a personal passion for a social cause, and learning from some of the world's greatest mentors while my friends and I built a charity.

The staff were a bunch of seventh-grade students in a Toronto suburb, determined to raise awareness about the evils of child labor on the other side of the world. Today, WE is a global movement that's empowered more than one million people to lift themselves out of poverty through sustainable development. At home, we empower millions more with service learning programs that enable them to discover their own cause, write their own journey of impact, and make daily choices that better the world. There have been many obstacles along the way

WE Charity launched more than twenty years ago with limited assets: a dozen kids around a kitchen table, a fax machine, and a Commodore 64 computer.

and more lessons learned in two decades of social entrepreneurship than anyone needs in a lifetime. One of the main reasons we wrote this book is to give you the blueprint and toolkit to make your own impact without having to repeat our mistakes. As kids, Marc and I couldn't find the support that we needed to give back. So we set out to help others, to show them that it doesn't have to be a struggle to do good. That's our purpose at WE: to make doing good, doable.

When I'm asked to describe "when it all began," I think of April 19, 1995. Back then I liked to begin my day with a bowl of cereal accompanied by Calvin and Hobbes, Doonesbury, and the Wizard of Id. But that morning, I never got to the comics because I couldn't tear my eyes away from the front page. A small boy was looking out at me defiantly, his arm thrust in the air and his fist clenched. The headline announced: "Battled child labor, boy, 12, murdered." It was his age that struck me. I skimmed the paper every day in search of the comics, which means I'd ignored plenty of other distressing headlines. But this kid was my age. The article said Iqbal had been sold into bonded labor, chained to a carpet loom, and shot down in the street after he escaped his captors.

Until that moment, my life had been pretty ordinary: TV, music, basketball with friends, Boy Scouts, and Taekwondo; I went to church every week and played floor hockey on Sunday afternoons. And I was a shy kid. Growing up, I suffered chronic ear infections and underwent various surgeries. I didn't hear certain sounds properly, and as a result, didn't recreate those sounds very well. Rs gave me particular trouble, so the name Craig was a trial. I didn't know it then, but Iqbal had just altered the course of my life.

As I stared back at the photo of Iqbal, I knew I wanted to help other kids like him, but I didn't know how. Over the next few days, I reached out to a few charities, making several calls to established nonprofit and human rights groups. Most of them didn't have time for a tween with no disposable income. At one well-known international children's charity, the guy who answered the phone asked if I knew where my parents kept their credit card. They wanted a Visa number, not my time. As a kid, this upset me, and frankly, as an adult, it still would. Old-school charities don't empower people to act. Instead, they make people feel guilty and then offer to alleviate that guilt by extracting their money. That transaction is usually the full extent of a supporter's involvement in the cause. When no established charities would help me, I turned to people who would. I asked my teacher Mr. Fedrigoni if I could make a presentation to my class.

On the bus to school, I clutched Iqbal's story in sweaty palms, my nerves getting the best of me. Terrified, I told my class about Iqbal, that he was just one among millions of enslaved children in the r-r-region. I said I was going to start a student group to investigate child labor, blurting out: "Who wants to help?" And then my stomach dropped. Middle-school kids don't make for the most forgiving audiences in the best of circumstances, and now a less-than-popular kid with a speech impediment was asking them to talk about world issues during their free time.

Eleven hands shot up. Never underestimate the desire of kids to make a difference. And there was one absentee vote that I'd already counted. My big brother, Marc, was instrumental in helping us get started. He was in high school, and thus by far the most qualified to write letters of protest to international governments.

The Tween's Guide to Starting a Charity

After my class presentation, we held our inaugural meeting during lunch period. Later that day, we set up an office in my parents' garage and installed filing cabinets, a bookcase, and a table, where we would build lemonade stands out of corrugated cardboard. The imposition on our parents and their home would soon extend far beyond the use of old office furniture.

We owe our parents a huge debt of gratitude. In the early days, they chauffeured us everywhere, taught us basic accounting, and offered in-kind donations, like frozen lasagna, which had a life expectancy of about four minutes. In the years ahead, my parents turned the entire house over to our fledging charity as office space, and they moved to the home that had belonged to our late grandfather. At our headquarters, pizza boxes stacked up like Lego towers; the backyard pool went wild and green and attracted frogs. It was a wonderful, chaotic place, a more charitable version of *Lord of the Flies*. Our parents turned their lives upside down for us. More than that, they gave us their trust and respect, enough to explore the world and our passions, something for which we will be forever grateful.

But I'm getting ahead of myself. The first turning point that grew us from a tiny after-school club to a global charity was a fateful trip. I harassed my mother until she let me travel to Southeast Asia to meet child laborers, and to find a charity on the ground that we could support.

"You're only 12," my mom had said with a sigh. "You've never even been on the subway alone, you're not going to Asia." It was classic mom logic. Eventually, after many months of pestering, finding a suitable chaperone in a family friend who was 25 at the time, and shoveling driveways to fund my journey (thank God for Canadian winters), Mom relented to the idea of me and our family friend visiting potential charity partners in Asia. That journey would have profound impacts on the rest of my life.

About seven weeks into my journey, I read in the newspaper that Canada's Prime Minister at the time, Jean Chrétien, was traveling to

Southeast Asia with a trade delegation. Our organization had twice asked Chrétien to meet with me to discuss child labor, to no avail. This time, our itineraries happened to match up. The newspaper had printed the name of Chrétien's hotel in Delhi, so we decided to write a letter to him and slide a photocopy under the door of

"You're only 12," my mom had said with a sigh. "You've never even been on the subway alone; you're not going to Asia."

every guest room, hoping to reach him. Before I made it to every floor, an amused security guard stopped me, but gave me the idea to hold a press conference. He explained that the trade delegation press corp was staying at the same hotel. Why not write them a letter instead? Looking back, I'm thankful for his cease and desist and his much better idea.

The next day, we found two dozen senior political reporters, curious about a Canadian kid who claimed to have something important to say. They looked every bit like journalists, with flip pads and equipment weighing them down. I spoke briefly, then introduced the child slaves that I had met during my travels. Mohan, a nine-year-old boy, had been working twelve-hour days in a carpet factory since the age of five. He told the press about going without food or bathroom breaks. He was often beaten for falling asleep on the job. Another boy, Nagashir, could barely speak from injury. He wasn't sure when he was sold into slavery at the factory, but he imagined he was around seven. Then 14, he told the story of an attempted escape—not for himself, but for his younger brother. They were both caught and badly beaten. Nagashir was branded with a hot iron. He lifted his arms and turned his neck to reveal the scars from where the iron had cinched his throat, making his speech painful and difficult.

It wasn't until a few days later, on the next stop in my travels in Karachi, Pakistan, when I learned that our impromptu news conference had caused a major stir, both with the Prime Minister and my mom. Already upset with me for not calling enough, Mom was shocked to see me at the top of every Canadian newscast and even CNN. Calling collect from Asia was a laborious process at the time, and it would be a few years yet before Internet cafés made their debut. When I finally called home, Mom had no time for small talk.

WE

It's our mission, our community, and our name.

Our purpose? WE makes doing good, doable.

WE is not a traditional charity with the old-school model of a one-off donation at tax time. The WE Movement makes changing the world part of everyday life.

Our social mission launched in 1995 when I was a 12-year-old cold-calling charities to ask how I could help. When "send money" was the only answer, we realized that people needed more accessible and meaningful ways to make an impact. Small actions could add up to big change, if only people knew what to do. We had an epiphany: to launch a movement of ordinary people and create a tidal wave of positive social impact through seemingly small, daily choices. Our mission was born: WE makes doing good, doable. No one—12 year olds or otherwise—would feel powerless.

WE became our driving mantra in the early 2000s. In 2006, we published Me to We: Finding Meaning in a Material World. *When the book became a* New York Times *bestseller, we realized that millions of people felt connected to WE.*

Today, the WE Generation is embracing choices that better the world. It is more than an age demographic, but a shift in perspective about our daily choices—how people give, shop, travel, live, work, and use technology. The WE Community is comprised of over four million people who actively engage with this movement every year through WE Schools, WE Families, WE Companies, and WE Living.

WE Charity helps people discover the causes they're passionate about to drive social change locally and globally. Our domestic programs in North America and the UK provide resources and support to enable millions to take action and make a difference in their communities, helping more than 2,500 charities. On a global scale, our WE Villages sustainable development model helps people lift themselves out of poverty in developing countries by providing education, water, health, food and opportunity. Our social enterprise ME to WE offers socially-conscious products and life-changing experiences which transform consumers into world-changers. All ME to WE products financially support the work of WE Charity, making a massive impact by giving back.

WE exists to help you on your own journey to change the world.

WE Families engages millions of parents, extended family, and children to teach the next generation to care and contribute.

WE Schools provides 15,000 partner schools with free, classroom-ready service learning programs and curriculum, and brings WE Day to cities around the world to celebrate young leaders.

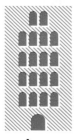

WE Companies partners with Fortune 500 companies, startups and mom-and-pop shops, offering turnkey programs that connect partners' employees and customers to causes.

WE Living empowers consumers at 12,000 partner retail stores with socially conscious products and experiences to better the world.

The WE Movement has hundreds of staff, as well as coaching resources to support you to take action on the service cause of your choice. WE also invites you to engage in our own local and global programs. For example, internationally, our WE Villages model enables sustainable development in Asia, Africa, and Latin America, empowering one million people around the world, and welcoming thousands of global volunteers.

We believe that people are looking for authentic, purpose-driven means to make a difference. Ever since a bunch of kids convened in the suburbs over twenty years ago, WE has empowered millions to make doing good, doable.

"Where are you!? I saw you on television—have you lost weight?! What have you eaten today?!"

After much reassurance from me, she followed up casually: "By the way, the Prime Minister is trying to reach you."

Talk about burying the lead.

It turns out that the next stop on my itinerary also happened to match with his. We met in Islamabad, and after a 15-minute conversation with the Prime Minister, he promised to raise the issue of child labor with the business delegation traveling with him, in addition to the President of Pakistan.

When I returned home, a crush of journalists waited at the airport. *60 Minutes* trailed me through my high-school cafeteria. Like a scene out of an old (pre-Internet) movie, the mail carrier delivered bags overflowing with letters of encouragement, and messages from other children who wanted to join this organization. Single dollar bills from allowance and birthday money were sent by kids who wanted to help. We soon had raised enough money to build a rehabilitation center for freed child slaves, along with 22 primary schools, in Asia.

Our tiny charity had started with a leap, but the real learning curve was still to come.

Schooled by Oprah Winfrey

The *Oprah Winfrey Show* asked me, at 16, to appear on an episode featuring young people making a positive difference in the world. Oprah, being Oprah, had prepared a surprise for each guest. I was introduced to a young New Jersey boy whose school had held a fundraiser; he presented me with a giant novelty check for US$3,378 to help build a school in Nicaragua. We both turned to Oprah to wrap up the segment.

"You know what?" she announced. "I want to build a hundred schools with you."

After interventions from lawyers who tried to dissuade her (she hadn't fully vetted us, yet she'd made a very public promise), Oprah had made up her mind. This would be her first major overseas investment. A few days later Marc and I flew back to Chicago to meet with Tim Bennett, the president of Harpo Productions at the time, who warned us: "You have no idea what's about to happen when this goes to air." Then he asked us three questions: "Do your schools have paraseismic engineers? Do you do currency hedges to make sure fluctuations don't affect the final price of your projects? Do you have a third-party governance and evaluation system in place?" Marc and I looked at each other—para-what? Clearly, we did not fully understand the power of Oprah. We had a passionate group of young people and the eyes of Oprah's viewers upon us, but we didn't really have the infrastructure to support her generosity. We quickly learned how Oprah ran her empire. She and her team were the ultimate business professionals, and in return for her investment, they acted like venture capitalists who expected us to grow and deliver scalable social change in a model similar to a successful tech company, not a fledgling charity.

Suddenly, we had the equivalent of what the for-profit industry would call "series A/B/C" funding rounds to secure world-class designers, builders, and engineers. Our school buildings have since survived earthquakes in Haiti and China. Marc and I reported to Oprah's board of directors, which she chaired, on risk assessment, cost evaluation, long-term sustainability—factors we didn't realize applied to charitable leadership but have since become hallmarks of all our programming. With me in high school and Marc a college undergrad, we were getting schooled at the unofficial Oprah Winfrey MBA program. At the time, it was all a bit terrifying. We would leave board meetings drenched in sweat and searching for a dictionary.

When we first stood in front of Oprah's team, we were kids, earnest young people with a desire to "help children." Although we had no shortage of good intentions, we quickly learned that it's much harder to achieve lasting impact. Over time, we understood the difference between doing good and making scalable, sustainable change. We learned how to act on the best strategies to streamline efficiencies and reduce costs to achieve the greatest impact-per-dollar, lessons and tips we'll discuss in Part Three.

In the beginning, before Oprah's intervention, we funded Bal Ashram, a counseling center for freed child slaves in Rajasthan, India. Raids meant descending on brick kilns or kicking down doors to back-alley factories to find dark rooms filled with bewildered children; rescue workers led them dazed into the sunshine. Our mission back then was to free child slaves, which we took fairly literally to mean removing them from the workplace. But when we started to "free" the same children again and again, sold back into slavery, we realized we'd become a stop-gap measure. After consultations with locals, we shifted tactics. We started to build and repair schools, in order to provide the skills and economic opportunities that would become alternatives to bonded labor and raids. Each new school was a cause for tremendous celebration. Every child in the village streamed through the doors and sat two and three to a desk waiting for class to start.

It was around this time that Oprah started to fund us, and challenged us to more rigorously measure the effectiveness of our programs. So when we returned to our schools months later on follow-up visits, we found empty seats. Girls were dropping out in virtually every country in which we worked. We could build a school, but we couldn't keep it filled with students.

In many developing communities, girls make daily treks to fetch water, often miles away, a task that can consume an entire afternoon— the school day. So we built rainwater catchment systems, dug boreholes, and installed water pumps next to our schools, so girls could attend class and return home with water.

Still, some of our best students missed long stretches of schooling. They were battling bouts of malaria or tuberculosis; others dropped out when their parents fell ill. This was the genesis of our health programming, which now includes mobile and permanent clinics and hospitals, along with wellness education.

Once we had full classrooms, some of our students couldn't focus. It's tough to solve science or math equations if you haven't eaten a proper meal in several days. Malnutrition in some of our overseas partner communities is extreme. We implemented school lunch programs and planted vegetable gardens on campuses, making agriculture and targeted drip irrigation part of the curriculum. Children now learn farming techniques at school from local specialists, taking the findings home to their parents' fields.

When people are healthy with full stomachs, free from the burden of carrying river water for miles, they have more time to work and provide for their families. Our final pillar of opportunity helped create alternative income programs, business education training, and community-led micro-loan groups. Tens of thousands of small businesses were seeded and grew, giving villages the tools to lift themselves out of poverty through employment.

We learned that we needed to help communities become sustainable and economically self-sufficient. With this five-pillar development model, partner communities become self-sufficient after about five years. It's not a hand-out, but a hand-up that breaks the cycle of poverty.

That watershed realization led to a cycle of constant innovation and learning. Eventually, we would further hone our geographic focus to countries in which we could make the most impact.

We have since realized that when it comes to doing work in developing countries, especially in some of the poorest and most politically challenging of the world, there is still much to learn. The hardest part of development is not identifying what works through research-driven models, but operating within cultural contexts that are often vastly different, and complicated by extenuating circumstances of dire poverty and weak rule of law.

We know, of course, that donor and business partners in the West expect charities to be run like solid businesses with efficiency, transparency, and sustainability. Building world-class processes and procedures in nations with nascent democracies is the most challenging aspect of our work, yet at the same time some of our most important.

The first 20 years of our international development work was focused on researching and developing the model to lift people out of poverty. The next 20 years will be focused on long-term succession planning, building local capacity, and scaling models for impact.

If any of these solutions seem obvious or to have appeared too quickly, keep in mind I've condensed years into a few hundred words. And at every stage, we got flak from consultants and old-school charity experts who warned us that our holistic model defied the 30-second charity soundbite plea to attract donors. Anything more is too complicated, they said. Tell people you just build wells. Tell people you just build schools. How could we do that, knowing that building schools isn't enough on its own to create sustainable change?

Oprah was the first to teach us that visionary philanthropists are acting more like venture capitalists, with more sophisticated goals and metrics. They are willing to listen, do their research, and they want more than a picture of a smiling child. They want measurable results: reduced infant mortality rates, increased graduation rates, and long-term economic improvement.

WE Charity by the Numbers[1]
North America and the United Kingdom*

15^K

15,000 WE Schools engaged in our service learning program.

3.4^M

3.4 million people involved in WE Schools, WE Families, and WE Companies.

40^M+

40+ million volunteer hours logged by students to earn their way into WE Day.

250^K

250,000 annually attend WE Day stadium celebrations, bringing together the movement in 16 stadiums.

Around the World

1,000

1,000 WE Villages schools and schoolrooms built around the world.

30^K

30,000 WE Villages businesses owned and operated by women around the world.

200^K

200,000 WE Villages children graduating primary school.

1^M

One million people in WE Villages with access to clean water and health care overseas.

*As of June 2017

With our global development programs on stable footing and continuing to rapidly grow, our senior team and I paused to consider the next step in our mission.

As we entered our 20s, we realized just how much we benefited from our journey. In addition to finding our purpose, we were fortunate to forge lasting friendships and develop relationships with life-long mentors. Marc and I weren't particularly close when we were younger given the nearly six-year age gap, but our love for our work brought us together to forge a deeper bond. People speak of helping others as a thankless task; I don't understand that, having experienced an incredible journey. We realized we wanted to share those same opportunities with others.

In countless conversations, I've heard that my own desires to better the world are far from unique. But it's not easy for people to meaningfully engage with the old-school model of charity that, for the most part, is just a transaction. We wanted to empower individuals to make a real difference through everyday actions. In many ways, it would be a gift for the next 12-year-old who encounters injustice and wants to help be that change.

We continue our WE Villages global development programs, but we've also launched initiatives closer to home. We started a program for families to help raise socially conscious children, called WE Families, because our parents were our biggest champions. We created one for teachers, WE Schools, to bring service learning into the classroom, since all of our educators—Mr. Fedrigoni especially—changed our lives. We built WE Companies to enable social impact because we believe business is responsible for doing good, and will benefit by embracing purpose.

Now people come to the WE Movement to discover their cause and take more meaningful actions with educational resources, global service travel opportunities, inspirational events, and socially responsible products that support causes. Every year, more than 2,500 charities are helped by the millions of people who engage with WE.

During the course of writing this book, people have asked me what a business might possibly learn from a charity: why include our story here? Any company could learn from a startup (okay, school club) that grew into an organization with over $50 million dedicated annually to charitable projects. More fundamentally, purpose is the lifeblood of charity, and we can teach you how to leverage the power of purpose to make incredibly far-reaching social impact—and in the process achieve your business goals, even surpass them.

Likewise, some in the nonprofit sector have questioned why they should reach beyond the traditional charity blueprint. When studying the most pressing social issues, the world does not need small change; it needs massive impacts. Charities and social enterprises can learn from certain corporations that have built models to exponentially scale positive change, leveraged technology as accelerators, and driven massive innovation to transform our daily lives.

Building the WE Movement taught us that business is not the opposite of charity. A well-run charity is similar to a well-run business, the difference being that a charity measures success not in terms of dollars, but lives improved.

Business is not the opposite of charity.

Oprah first taught us the power of cross-sector partnerships. Using the best elements of purpose and profit from both camps, it's a lesson we have since used to develop many successful inter-sector marriages, including with KPMG, Microsoft, Allstate, Virgin Atlantic and many others. Through these collaborations, we created massive impact on pressing social causes, while also helping our corporate partners achieve their business objectives. You'll read about many of these partnerships here, throughout this book.

Frequent Flier Finds His True North

That was my childhood, more or less. If I sacrificed the ordinary, it was for extraordinary adventures. I traveled to the Middle East to deliver school supplies to Bedouin children. In Taiwan, I lived for a time in a Buddhist monastery where every morning we converged at dawn on a central temple lit by hundreds of candles.

After six years of dodging and then delaying completion of high school because of global travels, I was anxious for the next phase of my life to begin. I decided to pursue peace and conflict studies at the

University of Toronto and, later, an executive MBA at Northwestern University's Kellogg-Schulich school of business to match Oprah's teachings. All the while, I volunteered full-time at WE (I was lucky to have full scholarships and fellowships throughout my undergraduate and postgrad studies). The organization is responsible for all the most important moments in my life. I first met my wife Leysa through WE Charity, and our friendship was built on our shared passion for social causes.

We started dating while she was living in New York, where she was working at Bellevue Hospital's Program for Survivors of Torture. She was pursuing her PhD in psychology, and I was crisscrossing the globe, making our time together rare and cherished. On our first official date, I took her to see the legendary Canadian poet and songwriter Leonard Cohen.

Our lives have never been normal; punctuated by my two failed attempts to propose due to flight cancellations. When I finally managed to get my act together, I spelled out "Will you marry me?" in flowers on the floor of my apartment, and I told her that no matter where I was in the world, she was home. Amazingly, she said yes.

Geography aside, Leysa and I have the most important things in common. We both work in the nonprofit sector and wrestle with our desire to make a positive impact around the world while trying to balance the need for a stable life—and a somewhat normal schedule. Finding that happy medium has recently been put into clearer focus as we welcomed our first child in the summer of 2017. Our boy Hilson was named after Leysa's great-great uncle, whose family immigrated to Canada from Ireland in 1810. More than 200 years ago, he established the now sixth-generation dairy farm where Leysa was born and raised. While we better understand the need for stability, we are more committed than ever to bettering the world our child will inherit.

"The way I saw it back then, society gave
two choices: I could harm the planet
at work and give back in my spare time,
or I could follow my dream of social impact
and forfeit job security."

FROM THE SLAUGHTERHOUSE TO SOCIAL ENTERPRISE

By Marc Kielburger

After a few detours, I was set to graduate from Oxford with a law degree. Debt weighed on me like a stack of used textbooks, and I was tired of eating instant ramen noodles atop furniture I'd rescued from the street. Thankfully, I was entertaining several job offers. I could accept the very lucrative gig I'd been offered by the jet set, or I could help run a small charity out of my parents' living room with my little brother. I mean this sincerely: it was one of the most difficult decisions of my life.

Most of my classmates were taking offers in Manhattan or London with Lehman Brothers, Goldman Sachs, or JPMorgan, heading up the kind of acquisitions chronicled in the *Wall Street Journal*. Others went to Silicon Valley and sold software to other companies that sell software, working on multimillion-dollar patents. In those days, everyone wanted to be Steve Jobs with more wardrobe variation. Meanwhile, our charity's entire staff fit into two rooms; everyone shared one phone line. It was a long way from Wall Street.

I'd been involved in the WE Movement from its earliest days. I'd written grant proposals, traveled to visit the U.S. Congress in Washington to denounce child labor, and led teens on volunteer trips to India and Kenya, where I taught my then 13-year-old brother how to drive a Land Rover as nearby elephants headed for the hills. On top of that, I'd spent my undergraduate tenure frequently flying home to Toronto from Harvard's Boston campus to help run the charity. Later, at Oxford, I condensed my law studies into shortened semesters so I could travel home as often as possible, keeping one foot on each continent. I was heavily invested in the charity's future, and a job there offered the kind of personal and professional values that I aspired to. But the pay was . . . well, there would be no pay. Taking up an official role with the charity would mean turning my back on the consensus definition of success.

Still, only one for-profit job offer had really tempted me. A U.S. multinational had launched a full-court press to get me to sign on as junior executive, flying me to and from New York, putting me up in swank hotels and taking me to five-star restaurants. But they wanted me to sell boxes. Literally—cardboard boxes. Despite slick job perks, I wouldn't be fulfilled by cardboard. I wanted to do something meaningful while I was still young, not wait until I was a rich, old box executive. Was that naïve? It struck me that creative fulfillment and "making a difference" at work wouldn't even have occurred to my grandparents' generation and, to a certain extent, to my parents'. There would have been no choice for them: take the well-paying but likely unrewarding job at the box factory. Find your purpose off the clock.

My generation has a different perspective on meaning at work and the impact of business. Mine was the first cohort to grow up with 24-hour news as an afterthought. CNN and its unceasing news cycle didn't launch until 1980, if you can believe it. As I grew up, information and technology expanded public awareness on an unprecedented scale, and increased transparency, both in terms of world issues and of corporate misgivings. We regularly discussed global events at the family dinner table, and I understood the pitfalls of traditional business as consumer boycotts gained media traction. Major brands had been raked over coals in the mid-1990s for using sweatshop labor, some of which had been my favorite logos as a teen. Many companies were destroying the very things needed to sustain them, and the public was starting to pay attention.

The way I saw it back then, society gave two choices: I could harm the planet at work and give back in my spare time, or I could follow my dream of social impact and forfeit job security. A decade or so later, this is still the prevailing value system, with purpose and profit treated like separate prospects. Back then, when I was weighing my career options, I wondered if it was possible to earn a living and support a family while changing the world, but pushed that notion out of my head as improbable.

What I know now is partly why we're writing this book. We believe in the power of business to make the world a better place. Companies, with their vast resources and networks, have an unparalleled ability to scale solutions. What if they could mass-produce solutions to the world's biggest problems? Business can be so much more than a do-no-harm mentality. In the WEconomy, we're borrowing the fine-tuned elements of corporate instruments, using each mechanism to move the needle on a pressing issue. If every company makes a social mission part of its core operating procedure, leveraging each and every asset, imagine the sheer weight of forces working for change. Every employee would feel connected to a cause larger than themselves, bigger than their company and part of the greater good. Purpose and profit wouldn't be two ends of the spectrum. No one would have to choose.

> *When leveraged properly, capitalism can be one of the greatest forces for social change.*

We believe in the power of business to make the world a better place.

It's starting to happen now. You can earn a living and change the world. And you can do it within the confines of your job. When leveraged properly, capitalism can be one of the greatest forces for social change. Further pushing this evolution, the emerging social enterprise sector can work like business, earning a profit with a core mandate to make the world better. Partly, this book is about finding more options across the spectrum of purpose and profit—to find meaning, make a decent living, and help change the world.

Of course, I couldn't articulate this as a wide-eyed youth in the suburbs.

Growing Up Kielburger

During my childhood in Thornhill, north of Toronto, we were expected to chip in as soon as we could hold a paintbrush. Our parents flipped properties before there was a cable channel devoted to the process—buy house, renovate, repeat. We were the only kids our age who became accomplished at painting, plumbing, and drywall, more familiar with the local Home Depot than with any of our childhood homes. Mom and Dad, both school teachers, believed firmly in the value of hard work and entrepreneurship.

When my mother, Theresa, was nine, her father died suddenly, leaving my grandmother Mimi to provide for the family. With just an eighth-grade education, Mimi cleaned houses to make ends meet. And when ends failed to meet, as they did one especially tough summer, the family was forced to live in a tent. One day, Mimi read about a local high school burning down, years of academic records destroyed by flames. Buried in the classifieds, she also spotted an opening for a secretarial job at one of her hometown's biggest employers, the Chrysler Corporation. Only high-school graduates were eligible. Lucky for my mother and her three siblings, Mimi had moxie. Mimi bought a typewriter and, painstakingly, taught herself to touch-type late at night and on her rare days off. Then she applied for the secretarial job. When asked about her high school credentials, Mimi replied, "Oh dear, did you hear about my high school burning down?" Her typing skills were so exceptional that no one had reason to doubt her. Eventually, Mimi worked her way up to head the secretarial department.

My dad, Fred, is the son of a German-Romanian immigrant who came to Canada with next to nothing during the Great Depression. A cook and a musician—my dad's dad could play eight or nine instruments—he didn't speak more than a few words of English. There weren't many job openings for foreign-language chefs or multi-instrumentalists. He literally fought to survive, boxing for money in what he described as "suicide matches." Eventually, he found work as a servant in Toronto's upscale Rosedale neighborhood, saving enough to open his own corner store. In more than 20 years, it closed for exactly one day, so the family could enjoy a brief holiday in Niagara Falls.

My parents feel the meaning of struggle and sacrifice in their bones. And like all parents, they wanted more for their children. Their own tough childhoods heightened that desire, and so they encouraged my brother and me to consider distinguished careers in medicine and law, respectively. At the same time, our parents have always been sensitive to the struggles of others. We will be forever grateful for the lessons in tough love and drywall repair, mixed with those about compassion for strangers. Before we were born, my mother left teaching for a few years to work as an outreach worker, helping homeless youth escape drugs, alcoholism, and prostitution. Dad volunteered one summer at the original L'Arche, a home for adults with developmental disabilities in Trosly-Breuil, France. He slept on the couch of the organization's visionary founder, Jean Vanier, who subsequently built L'Arche into a worldwide support network. But our parents didn't talk much about their own activism when we were young. In fact, as teenagers, we had no idea about this part of their past. It wasn't their style to tell us how to do it, and so we found our own way.

Water Boy to the Prime Minister

My path in grade school and in high school meandered toward service. It seemed to me, as a high school student anyway, that to change the world, I had to go into politics. I had always been fascinated by the power and drama of politics, and chose the University of Ottawa in the nation's capital, and the center of Canada's political arena, for the first year of my undergrad. I was thrilled to win one of 40 coveted spots in the House of Commons Page Program in Canada's Parliament.

Pages in Canada's House of Commons, akin to pages in U.S. Congress, ferry secret notes back and forth across the plush green carpet, and deliver water and stationery to Members of Parliament. It was important, we were told, that then–Prime Minister Jean Chrétien took his water without ice, while then–Finance Minister Paul Martin took his with ice. With all the shouting across the chamber, it was critical that each politician have his or her throat moistened to an exacting standard. The work was hardly glamorous, but it did afford an intimate view of the cut and thrust of politics. And there was one other job perk.

Roxanne Joyal was a page from Winnipeg, Manitoba; a striking, brilliant young woman with a fiery French-Canadian accent who wouldn't give me the time of day. I managed to insert myself into her life by dating her roommate. My plan to woo her makes me sound like the antihero in a Woody Allen movie, I know, but it must have worked because she agreed to marry me years later.

After we'd been dating awhile, Roxanne and I took a break from our studies to volunteer in Bangkok, a shock to the senses with its landscape of gold-plated skyscrapers dotted with forests of construction cranes. Klong Toey, the district where I lived, was a maze of densely packed streets; people spilling onto sidewalks from dark, misshapen houses fashioned from shipping crates and corrugated tin. The neighborhood was known as "the slaughterhouse," named after the abattoir in the stretch of slum next to the Chao Praya River. Sometimes I lay awake at night listening to the pigs screaming in their final moments. During the day I volunteered at Bangkok's only free hospice for AIDS patients. Roxanne was stationed in another part of Klong Toey, where she worked with new mothers with HIV and AIDS. At the time, AIDS did not officially exist in Thailand. Those dying of the disease were referred to only as the "very sick." For six months, I held the hands of patients as they took their final breaths, consumed by an unspoken illness. The work was emotionally exhausting and infuriating. I was enraged at the thousands of deaths that were being ignored by the government, and resolved to learn everything I could about HIV/AIDS prevention and support.

Inspired by my trip, I moved closer to my purpose. With a full scholarship, I veered from politics and transferred into the international development program at Harvard University. Looking back, this was a further step away from the traditional corporate route toward an exciting, if uncertain, career path in the charitable sector. I knew I couldn't spend my life selling boxes, even if I was well-paid to do so.

Enterprising for Good

At law school across the pond in Oxford, it was easier for me to travel to the expanding WE Charity projects in Africa, which I visited frequently. No place struck me more than Sierra Leone, which is the most damaged country we've ever worked in. An 11-year civil war fueled by blood diamonds brought terror to every corner of the tiny West African nation. Thousands of boys, some as young as seven and eight, were forcibly recruited to the rebel ranks. Those who refused had a hand chopped off to stop them from fighting for the enemy. Young girls were taken as war brides. As the civil war approached its end, our organization began to build and repair schools, but reading and writing took a back seat to more remedial lessons. Kids with prosthetic limbs were taught how to hold pencils. If a book fell to the floor with a thud, students would collapse in tears or dive under desks, the sound like gunfire, a trigger for PTSD.

"A little bit of good can turn into a whole lot of good when fueled by the commitment of a social entrepreneur."

—Jeff Skoll

Two years into our work there, everything changed. Then-U.S. President George W. Bush had launched an aerial strike in Afghanistan in response to the 9/11 terrorist attacks. A huge amount of aid was poised to flood into that country. Sierra Leone was old news, and NGOs were preparing to ship out en masse for the next stop on their global poverty tour. Many had no choice. Governments and media lurch from crisis to crisis, and donation dollars follow. As ships streamed out of port, we worried about our own projects in the face of news cycles and fleeting attention spans. We are not an emergency aid organization. Our model is built to last, and to withstand the whims of governments and media attention spans with sustainable, community-driven projects. But it takes time, an average of five years, to build relationships so that locals can sustain projects, taking them over from our team— education, health care, clean water, increasing crop yields for farmers, and small job creation. Real change requires a lasting commitment and investment.

We sought the guidance of a long-time mentor: Jeff Skoll. We first met Jeff in Los Angeles through a mutual friend who wanted to produce a film about WE's founding story. At the time, Jeff was at work on his fledgling film company. He had helped build eBay, and used his newfound wealth to launch The Skoll Foundation and the

Social Enterprise: A Not-So-Clear Consensus

Social enterprise is a relatively new term for a model that, depending on your definition, can be traced back centuries. Broadly, it is a blurring of the line between business and charity, using commercial strategies to solve social problems. Of course, that could mean anything.

We've narrowed the definition of a social enterprise to a business that generates revenue through sales of products and services with the fundamental purpose to make the world better.

Allow me to explain why we feel this way.

There are many great, ethical companies. The Body Shop is a socially conscious company, but its foremost driving goal remains profitability for its publicly traded parent company, Natura. This is a traditional business.

Similarly, there are high-performing charities that earn revenue through sales, like the Salvation Army—but it also receives donations and tax breaks. Legally, it remains a charity.

A small number of countries have started to build legal designations for social enterprises, allowing these entities to access the traditional capital of business, but granting special incentives to enable their purely social mission.

Perhaps the world's most famous social enterprise is Grameen Bank, a for-profit that seeks to provide micro-credit to lift people out of poverty. It was founded by Muhammad Yunus, Nobel Peace Prize winner.

This same value set is applied at ME to WE

In sum, social enterprise is a hybrid sector, the love child of charity and business.

As more and more innovation is spurred by social challenges, social enterprise could be the future of both capitalism and social impact.

Skoll Centre at Oxford University, both devoted champions of social entrepreneurs, as well as the annual Skoll World Forum on Social Entrepreneurship.

Jeff told us about the origins of his high-octane philanthropy, that he'd donated to traditional charity after coming into wealth. But after spending tens of millions without proof of positive impact, the entrepreneur in him grew frustrated. So he started asking for proof of returns on his donations, like a social impact investment.

We told Jeff about our Sierra Leone problem and, candidly, quietly, hoped that he might solve our funding shortfall with a donation. Instead, Jeff asked a series of questions that had a far more profound and long-lasting impact on our social mission: "Between you, you have a law degree and an MBA, correct?" We nodded, unsure why that mattered. Neither of us was a practicing lawyer or corporate executive.

Jeff pointed out that with our educational background, we should be able to come up with a solution. He told us that our funding challenges in Sierra Leone were only a symptom of a larger problem in the economics of the charitable sector.

Most charities struggle for stable revenue, and this limits their ability to invest in the most effective long-term projects. The entire sector is often unable to scale because donors don't want to dedicate resources to accelerators like technology or research and development of new impact models. Jeff challenged our longstanding assumptions that the business world makes the profits and then shares a little extra with a beholden charitable sector. He cautioned us that the charitable sector was often caught in a cycle of wasteful fundraising techniques, like for-profit firms that take up to 90 cents on the dollar for mass mailings, telemarketers, street canvassers, and those Sunday morning commercial pleas to send money.[1]

As social entrepreneurs, we could create financial sustainability for our projects. We were missing untapped opportunities by limiting ourselves to only traditional charitable models. Jeff planted the seed for a socially conscious revenue driver.

Over the years, we had dedicated profits from our book sales and speaking honorariums to fund the charity. With Jeff's coaching, we

ME to WE by the Numbers[2],*

20^K

Travelers

20,000 travelers to development projects in communities around the world.

140^K

Students

140,000 students receive leadership training annually.

1,500

Artisans

1,500 women entrepreneurs in Africa and South America employed full-time as artisans.

10^M

10 million social impacts funded and delivered through product purchases, including clean water and school supplies.

$13^M

$13 million in cash and offsetting in-kind donations to WE Charity.

*As of 2017

decided to build on these early revenue models to launch a fully fledged social enterprise, a type of business that doesn't have a developed national framework in Canada, although it's a model used throughout the UK and the U.S.

As the early catalyst, Skoll agreed to become our backer and provide the startup funds. We codified a series of founding principles to ensure that ME to WE Social Enterprise would always exist to serve a social mission. Most important, ME to WE would donate half of its profits to WE Charity, and reinvest the other half to grow the social enterprise by launching new ventures to increase the overall impact. ME to WE has one simple purpose: to better the world.

Since ME to WE couldn't ever go public on the stock exchange like a traditional company, we joke that in exchange for his funds, Jeff got "stock options in a better world." We were unbelievably lucky to find someone who didn't care about monetary returns—only rigorous, evidence-based social impact (more on this later). We cannot sufficiently express our deep gratitude for his social commitment, as Jeff redefined the term "angel investor." He joined our board of directors, injecting precision and reporting governance in addition to funds. With Jeff's championing, we set ambitious goals to generate revenue for WE Charity to scale impact, achieve stable funding, and invest in the hardest-to-fundraise-for projects in remote countries around the world. To achieve this vision, we started with global travel and socially conscious retail.

ME to WE Trips, one of these ventures, now operates in six countries, where thousands of individuals, school groups, corporate teams, and families travel with us each year to engage in cultural immersion and eco-friendly travel. In the pink hills of India's Aravalli Mountains, you'll be welcomed into village homes to make chapatti with the local women. In the Amazon's cloud forest in Ecuador, you'll visit a cocoa farmer to help with the harvest. In Kenya's Maasai Mara, you'll walk with the mamas to the Maasai River to collect water. WE has an ongoing partnership with each community, so travelers are welcomed like friends and partners in social impact, not temporary visitors.

Inspired by Jeff's early guidance, every ME to WE project is filtered through two lenses. First, it must do good in the world in and of itself. For instance, we create jobs in our trip locations, where we need local architects and engineers, chefs, drivers, interpreters, and guides. And second, it must make money to fund the organization's charitable projects. Revenue from trips is funnelled back into WE Charity to fund development projects in those same communities. Every trip participant is part of the sustainable development process; you do good just by staying with us. Not only by mixing cement and laying bricks for a new school or water project, but because the cost of your trip itself helps to fund the very same projects you're building.

Our social enterprise helped solidify the idea of purpose and profit, or in our case revenue, coming together to change the world.

Within seven years of starting up, more than $13 million in cash and offsetting in-kind donations has gone to support the charity (for instance, ME to WE pays the rent for WE Charity offices). This financial prop keeps our charity administration rate as low as possible, at an average of 10 percent, meaning 90 percent of every public donation dollar goes directly to the projects—a very efficient rate given the average among U.S. charities of our size is 25 percent spent on administration and fundraising.[3] Most important, we're able to invest in key drivers like measurement, research, and continuous project improvement. This financial stability allows us to plan for the long term to achieve the greatest, most sustainable impact.

With our model in place and running successfully, we had solved a problem for the charity and opened a new door for me and our senior staff.

From day one, many of the original founding team, along with Craig and I, had decided never to take a salary from WE Charity, even though we dedicate most of our time and efforts to growing the charity's impact. Like many who want to work in the social impact sector, we struggled with the idea that we didn't want to be a financial burden. We so deeply believed in our mission that we wanted as much of the money raised as possible to go directly to our projects.

Without a salary, we embarked on some very thoughtful planning about how to sustain ourselves. While in university, Craig and I pulled many all-nighters applying for every scholarship and fellowship available to cover our studies and campus living expenses. When we graduated, we faced some difficult choices between following our passions or managing to pay the bills.

Our parents' own childhood hardships made them fiercely committed to social justice, with a belief that serving the most vulnerable is life's highest calling. When they achieved financial success through their real-estate entrepreneurship, they paid it forward—for us and for WE.

After our studies, as Craig and I struggled to continue with the charity, we had a series of heartfelt conversations with our parents that we'll never forget, and for which we're forever grateful.

They offered to assist us, to the best of their ability, by supporting our life calling. They decided to unlock our early inheritance, and committed to providing financial support over the years through small acts and larger gifts, such as our first mortgage down-payments.

Our parents have always been our greatest champions and most generous benefactors, both personally and professionally. From the earliest days when they moved out of our childhood home so that our office could move in, to their continued support, we are forever indebted.

Years later, with ME to WE growing, Craig and I felt for the first time that we could start drawing a salary from the revenue generated by the social enterprise. This gave us the security to continue our own career paths in social impact and still allow us to start our own families.

Reflecting on my journey, I'm aware that I have been privileged to benefit from a mix of exceptionally supportive parents, opportunity, hard work, and luck. My grandfather used to say that capability is spread more evenly than opportunity, meaning that everyone can succeed, if given the chance. I'm very aware that there are so many other people whose incredible skills and dedication would benefit the purpose sector. It's odd, perhaps even unfair, to think that changing the world for the better has not been considered an esteemed career, but something that should be done as volunteers or for a pittance. Craig and I have seen our friends reluctantly leave the nonprofit sector for more lucrative careers so they can buy a house and start a family. We've also seen how hard it is to recruit talented employees when nonprofit salaries are so modest, and so many young people are overburdened trying to pay off college debt. We want the best, brightest, and most dedicated to form lifelong careers out of solving the world's foremost challenges.

That's why we started the WE Incubation Hub, to support young social entrepreneurs. We don't want future generations to have to struggle so hard to marry purpose with profit. It connects young social entrepreneurs with the accelerators of space, mentorship, technology, and venture capital. We support them to scale the best new ideas to tackle the world's foremost challenges such as hunger, poverty, and climate change.

Entering my forties, I may not have the fancy corner office of a cardboard box executive, but I have personal gratification, stability, and other job perks. My family travels with me to our projects, and together we've been around the world. My girls already have an appreciation for other cultures and an extended family in Kenya. My oldest, Lily-Rose, speaks a few words of Swahili with a Kenyan accent. Take Your Daughter to Work Day is a whole lot more interesting than it might have been.

How many hoops do you have to jump through to do a good thing?

The answer is: We hope fewer, thanks to our struggles.

A charity that starts a business to support itself was an idea that was ahead of its time—too far ahead, as it turned out, for some governments to process. Earning revenue to offset costs ran completely counter to the long-standing concept of a "nonprofit."

In the United Kingdom, charities can form separate for-profit trading companies to generate revenue to meet charitable goals. But in other countries, like ME to WE's home of Canada, not only was social enterprise a new concept, there were simply no regulatory models for us to follow.

Two of Canada's top law firms, Torys and Miller Thomson, were willing to help us, pro bono. Together we worked to establish a legal structure governance model and reporting requirements.

For added checks, the model was reviewed by a retired Supreme Court justice and a former Canadian Prime Minister and his law firm.

In the end, the law firms told us that the costs of these services would have reached hundreds of thousands of dollars (did I mention we're really grateful for that donated time?).

Here's the deal: We did it, but it shouldn't have been that hard.

With public donations and charitable transfers from governments both in steady decline, social enterprises are trying to fill the void and provide a stable source of funding to create innovative, sustainable solutions to the world's most pressing challenges.

We need to fundamentally change our thinking, and that of our governments, when it comes to how we view organizations that set out to solve some of the world's biggest and most persistent challenges.

Governments around the world have an obligation to work with social entrepreneurs to establish reasonable legal and taxation frameworks to approve social enterprises and encourage their development and growth. While the UK is coming around quickest, all countries—particularly Canada and the U.S.—need to do more to facilitate and support the social enterprise sector.

PURPOSE AT WORK: WHY BUSINESS SHOULD GET INVOLVED

By Craig Kielburger, Holly Branson, and Marc Kielburger

Now that you know a bit more about us, our career paths, and our childhoods, you're probably wondering about your own personal and professional journey to purpose and profit.

Not everyone can leave a day job on principle or pack up and move to Bangkok to volunteer, and luckily, you don't have to. Maybe you want to inject a social mission into your business, as long as it doesn't hurt the bottom line. Maybe you want to change the world, but can't afford to spend all your time volunteering (that's why everyone wants to be Oprah and not Mother Teresa—the vow of poverty is less appealing). There's no shame at either end of the scale; but today, everyone is searching for some combination of money and meaning.

In Part Two, we'll prove that purpose is good for you and good for business. Some of the world's biggest brands are implementing social missions that boost bottom lines, and we've chronicled a variety of them here. (We'll also draw from the companies and social missions we know best—our own). These case studies can be used as blueprints to help your organization. They'll provide the ammunition you need to convince your stakeholders and colleagues that purpose pays. If you're an entry-level employee, we'll show you how to inject purpose into your current job to get more meaning from your nine-to-five while advancing your career.

The corporate landscape is already shifting as companies start to compensate for social problems. Businesses don't thrive unless their ecosystems thrive, and not just in the environmental sense. Companies need solid roads for supply routes; they need to raise capital through secure banking systems. Functioning electrical grids power factories and the education system brings talent into the pipeline. Today, companies are waking up to the fact that business not only relies on this infrastructure, but should be responsible for its welfare.

No company is an island, immune to the systems that keep society functioning.

The WEconomy is about bettering this ecosystem. Companies can no longer do the bare minimum, maintaining only the systems they directly rely on. They must consider the planet's limited resources, the welfare of their workforces, and how savvy customers will react to shortcuts that do harm. It's now the responsibility of traditional companies to use their resources and scalability to solve some of the world's biggest problems. By extension, individual employees now have the chance to flex their personal values on company time. Business is clamoring for the kind of innovators we'll highlight. You can be one, too.

But first: Why now? And why you?

Now More Than Ever, We Can Afford to Care

In the West, we live in an age of relative prosperity. Once upon a time, not that long ago, Americans dreamed of a "chicken in every pot"— the prospect of families eating meat at least once a week. Today, there's a fried chicken franchise on every corner. With massive wealth creation in the West, the basic survival motive has been satiated for a rapidly growing middle class. The Brookings Institution estimates that 1.8 billion people globally belong to this middle class, and it expects that number to rise to 3.2 billion by the end of 2020, and 4.9 billion by 2030.[1] Of course, we're oversimplifying, as wealth distribution and a gap between rich and poor, even in the West, is a significant and growing problem. But for a large part of the middle class, motivations have changed along with consumption habits and resource investments. This new workforce is looking for more than a paycheck. Now more than ever, they can afford to care. And businesses can't afford not to care.

As consumers and employees, now more than any other time in modern history, we can afford to think about how we shop and where we work in terms of the greater good.

We Want Our Voices to Be Heard

Social consciousness is seeping into the work and home lives of students, digital natives, mid-career professionals, and baby boomers alike. Because of social media and the unprecedented access to information, ordinary people are more enabled than ever before. We call them WE Generation—spanning all age demographics and professions, these are the people connected by the desire to make a difference—rather than birth order. They want to be the heroes of their own stories in which they right the wrongs they see in the world. Whether taking an action as small as clicking their signature onto an online petition, or purchasing an eco-friendly product, people today feel empowered to effect change. They don't trust governments or faceless corporations to fix the world's problems; they want to be part of the solution themselves, in every aspect of their lives.

In the WEconomy, employees want to find more meaning at work, and consumers want to spend their dollars on companies that not only care, but that are working to make a difference. Shareholders are demanding profits and social impact.

Increasingly, workers demand that their jobs and their companies reflect their values. They no longer accept the model of clocking in just for a paycheck, then giving part of that income to charity or religious groups, expecting them to address the world's social challenges. They want to make their mark by adding a social mission right into their workday, and by giving back through their purchasing and consumption habits. Studies show that workers, especially young workers, are willing to take a pay cut for a position that packs a purposeful punch. Companies will have to adapt to these new motivations that have employees using their day jobs to support causes, or risk losing top talent—and a huge customer base.

CEOs today want to be seen as titans of business, but also as champions of social causes in their communities and among their peers. And increasingly, business people want to create companies that do good. Elon Musk could have sat on his PayPal fortune and never been heard from again. But he wanted to change the world for the better—and so we have Tesla and SolarCity and talks of colonizing Mars. Bill Gates could still be rolling out Windows updates, but instead we have the Bill and Melinda Gates Foundation.

The Most Connected Time in History

The past four decades have seen unprecedented leaps forward in the dissemination and availability of information. CNN, the first network to run a 24-hour news cycle, launched in 1980. Now we have FOX, BBC, MSNBC, Al Jazeera, and countless other networks bombarding us with an endless stream of problems from around the globe.

The Internet has only been widely available in the West since the late 1990s, yet its impact on how we live our daily lives is incalculable. Beyond changing almost every aspect of how we work, interact, travel, date, and shop, the information age has created a generation that is plugged into social and environmental issues like never before.

We are constantly plugged into an ever-changing, confusing, and at times frightening world. Democratic decisions made by disaffected voters around the world have plunged us into an era of uncertainty and, for many, intense anxiety.

With the onslaught of information comes empowerment. The capacity of one individual to influence positive change is stronger than it has ever been.

Divisive and aggressive rhetoric are the norm on many political stages and an overriding sense of unease dominates the news media landscape. But with the onslaught of information comes empowerment. The capacity of one individual to influence positive change is stronger than it has ever been. The ways in which people achieve purpose are changing and expanding as our compassion grows for a global community made smaller every day. When you experience the world through your smartphone, you see boundaries differently; it's easier to view your own identity within this global context, and to feel more connected to the world and its problems.

The technology revolution has made it easier to speak out, mobilize, and rally millions of people around the world. Just look at #BlackLivesMatter, #Pride, or the historic Women's Marches in January 2017. By coming together across diverse groups and setting aside individual agendas, we can stem the tide of negativity.

This sense of global community now extends to brand identification and purchase decisions. If we want to see ourselves as agents of change, we want that reflected in the brands we buy, and in our own curated lives on social media. Shoppers vote with their dollars for products packed with positive impact. Consumer surveys show that, price and quality being equal, brand loyalties lie with a company's social and environmental mission.

People flock to social media to praise people and companies that do good—or call out the ones who don't. Careers and companies can be decimated overnight by Twitter campaigns or Facebook warriors. And yes, people love to share their own good deeds or impactful purchases. As a business, this presents a huge opportunity for free advertising that resonates far more with consumers than a 30-second TV commercial.

Purpose must be factored into the economy to account for our changing attitudes and expectations of companies.

What Does It All Add Up To?

So we can afford to care more than ever, we want our voices to be heard more than ever, and we live in the most connected era in human history. How do we leverage this knowledge to improve our lives, improve our job satisfaction, get promoted, and make our businesses more profitable—all while contributing to the greater good?

Those are the questions we're going to answer here, in Part Two.

In the chapters ahead, we'll show you how world-leading companies have used purpose as a launch pad to build new products, differentiate in a competitive market, increase employee engagement, and secure more loyal brand ambassadors. If you're leading a company, here's your purpose incentive. If you're an employee looking to shake things up at your office, here's a blueprint to take to your boss. If money and meaning are what you're after, adapt purpose to your current role by appealing to the company's best interests. Make the business case for your current employer. Show how injecting more social purpose into your nine-to-five will benefit your company.

We will help you succeed in this new normal.

The Water Cooler: Get to know the players

Baby Boomers born between 1946 and 1960

- *Delayed their retirements to pay for their kids' college tuition, or took positions with more flexibility. Regardless, they are still at work.*

- *Reinvented retirement by shifting to part-time positions—career makeovers that cater more to interests and values as they start to think about legacies, both professional and personal.*

- *Many volunteer in their free time or take positions on charitable boards.*

Gen Xers born 1961 to 1980

- *A powerful force for a purpose-driven economy. And they're running things.*

- *In 2014, 68 percent of Inc 500 companies were run by Gen Xers.[2]*

- *Time magazine called Gen Xers "the future of work," with the first of their cohort turning 50 in 2015, and the average age of an S&P 1500 CEO being—you guessed it—50.*

- *This cohort volunteers more than any other generation.*

Incoming generations—Millennials born 1981 to 1995 and Gen Z born after 1995

- *They will withhold their talents and spending power from companies that don't live up to their expectations.*

- *60 percent of Gen Zers want jobs that have a social impact.*

- *They are 'entrepreneurial' (72 percent want to start their own businesses) and community-oriented (26 percent already volunteer).[3]*

- *They now number some two billion worldwide.[4]*

- *They are the most educated generation in history.[5]*

"If you embed purpose in
the very DNA of your business, the
rewards can be invaluable."

PURPOSE 101

By Holly Branson

"Even if we launch Virgin Sport and it doesn't make any money— it really doesn't matter."

"I don't understand what you mean, Richard.? Why would we launch a business and not care if it makes money or not!? No offense, but that doesn't make business sense."

This is an actual conversation between my husband and my dad in South Africa a couple of years ago. They had just competed in Cape Town Cycle Tour, the largest timed cycling event in the world. Dad and Freddie had an amazing few days cycling hard, more than 100 kilometers through mountainous Cape Town, and the rest of the family joined them to cheer them on.

Freddie was buzzing; he's always loved sports, and is always training for something—the next Strive Challenge, the next triathlon. He has the bug, big time! He'd often wondered why Virgin didn't have a business under our Health and Wellness arm to put on these incredible events. Surely they were huge moneymakers. Having come from a suit-and-tie job in the financial heart of London, Freddie was still coming to terms with how to do business the Virgin way, which is much less rigid and formal. So when he discussed his idea with Dad, he was shocked by the response. Freddie tells it better than I can:

"Richard said: 'Don't make it about the money. There's got to be a reason you're setting up this company, an underlying issue you're trying to tackle.'"

Easy to say when you own a hugely successful global brand and don't have to worry about money, right? But Dad has been a believer in purpose and passion as the driving force for business since his very first venture, before he made a single penny.

Freddie admits he never truly believed in the concept until he launched Virgin Sport.

"I always thought the reason for starting a company was to make a phenomenal business out of it; to make money. But when we set up Virgin Sport, we knew that our purpose would be absolutely vital to getting it right. We listened to Richard and made it our first priority to agree on our purpose. It changed and evolved, but ultimately became: Inspiring People to be Fit, Active, and Healthy. It defined our business model and strategy. I know that Virgin Sport will be successful financially, because putting purpose at its core has made it a valuable business proposition and investment opportunity. Don't you just hate it when your father-in-law is right?"

What Is Purpose?

When you think just two decades ago, corporate social responsibility meant writing a check for the local little league team—a nice gesture, but hardly enough. Now the acronym CSR is banned at Virgin Management Ltd., because it hearkens back to the days of a single office or unlucky person tasked with reversing the negative effects of big business on the planet—sort of an apology for turning all of Earth's resources into products. For the longest time, business has used resources as if they were limitless, with no consideration for the environment or for what it might mean for future generations. But resources are running low, and companies are already feeling the burden on their supply chains. This is more obvious for those in manufacturing, and more challenging for those in the services sector, who don't build products out of raw

Virgin's Purpose Pointers

What purpose is:

- Why you exist—the role and meaning you have in people's lives
- Enduring—a much longer-term view
- Insight-driven and co-created
- Distinctive and differentiated
- Aligned with values and incentives
- Embedded in every aspect of the business
- A driver for all decisions
- Something all employees have a role to play in delivering
- A compass when making difficult decisions
- A driver for innovation

What purpose is not:

- How and what you do
- An annual plan or quarterly campaign
- A strapline that is not informed by key insights
- Desirable, rather than essential
- An afterthought when decision making
- Solely a leadership initiative
- A separate project or business unit
- Something you discard when times are tough
- About maintaining the status quo

Purpose statements:

Patagonia

Build the best product, cause no unnecessary harm, use business to inspire, and implement solutions to the environmental crisis

Unilever

To make sustainable living commonplace

Tata

To improve the quality of life of the communities we serve

Google

To organize the world's information and make it universally accessible and useful

Virgin

Changing business for good

WE

Making doing good, doable

Tesla

To accelerate the world's transition to sustainable energy

Microsoft

To empower every person and every organization on the planet to achieve more

materials, to understand. But if you're in retail and believe dwindling resources don't affect you, you're wrong. Today, myriad companies should be examining every link in their supply chains, measuring environmental impacts to improve efficiencies, and leveraging core skills and assets to move the needle on social change. They can do all of this and make a profit.

In the WEconomy, purpose is your barometer for the greater good. Where does your business fit into your local and global community? Does it help or harm it? How does the welfare of the community shift the priorities of the company? Does the welfare of the community even register as a priority? Ask the same question about the welfare of your most valuable asset—your workforce. If your "purpose barometer" swings toward the negative—you know you need to take steps within your company to reverse that trend. Part of a company's mission today must involve social purpose, both for the greater good and for the good of the business. This bears repeating, because it's important: social purpose should be embedded in the business model as much as any other value proposition.

Before you raise an eyebrow, know that we're not peddling magic beans. We have proof that purpose is a value proposition. We've gathered case studies, many from our own partnerships and experiences and many from other leading organizations around the world, that show how firms of all sizes have implemented and profited from purpose. We'll show how companies now employing the triple bottom—people, planet, purpose—have saved money in a whole range of industries with razor-thin margins. The Royal Bank of Canada (RBC) appealed to a young demographic rarely seen walking into financial institutions by processing pennies during a nationwide charitable coin drive. This purpose drove 55,000 unique customer walk-ins through the doors of the bank.

Purpose is also good for individual workers. Even if you don't run your company—and your boss's boss only speaks to you to ask for a coffee—purpose can be a form of personal development, a method to advance your career and build social capital at work. What better way to create meaning in what you do every day? What better way to nab attention from the higher-ups than with leadership on a program that's good for the planet and good for business? Executives love to celebrate those types of initiatives in a public way. And when you make the boss look good, you look good—you get noticed, you get access to senior leaders. Here we'll show you why companies and employees should be solving social problems at the office.

Purpose is the new currency; it's one of the greatest untapped forces in the for-profit world. Without purpose, your business model is incomplete.

In a nutshell, No. 1 on your agenda should be "Define Your Purpose." This is a fairly new concept. Embedding purpose into the very DNA of your business is, for now, still an emerging paradigm.

Still, it was only about 70 years ago that more than just a handful of companies started to talk about the importance of branding. Today, if you don't have a brand, you don't have a business.

It was only 40 years ago that "people metrics" were being considered in company performance and much more recently that the well-being of people was factored into company performance and therefore the bottom line.

In the words of my Dad: "Happy staff result in happy customers, and happy customers result in happy shareholders."

We predict that within a decade "Purpose" will sit alongside "Brand" and "People" as the three most important principles guiding the launch of new companies and business models.

So where to start?

> *"Your Purpose encapsulates why you exist. It drives every decision your business makes. Your people live and breathe it, and over time it will be the reason your customers keep coming back. Get your Purpose right and it will secure business health, profitability, and future value."*
>
> —Charlotte Goodman

Purpose 101 (the Virgin Way)

Embedding purpose into the business was an interesting journey for us at Virgin and, at times, far from easy. Historically, Virgin has always launched businesses to champion the consumer, introducing competition and breaking up monopolies and duopolies to bring fairness and value. But we knew we could do it better. We knew if we got it right, we would be one of the first companies to say that people, purpose, and planet truly described our brand.

LESSON **01**: INVEST

It all starts with People. You have to throw resources (financial and talent) to develop, grow, and sustain your purpose. If you continue to think of it as CSR—as someone's part-time job performed over their lunch hour—you'll get nowhere fast. Purpose should not sit within a separate department, but rather be at the heart of everything your company does. The talent driving your purpose should have access and influence within every department, work stream, and member of staff within your organization. That's the most effective way to ensure your purpose is the lifeblood of your business. We were lucky—we had Jean Oelwang and Charlotte Goodman and their team at Virgin Unite, our foundation. We didn't force this on an unwilling or unsuspecting group— we devoted some of our best, most passionate, and inspired people to the task of putting purpose first. We called them the Business Innovation and Purpose Team. In the beginning, their role was to spur Virgin companies to think more about their impact in local communities and the wider world, and to leverage the power of their staff to ensure that impact was positive. The team was there to encourage the businesses to think bigger than a one-year partnership with a local charity, to get them thinking creatively about impact on a bigger scale, with longer time horizons, and to leverage all assets of the business—including all partnerships. Here is where the magic truly happens—when you devote an entire team and its resources to finding a purpose that fits your core business model. Having the right people holding the wand will make all the difference.

As you and your team start to articulate your purpose, it may help to ask the following questions to get your purpose juices creatively flowing:

- *Does it articulate why you exist?*

- *Does it capture the essence of your business?*

- *Does it emotionally engage people?*

- *Is it simple, distinctive, and differentiating?*

- *Does it explain a big, bold ambition?*

- *Does it highlight the positive change you will create?*

- *Will it stand the test of time?*

- *Does it lend itself to driving every decision you make as a business?*

Take Virgin Money (VM, our bank), one of the first Virgin companies to embrace purpose and run with it. VM distilled their purpose statement down to three simple words: "Everyone better off." Everyone consists of their five Cs: Community, Colleagues, Corporate partners, Customers, and Company. The company won't make a single decision unless they determine all five Cs stand to benefit. A few more examples of clear and simple purpose statements are Virgin Mobile Australia's "Making Mobile Better" and Virgin Hotels' "Everyone Leaves Feeling Better." You don't need to overthink it; a purpose statement should be concise and punchy. Don't confuse it with your business mission statement; this is your clear and defined purpose statement.

A quick example of how Virgin Money implemented their purpose statement is to look at how they tackled their sponsorship of the London Marathon (that comes under C for Community). At the time, many of the millions raised by the London Marathon were processed through an online donation site, JustGiving, a for-

30 percent of a company's value is based on its relationship with society.

—McKinsey

Where to start?

Writing a purpose statement can be a challenge. Charlotte Goodman, the Virgin Group's director of Changing Business for Good, advises you start with the following steps:

Insight is everything: The first step in articulating your purpose is to consider your stakeholders— employees, partners, and customers. Find out why they think your business exists, what they think would make your business stand out from the crowd, and what role they think your business can play in people's lives now and in the future. A critical and forensic insight is absolutely key to helping truly differentiate your proposition and your purpose.

Bring your senior team on board: Senior buy-in is essential. Make the case for purpose by demonstrating the long-term benefits. Involve senior team throughout the process so they can lead the effort across the company. Remember, while leadership is critical, everybody in the business should be involved in delivering the purpose.

Co-create: The development of your purpose is a great opportunity to collaborate and co-create with colleagues across the business. Get their input on how to embed your purpose into every area of the business.

Create consensus: Set up a workshop to bring together key stakeholders to finalize your purpose. This is the opportunity to build on all your killer insights and to create the final articulation that will serve as your Purpose. Expect and encourage healthy debate; it represents engagement and passion.

profit business that charged a 5 percent administration fee and took 5 percent of your Gift Aid. Our team shook that up with Virgin Money Giving, which gives donors and charities in Britain a better deal. Drawing on the infrastructure and expertise of Virgin Money, the nonprofit offers the same service for only a 2 percent fee, to cover overhead costs.

It helped that Virgin Money was a sponsor for the race. Launching the digital fundraising service made that sponsorship more than just an act of corporate branding; it integrated Virgin Money into the experience of the event, it drove greater engagement and leveraged our expertise to enhance the business case for the sponsorship, it promoted our banking services and strengthened our brand. All this with a lower administration fee, which meant more money went to British charities. Over £560 million has been donated to charities via Virgin Money Giving since launch, resulting in an estimated £17.9 million more donated to charities due to the not-for-profit model.

Thanks to the Business Innovation and Purpose team and the passion and dedication of their colleagues across the businesses, by 2017 twenty-five Virgin companies had purpose statements at the heart of the business. The statements continue to evolve as the businesses do. While your purpose should be enduring, it is important to revisit your statement often to ensure you are still living up to it.

> *"I believe that with great wealth comes great responsibility, a responsibility to give back to society and a responsibility to see that those resources are put to work in the best possible way to help those most in need."*
>
> — Bill Gates

LESSON 02: BE BRAVE AND BE BOLD

Lesson two is a little trickier because it requires sticking your neck out. Be brave and be bold. Currently, there aren't enough companies out there doing this meaningfully that can be emulated, so you're going to have to be fearless and accept that you might make mistakes. Don't sit around talking about it for months—jump in and give it a go.

LESSON 03: IT'S (STILL) ABOUT THE BOTTOM LINE

Let's not forget that we run businesses, and that businesses need to make money to survive. You can start a company with purpose, but ultimately you need a plan to make a profit (no matter what my dad says to the contrary!).

At Virgin, we needed to prove to our operating companies that purpose and profit do go hand in hand. The best example of this is RE*Generation, a project tackling homeless youth issues at Virgin Mobile US.

RE*Generation started with the purpose statement: Empowering a Generation to Help Its Own.

Virgin Mobile, with the help of Virgin Unite, brought together organizations that care about homeless youth and connected them with customers who wanted to help. They donated via text and volunteered. Virgin Mobile provided a platform for their customers so they could easily make a difference and positively contribute to their community. The feel-good factor this created between customer and company was immense. Dan Schulman, CEO of Virgin Mobile US at the time, hired a consultant to assess the customers who had engaged in the RE*Generation project versus those who had not. They found that the customers who participated by using the platform were more loyal Virgin Mobile customers, staying with their plans longer and using more minutes. Dan proudly held up this finding as testament to the fact that purpose brings profit.

LESSON 04: SHAKE UP THE TEAM

At Virgin, we decided to take things even further—to integrate purpose firmly, and visually, into our core business strategy. First, we moved Charlotte out of Virgin Unite to sit with our investment team. Charlotte pointed out that it doesn't matter how much she works with existing businesses—if Virgin launches a new company or invests in a new company that lacks purpose, it will undermine everything we stand for. It's much harder to reverse-engineer a social cause than it is to start with it. We made the strategic decision that Charlotte's team should sit at the heart of our investment portfolio.

I cannot underestimate the importance of this new seating arrangement—Charlotte, tasked with bringing purpose into every business, sat next to the numbers-driven investment team. Every potential investment at Virgin came under the microscope of purpose.

> *"Being good is good business."*
>
> — Anita Roddick, founder of The Body Shop

The establishment of a Purpose Board came next. I chair the committee, which receives input from all staff. We have representation from Virgin Unite and from the Heads of Virgin Management covering people, brand, investments, and corporate communications. We meet six times a year to ensure we have the right governance in place, that purpose is central to our agenda, and that it gives momentum to our strategies.

The Purpose Board, as the name suggests, determines the purpose priorities for Virgin Group each year. We identify key opportunities and best practices, and of course, we share them widely. We also consider any key risks and discuss how purpose is being used by businesses to navigate difficult decisions. A cause can be a very useful compass to keep you on track. The right track takes into account employees, customers, partners, investors, shareholders, society, and the environment. Central to our view is that the business must act beyond its own interests—the Purpose Board provides oversight.

Finally, the Purpose Board ensures we measure and demonstrate the benefits to business, people, and the planet of being more purpose-driven, like Dan Shulman did at Virgin Mobile US.

In a nutshell: to make change happen, you have to take it seriously and give it credence. This doesn't have to come in the form of a Purpose Board—all aspects of a successful business should be innovative, even when it comes to doing good. This means constantly reassessing what sort of purpose implementation works best for your company. A board may not be right for your company. But regardless, your people must

You know your "Purpose Barometer" is on the money when:

 You have a long-term vision, strategy, and budget to deliver your purpose

 The Board is reported to, engaged, and accountable—you have effective purpose governance

 The leadership team is engaged and accountable

 You have developed a measurement system to support the purpose strategy

 Incentives, rewards, and recognition are aligned to your purpose

 Your purpose is operationally embedded and is driving decisions

 Your purpose is considered and evident throughout your value chain

 Your risks are being effectively identified, mitigated, and managed

 You are using purpose to drive innovation across the business

 You are performing better than peers and are creating opportunities to become pioneers

see that the top brass take purpose seriously. In fact, why not ask them how you're doing? At Virgin, we ask the following questions of our people:

1. How can the business better embed purpose into everything we do?

2. How can the leaders better drive purpose?

3. How do you see your role in delivering purpose and how can we help you do better?

LESSON **05**: PURPOSE IS A JOURNEY

Discovering, developing, and embedding your purpose is a journey and not always an easy one. But if you truly embed purpose into the very DNA of your business the rewards can be invaluable. Use it as your compass during difficult times, for example, complex negotiations, in cost-cutting initiatives, or when performance managing people. Driving all decisions from your purpose will ensure that you are recommended by customers over competitors because you are purpose driven; you will be "employers of choice" because you offer people a greater sense of purpose at work; and you will positively impact lives in the communities you operate in and across your value chain.

Let that be Lesson 5 and the end of class: YOU need to get actively involved.

"Companies that do good are
more likely to be trusted. Trust and
reputation are precious commodities
in today's market."

INSPIRE BRAND FANATICS

By Craig Kielburger

The Beatles, Bieber, and . . . you? Purpose can make your customers superfans

Selena Gomez is casually perched on the edge of a stage, chatting with a stadium packed full of starstruck youth. It's WE Day Chicago 2015. At her side, a teen computer whiz types away on a Microsoft Surface. Gomez tells the rapt audience, "There is a brand new kind of world-changer out there and their first language is code. With me is Abril Vela."

Abril moves her fingers swiftly. "I just wrote this code while we were sitting here. Why don't you finish it?" Gomez reaches over, types in a few letters. The message I <HEART> WE DAY appears on the massive screen behind the pair. The crowd erupts in cheers.

Abril is an alumna with Microsoft's Youth Spark program, which encourages girls to use technology to effect social change. But Gomez isn't a Microsoft spokesperson; we don't even know if she owns a Surface. Frankly, it doesn't matter. On that stage in front of thousands (and on the TV broadcast that aired later to millions), the celebrity with the most Instagram followers on the planet was an unofficial brand ambassador.[1] Gomez showed young people how "easy" and "cool" (her words) it is to use technology to code, communicate, and change the world. Not a penny was spent on an endorsement deal and yet all parties benefited. Gomez followed her deep passion for a charitable cause and connected with her followers in a unique way. Microsoft created an association in customers' minds with one of the biggest stars on the planet. It was a win, win, win.

You Can't Buy That Kind of Press[3]

WE Day broadcast viewers were two times more likely than nonviewers to see Microsoft as a company that uses technology for social good.

Can Your Team Make a Difference?

In 2016, Microsoft employees:[2]

Raised US$142 million for charity

650^K

Hours

Volunteered 650,000 hours

For those of us over a certain age, allow me to introduce Selena Gomez, actress, multiplatinum recording artist, and producer who's bouncing a celebrity spotlight onto the causes she cares about most. Gomez granted so many wishes through the Make-A-Wish Foundation that the organization gave her an award in 2012. Working around movie shoots and concert tours, she granted more than 90 wishes from sick children, including hospital visits and concert invitations.[4] A UNICEF ambassador since 2009, Gomez has held charity benefit concerts, supported numerous campaigns, and traveled on field missions to Chile and Ghana.[5] These are just two of her higher-profile initiatives, as the star is also concerned with girls' education and animal welfare, among many other causes. Not to mention, she's one of the nicest and most genuine people we've met.

Gomez also happens to be social media royalty. As of this writing, more than 100 million followers are signed on for selfies and behind the scenes looks at her concert tour through her Instagram feed—with a few carefully considered product shots in the mix. AdWeek estimated that a single post across all of her platforms is worth more than half a million dollars. This is not what Gomez is paid per post, but the "ad-equivalent value," a metric calculated based on a number of factors, including the potential to create sales conversations. Added up, it amounts to "the statistically most influential person on social media."[6] Welcome to the age of the influencer. Any marketing consultant will tell you that teens don't want to be blatantly sold to. Instead, they look to their peers or role models to interact with products while they witness the experience. Fans relate to Gomez and her collaborations.

Increased access to technology has lowered barriers to entry and saturated markets, leading to a decline in brand loyalty and a growing distrust of companies among a well-informed public with more brand choices than ever. Customer allegiances are shifting. In Canada, roughly three-quarters of people surveyed said they had recently switched from a preferred brand.[7] In a global study, 84 percent of shoppers said they seek out responsible products whenever possible and a whopping 90 percent would boycott

The death of traditional advertising?

"Tesla Motors has no advertising, no ad agency, no CMO, no dealer network, and that's no problem," says **Advertising Age.**

Traditional ads are falling by the wayside in favor of word-of-mouth brand fanaticism or user-generated content. Inspiring brand fans means getting them involved.[8]

Consumers

93 percent of consumers find user-generated content helpful when deciding what to buy.

Millennials

82 percent of millennials and 52 percent of boomers favor referrals from friends and online social networks when picking a purchase.

Consumers

85 percent of consumers believe user-generated content is more influential than brand videos or photos.

a brand with deceptive practices.[9] Today, with so many purchases tied to our identity as social media channels effectively create our own personal brands, consumers want to feel they are buying into a cause or movement that's meaningful.

Brand fanatics—those who not only fall in love with your products, but also convince their peers to buy them, are not just harder to come by, but also harder to lure using old-school advertising. In the age of ad fatigue, showing customers you care about their issues is more effective than a billboard or pricey prime-time commercial. That's why companies are as eager as kids to get into WE Day and other social initiatives. These platforms demonstrate their business is committed to purpose.

WE Day 101

WE Day is our global youth empowerment event. I like to call it the Super Bowl of Social Change. Like the world's biggest football game, WE Day is a stadium-sized event. It was held in 15 cities in 2017, with smaller, community-run events in even more locations. It brings together world-renowned speakers and performers with thousands of young volunteers to honor their contributions and kick-start another year of change. The "price" of their ticket is paid in food drives, charity dance-a-thons, and bake sales. Every young person at every WE Day in cities around the world earns entry by supporting one local and one global cause. Annually, this adds up to helping more than 2,500 causes and charities. To support kids on their mission beyond the event, the WE Schools service learning program engages 15,000 schools reaching over four million students with free educational resources, service campaigns, and mentorship programs.

Youth in attendance might worship at the altar of teen idols, but they cheer just as loudly for Selena Gomez and Demi Lovato as they do for Malala Yousafzai and Archbishop Desmond Tutu. WE Day is the only stage in the world where you can find Prince Harry, Jennifer Lopez, and Jane Goodall rubbing elbows with local nonprofit heroes and tens of thousands of student volunteers.

Alongside celebrities and inspirational speakers, WE Day invites corporate partners onstage to showcase a cause, charitable organization, or service campaign important to them. People often ask us why we have sponsors at all. Well, to start, we could never bankroll a series of free events for 250,000 attendees in 15 cities around the world. The majority of the students in our U.S. program alone are from lower-income schools that need free or reduced-price lunch programs to feed students. WE believes that every youth, regardless of socioeconomic background, should have access to service learning as well as volunteer opportunities. Secondly, I've never met a chief executive who feels they get enough credit for doing good. And without positive incentives, what motivation do companies have to support social causes? Equally important, we want youth to start thinking about companies, their consumption, and their own future employment as mechanisms for helping the planet. We want them to understand that consumption and talent have power; they can vote for the good companies with spending habits and career choices.

We imagine a future in which logos and marketing gimmicks lose status while a robust social mission becomes the new measure of brand credibility. Just like a company's Super Bowl commercial becomes water-cooler talk in the days after the game, we want people to be buzzing about companies that are authentically doing good. We want teens to consider the cause and product impact, rather than the traditional advertisement, when buying clothes or coffee or a tablet. With the scale of WE Day—the 2017 broadcasts attracted 8.9 million viewers—we are making great progress to that end.

Purpose can create brand ambassadors by elevating the customer and manufacturer roles into a more fundamental relationship based on shared values. Companies that do good are more likely to be trusted. Trust and reputation are precious commodities in today's market.

Solving the Trust Deficit

Once upon a time, Don Draper swirled whiskey and burned through packs of Lucky Strikes while brainstorming new ways to manipulate housewives into buying detergent. We all miss *Mad Men*, but in real life, we've become wary of all things corporate, including ad messaging. Our trust in big companies is deteriorating, especially when it comes to innovation. It's widely perceived that companies aren't using the power of technology for good. More than half of global respondents in Edelman's 2015 Trust Barometer survey felt that greed, money, or growth were the primary motives behind business innovation—that's two times more than those who thought companies innovated in order to make the world a better place.[10] This puts Microsoft's impressive feat of reputation into perspective.

As we lose faith in large organizations and their ability to make the world better, we're experiencing a rise in business founded in grassroots communities, especially online. The explosion of the sharing economy, which is based on reciprocity and reputation between strangers, shows us just how much our thinking about trust has shifted.

Everything your parents taught you about not getting into cars with strangers has become obsolete. You can hail a ride through an app instead of a using a taxi service. You can bypass traditional organizational structures and rely on the kindness of strangers to buy almost anything (Craigslist, Etsy); fund your next venture (Kickstarter); board your pet (Rover); borrow power tools (Zilok); or support charity projects (Change .org, Crowdfunder UK). All of these structures have been broken down by building a community with shared values or a binding purpose. We trust in a group of peers with shared interests as much as—or more than—we trust in big companies.

Today, most travelers wouldn't dare book a hotel without checking online reviews. In fact, millions are choosing to stay in someone's vacant apartment based on referrals from people they've never met. As recently as five years ago, this notion would have been absurd, but Airbnb, the online apartment-swap tool that charges service fees for every booking, is reportedly valued at $30 billion,[11] more than most of the big hotel chains.[12]

Stranger danger aside, putting our faith into an aggregate of users makes complete sense. Sharing our lives digitally, including purchases, means consumers can look to other consumers for feedback, not just to the brand. We identify with other users as vacationers, startup enthusiasts, fellow donors, or petition signers because of an immediate and obvious mutual interest. We trust our community more than a company, and elect leaders by liking and sharing their content. We know what they value because we value it too.

No offense meant to your marketing department, but most consumers are more concerned with online reviews than with your multimillion-dollar ad-buy. Consumers aren't just buying from businesses anymore. They are buying from other people.

So the question becomes: How do companies replicate that peer-to-peer experience? It ought to be easy. Surprisingly, consumers already tend to view companies as people.

One of the leading researchers into the phenomenon of "human companies" is Susan Fiske. The professor of psychology at Princeton University has published widely on the topic of social cognition. With marketing consultant Chris Malone, she wrote *The Human Brand: How We Relate to People, Products, and Companies,* which argues that we apply person-to-person social filters to our interactions with brands. One of the first things people want to know when they "meet" a brand is "whether the company has their interests at heart and the interests of society, or are they just self-serving?" Next, we assess competence, or "how good are they at doing what they set out to do?"[13]

A few things struck me about this. First, our assessment of competence could explain why a product "working fine" doesn't get people excited to post on social media. You don't lure brand ambassadors with functional merchandise. This is the bare minimum.

Next, and more importantly: we're more likely to trust a brand that, we believe, prioritizes our interests and the interests of society.

A brand can become massively successful—trustworthy and competent by human standards—when it is no longer "us" selling to "them," but instead is recreating that peer-to-peer sense of community fostered online. If your business and your customer come to a mutual purpose rooted in values, like sponsoring a charity race to end breast cancer or raising awareness for mental health, then the relationship becomes about the greater good.

Companies tend to score lower in consumer trust if it's believed they are operating with self-interest instead of social good.[14]

Be clear about what your company stands for. If you don't know, your customers won't either.

Bullies vs. Friends Who Share with Friends

Sitting in an early morning math class, Lynelle Cantwell heard whispers and laughter from her peers. A list had been posted online, ranking the 12 "ugliest girls" at her high school, and she was one of them. "I realized I had a choice to make," she told an audience of 18,000 at WE Day Vancouver in 2016. "I could react with anger and negativity, or . . ." Lynelle chose option two, and penned a Facebook missive defending herself against the surface appearance her classmates had attacked. "I am funny," she wrote, "kind," "down to earth," "accepting," "easy to talk to." To those who created the distasteful list and callously ranked their peers, she wrote: "I feel sorry for you."

> *"In order to do well in business, we must do good in the communities where we live, work and serve as citizens."* [15]
>
> —Darren Entwistle, President and CEO, TELUS

Lynelle posted her response that morning; by gym class that same afternoon it had spread. Support streamed in online from readers across the country. Her story also resonated with representatives from Canadian telecommunications giant TELUS, who approached her about a partnership. The company had made a public commitment to end cyberbullying and create safe spaces online; Lynelle was recruited as part of its Rise Above campaign to speak at WE Day events across Canada. If it seems odd that a telecomm company headhunted an inspirational youth speaker, think about it a bit more.

Most customers don't have a sentimental attachment to their cell phone providers. They want a decent signal and an affordable plan that solves a basic need to communicate. TELUS went beyond the necessity of service, aligning with teens and their parents in a fight against the scourge of our digital era. If you don't work closely with youth, it's easy to forget that online bullying is brutal and debilitating, the schoolyard taunts that follow you home and everywhere you go, documented forever in public. Victims often become depressed, anxious, and even suicidal. Lynelle, a survivor of online abuse, reached a total audience of more than 6 million, including at various WE Day events and on the televised broadcast. Young people looked to her as a hero; she helped those kids understand that they are not alone. For a digital comms company, it's an authentic cause connection that resonates with customers and relates to the brand.

TELUS also partnered with us to co-create a WE Day app, a platform where young people committed to social change could share ideas and inspiration, issue volunteer challenges, and log their service hours. Digital natives who are connected, collaborative, and ready to come together to do good can now convene safely to share stories and tips about their journeys for social change. Among the app's features are peer-to-peer "challenges" that rally the online community to perform daily acts of kindness. More than 100,000 challenges have been accepted by users to date, including a call to plant trees and reach out to befriend a neighbor. One of the more unique ideas is a challenge to learn basic carpentry skills to support the trades and "make Canada strong by building it piece by piece." TELUS went from a cell phone provider to the creator of this supportive online community, especially in the eyes of many parents.

Partnering with purpose to drive results[16]

TELUS supported the very first WE Day event in Toronto in 2007, and has been a partner ever since— with benefits.

47%
Teens

47 percent of teens involved in TELUS-sponsored WE programs spoke positively about the company to their parents.

20%
Parents

20 percent of parents who were aware of the company's charitable work with WE purchased a TELUS mobile phone and plan.

In return, those parents became brand fans for a cause that helps their kid—and for the company responsible.

Consumer response to TELUS and its antibullying initiatives are proof that people respond to values-based outreach. Purpose programs can also gain recognition from third-party groups, accolades that will surely act as fodder for more brand fans. The company has been globally recognized as a purpose leader. In 2010, TELUS was named most outstanding philanthropic corporation in the world by the Association of Fundraising Professionals.[17] In its home country, it's consistently designated a "caring company" by national charitable watchdogs for giving more than 1 percent of its pretax profits to charity. Since 2000, TELUS has donated $300 million to charitable organizations, and staff have volunteered 4.8 million hours of service to communities across the country.[18]

Inspiring a network of brand ambassadors is much easier to do on a foundation of purpose.

Does Your Company Walk Their Talk?

A little girl brings her soapbox car to a boys' club. As she zips past all-male competitors, her proud father watches, adding a voiceover that makes her race more symbolic. "Do I tell her that despite her education, her drive, her skills, her intelligence, she will automatically be valued as less than every man she ever meets?"

The 60-second spot for a car company appeared during the 2016 Super Bowl. It was meant to be a very public call for gender empowerment during one of the most wide-reaching marketing forums in the world. And it flopped. Critics nailed the automaker because at the time of the ad, the company had no women on its six-member executive team, and just 16 percent female representation on its board, well below one of its major competitors (at 30 percent).[19]

Lifestyle branding has led to more experiential storytelling, with emotionally driven narratives and less overt product pushing. It's why a TV viewer can sit through an entire commercial, puzzled about what's being sold until a logo appears at the end. What seems like a public service announcement against impaired driving is, in fact, a beer commercial.

Brand fans will only respond to these efforts if the company's practices align with its message. When companies try to shoehorn their way into these conversations, it's called cause washing: the false advertising of purpose. And it has no place in the WEconomy. In the age of limitless information, customers will sniff out and call out cause washing like a bad smell. We're showing you how to infuse purpose in your company or career path because we want the good ones to succeed, to create a larger movement and to amplify social change on a massive scale.

Brand fans are not easily fooled, and a simple Internet search reveals stacks of information about the authenticity of a corporate cause. Simply posting a "mission statement" online without practicing the sentiment, or engaging in a random, one-time action won't make a meaningful impact. Before adopting causes and preaching publicly about your purpose, get your own house in order.

So, does your company walk the talk?

"Every company wants to invent the next big thing. Look for product opportunities in your biggest challenges."

BUILD NEW PRODUCTS

By Marc Kielburger

Impact through innovation: New products for the WEconomy

The savannah of Kenya's Maasai Mara is vast and beautiful. It is also home to some very dangerous creatures, most notably lions. So when you're sitting around a bonfire in the dead of night, the last thing you want to hear is something large crashing through the underbrush.

It was 2007, and Roxanne and I had invited the entire family along on our honeymoon to Kenya. As the noises drew closer, I feared we had inadvertently brought our loved ones to an untimely end. This was it—we were set to be dinner.

What emerged from the long grass was not a pack of hungry felines, but a jubilant crowd of Maasai warriors, mamas, and elders from the nearby community.

The chief stepped out from the throng. He explained that we were part of the Maasai family and needed to be married according to local custom. Speechless and a little choked up, we were placed back-to-back as the Maasai danced and sang around us. They placed grass on our shoes to symbolize that we were part of the Earth. Elders spit

THE WORLD'S
PROBLEMS ARE
INNOVATIONS
WAITING
TO HAPPEN.

fermented goat's milk at our feet—not the most romantic gesture, but a sign of great respect in their culture. Roxanne was presented with an incredible collection of beaded wedding necklaces. For the Maasai, a man's wealth is measured in cattle and children, while a woman wears her wealth and experience around her neck. All of the important events in a woman's life are marked with necklaces: marriage, childbirth, grandchildren. A Maasai mama's life is written in beads.

We didn't realize it in that beautiful moment, but the Maasai had provided us with more than just a lifetime memory. They had given us a completely new perspective on business and its power to uplift lives.

As I previously shared, charities often struggle to secure stable funding. We had been searching for predictable revenue streams for ages, looking for something that would generate funds and remain consistent with the purpose of the organization. With their exquisite beadwork, the Maasai had given us both.

Entrepreneurs struggle to find new product ideas all the time. We were no exception. The Maasai taught us that some of the best ideas come from nontraditional thinking: no whiteboard or expensive consulting groups required. I'm not suggesting you need to fly to Kenya to generate new product or business solutions. But in the WEconomy, innovators need to step outside their comfort zones.

Don't just scan the Business section of the newspaper (or your favorite online news hub), read the front page.

The News and World sections are full of stories from every social and economic sector, with no shortage of intractable problems seeking

Did You Know?[1]

40%

40 percent of social enterprises are run by women, versus.

18%

18 percent of traditional small and medium-sized enterprises.

innovative solutions—how many of those can be product solutions? Climate change, water scarcity, poverty . . . sadly, the list of problems is long. But so are the opportunities for developing solutions.

While we're on the subject of reading materials, business books will tell you about finances and accounting and management. Very few offer insights about the state of the world. Current affairs and business are not separate subjects. The world's problems are innovations waiting to happen. Look for titles that explore the intersection between global issues, politics, and business. For that matter, extend your traditional learning platforms and look for networking opportunities at nonprofit seminars, where academics and charity leaders gather to discuss the electrification of urban dwellings in slum areas, or the distribution of medication to remote regions, or weaving mosquito netting out of recycled bottles.

The nonprofit sector will happily welcome reinforcements. Charities often develop small-scale models, while businesses are frequently better suited to scale those solutions by attracting a large inflow of capital. Businesses can leverage this power to help solve society's most pressing problems, and earn profit in the process.

Years before the wedding, Roxanne graduated with distinction from Stanford University's international relations program. She went on to win a Rhodes Scholarship and earn a law degree from Oxford. Returning from the UK, she landed a position as a clerk in the Supreme Court of Canada. At the same time, she also moonlighted as coordinator for what was then our volunteer travel startup. On any given day, she would draft precedent-setting decisions for a judge, then draw up travel itineraries for the teenagers headed overseas to help with our projects. On her holiday breaks, she returned to Kenya to help us establish schools in the Maasai Mara.

Though a promising career in law stretched out before her, Roxanne's true passion was elsewhere. At Stanford, Roxanne wrote her thesis on women's economic empowerment and became immersed in the study of traditional Maasai gender roles. She traveled regularly to Kenya, meeting with the women to hear their stories. Soon, her research trips became social visits with friends, where she established herself as a trusted

The Closed Loop Model

We wanted customers to purchase beautiful, handcrafted necklaces that would support mothers in rural Kenya. ME to WE Artisans would offer steady employment and small business training for extremely marginalized women, a source of income to support their families. Plus, partial proceeds from the purchase of Artisans' goods would support development programs, like building schools and clean water systems in the very region where the women live and work.

We call this a "closed-loop system" because profits from purchases of socially-conscious products made in our partner communities return to those same communities.

When we enter a closed-loop process, there are many considerations: Is the product scalable? Can we price competitively? But the benefits are overwhelming. The community achieves much-needed stable employment, and proceeds fund social empowerment programs. The consumer gets transparency on multiple planes. You know where your impact is being generated, both in terms of economic development (job creation) and community development (donations). You can track it online, and even visit the Kenyan Mamas who work as artisans on a ME to WE Trip.

It sounds simple, but it was revolutionary to deliver impact at this large scale.

voice and member of the community. The Maasai gave her a traditional name, Nalatwesha, or "little rainmaker."

With their bright red shukas, elaborately beaded jewelry, and elongated earlobes, the Maasai are among the most recognizable tribes in all of Africa. They are also among the continent's poorest. These rural communities remain challenged by malaria, tuberculosis, drought, and encroaching development, and it is increasingly difficult to maintain pastureland for their livestock. For pastoralists like the Maasai, cattle are their livelihood. With little economic power, Maasai women were dependent on their husbands, and maintained no financial or social autonomy.

Evidence shows that the more women are able to work and earn an income, the faster local economies grow.[2] We know from experience that when women contribute economically to their families, their status, equality, and inclusion in decision making within the family and the larger community rises significantly. There had to be a way to empower women to work outside the home in a way that was consistent with each community's cultural norms and family traditions.

Beading was already a source of income that didn't disrupt the social structure. Maasai men are responsible for their cattle, but the women fetch water, collect firewood, milk cows, wash

There Was a Problem

These social enterprises had a solution

Evaptainers make zero-energy refrigeration systems, using mobile units to reduce food spoilage in the developing world.

Wellowater created a rolling container that transports 50 liters of water in one trip, relieving women in developing communities of multiple trips with smaller jugs carried on their heads.

Toilets for People sells affordable composting toilets and sanitation services for charities working in the developing world, where pit latrines and flush toilets can fail.

clothes, cook, clean, and look after the children. Mothers and grandmothers have little time to themselves, but beading can be done anywhere. It often brings women together under the shade of an acacia tree to socialize, and to train a few extra pairs of eyes on young children. Roxanne had spent long hours in their company. It was under an acacia tree that she started to wonder: What if the process could be scaled? Could we maintain that handmade quality with larger distribution? Could we find a place in the competitive jewelry market in North America with traditional crafts? Would Western women wear African wedding necklaces? Could the necklaces become an alternative source of income for the mamas?

"Millennial women see their buying power as the strongest way to show support for companies addressing issues they care about. 64 percent of millennial women have bought a product associated with a cause in the past 12 months (vs. 54 percent of millennial men)."

—2015 Cone Communications Millennial CSR Study

If the idea worked, it could be what we in the development world call an "asset-based solution," one that relies on resources rather than handouts. In business, it could be a product origin story.

If you'll allow me to be the gushing, loving husband for a moment, I'll tell you that Roxanne could have taken her talents anywhere. But she chose to help build and lead a social enterprise with a business-based solution to women's empowerment. So with that, we had our first ME to WE Artisans product: Maasai beadwork adapted for shoppers in the West.

Of course, devising new product ideas isn't a concern limited to charities looking to make their mark. Massive companies like Unilever and Procter and Gamble (P&G) spend billions on research and development alone. For Unilever, it was more than $1 billion in 2015, and for P&G, it was $2 billion that same year.[3]

Unilever's history of social-based product innovation dates back to 1884 when the company developed the first commercially available soap, Sunlight. William Hesketh Lever was concerned about hygiene in Victorian England, and addressed a social challenge with a product solution.[4] Today, Unilever has more than 20,000 patents and patent applications, from Dove products to Q-Tips.[5]

The parent company of P&G staffs 8,000 in its 26 R&D facilities around the world, 1,000 of whom have PhDs. Historically, these have been the minds responsible for fluoride toothpaste (Crest in 1955) and synthetic detergent (Dreft in 1933).[6] This devotion to invention is the reason its brands like Bounty and Old Spice are still relevant 170-odd years after the company was founded. Product innovation is the not-so-secret weapon.

In the eight years from prototype to development, Gillette spent $750 million to create the Mach3, a men's razor with three blades.[7] That's a good chunk of cash by today's standards, but this was back in 1998. P&G then acquired Gillette in 2005. Razors are among the most patented consumer products on the market, with more than 50 protecting the Mach3 design.[8] Engineers considered the ergonomics of the handle and pressure distribution among the blades for the highly competitive market.

The point being: companies muster significant resources to invent the next big thing. Why not exhaust all avenues by looking for innovation opportunities that also give back? Some sectors have already started in on this: Imagine the windfall for whoever discovers a formula to put biofuel in every gas tank.

With Artisans beadwork, our initial challenges were slightly different than a corporate innovation think-tank. But we did have some inkling of what we were up against, making beaded bracelets, necklaces, and earrings for a saturated market. And we weren't just innovating our product, we were innovating our business model. Artisans started with a handful of Maasai mamas, in part because we didn't know whether we could establish consistent quality, meet production deadlines, or successfully modify Maasai designs for a Western consumer. Other obstacles unique to the region—droughts, floods, the occasional elephant herd—also disrupted work. And there were cultural hurdles, such as resistance to the idea of women working outside the home. The community held many meetings, but ultimately, the village chief was in favor of the economic opportunity, and he won over the dissenters.

> *"[ME to WE Artisans] empowers the family to be able to earn more collectively as a group and send more kids to school, eat better, have better health care and better shelter, and generally improve their family's position."*
>
> — Academy Award–winning actor Natalie Portman

Roxanne consulted with some 250 women to determine what the artisans would be paid for their work. With no established living wage in rural Kenya, and none of the women having ever experienced fair pay, everyone was shooting in the dark. In the end, as a group, the women worked out what each artisan would need to run her household, send her children to school, and to save for larger purchases. Working backwards, weighing those factors against operational costs, we arrived at a pay structure. The mamas would be paid per piece, which was assessed based on the time and skill involved in each product design. It amounts to four times more, on average, than what the women used to make. The mamas had always sold their jewelry, but had access only to a few local tourist markets, so saturated that everything sold at a steep discount. Roxanne found new buyers an ocean away. In North America, Artisans tapped into a ready market of socially conscious young women. We didn't have to "sell" the products, we just had to tell

Look to markets of the future

The market for capturing waste carbon and preventing it from entering the atmosphere was valued at over US\$2.2 billion in 2015, and is estimated to be worth more than US\$15 billion by 2023.[9]

The global sulfuric acid market was valued at US\$70 billion in 2014 and is projected to reach US\$85 billion by 2023. What is the sulfuric acid market, you ask? Fertilizer. Demand is particularly high in Latin American countries like the new farming powerhouse of Brazil.[10]

$52.4B

Diminishing supply and increased demand for clean water is driving the global market for desalination technology, which turns seawater into potable water, expected to reach US\$52.4 billion in value by 2020.[11]

our story; women in the West felt a kinship with the mamas, and wanted to support them.

We thought we'd ship 3,000 units a year, if we were lucky.

"The Maasai Mamas are amazing! They are incredibly hard-working women who are truly inspirational. The whole experience of meeting them and getting to know them was truly rewarding because they pursue their dreams while still supporting their families and taking care of their households."

—Singer/songwriter Demi Lovato

In 2015 alone, the most popular Artisans piece, a bracelet called the Rafiki (Swahili for "friend") sold 1.1 million units in North America. Thanks to that one product, we were able to fund and deliver 1.1 million impacts, including clean water, medical supplies, and school lunches, to empower communities to lift themselves from poverty. It's a single string of beads in the competitive accessories market, and yet leading fashion retailer Nordstrom leapt onboard, partnering with ME to WE to sell Rafiki bracelets in its 115 large-format stores across the U.S. and Canada—our first American retail partner. Now, the mamas are hand-stitching colorful beads onto Fossil watch straps for the U.S.-based retailer, and beading Rafikis created in collaboration with international YouTube sensation and women's empowerment advocate Lilly Singh. Demand from these and other contracts, including Macy's, Bloomingdale's, DAVIDsTEA, Walgreens, and Mastermind Toys, help employ more than 1,500 Maasai women—most of whom are now the top breadwinners in their home.

Our corporate partners aren't drawn to jewelry that they could manufacture anywhere in the world. They want to be part of the solution. They want their brand associated with a movement that empowers women in emerging economies. The likes of Natalie Portman, Jennifer Hudson, Nelly Furtado, and Selena Gomez have all been known to sport Artisans designs. Singer and songwriter Demi Lovato approached us to collaborate on a special Rafiki bracelet she designed to sell on her world tour. How many pop stars approach traditional companies to offer free product placements at their concert venues? Probably not many!

What's important about the Rafikis is not the actual bracelets, but the closed-loop process whereby consumers can directly support the Maasai women and their families. After all, the best kind of charity is a steady, empowering job.

Our latest closed-loop venture is a partnership with Ecuadorian farmers of cacao, the key ingredient in chocolate. Any chocolate aficionado will tell you that Ecuador produces the finest cacao in the world, called "fino de aroma," prized for its rich, deep aroma and complex taste. Despite its unique attributes, the local farmers who grow and harvest cacao are often paid a pittance for their hard labor. WE brings their product directly to North American and European markets, cutting out the multiple distributors and middlemen, ensuring that farmers receive a fair price. WE Charity has a long history in Ecuador, working in rural communities building schools, initiating clean water projects, and delivering other social programs. Profits from the chocolate sales allow the community to sustain the WE Charity development programs, such as funding maintenance and future repairs on the water treatment systems. It's not a hand-out, but sustainable empowerment.

We didn't reinvent the wheel—we didn't even reinvent the bracelet. We simply started with a social problem instead of a product category.

Roxanne's wedding beads helped us discover a product opportunity, and taught us that profitable product development can be found in solving a social problem.

We were hardly the first to do this—nor will we be the last.

Is There Anything You Can Do?

It was March of 2002. A gas-sniffing epidemic was spreading among aboriginal youth in Australia's outback. Social worker Chris Tangey watched as the kids he worked with, "bright-eyed and full of life," started sniffing gasoline to get high and turned into "the walking dead."

To many, this would be a problem for government social agencies or charities. But Tangey went straight to the source: Big Oil. He sent the same email plea to every major fuel company in Australia—Is there anything you can do?—convinced that no one would listen but desperate from a lack of options.

The email landed in the inbox of Mark Glazebrook, BP Australia's then-new manager of corporate responsibility, still getting his bearings. Glazebrook's bosses were wary when he explained the situation in the outback, telling him the company should only get involved if it could actually make meaningful improvements—if it could really help solve the social problem. With that remit, Glazebrook arrived in Central Australia to visit affected communities. He met a 15-year-old sitting on a bicycle, a typical teenage pose but for the can of gasoline strapped around his face. The boy did not have great expectations. "Well, I'm sniffing petrol now," he said, "then I'll go onto the grog [alcohol], then I'll probably go to jail and die." The problem seemed insurmountable to Glazebrook, while his bosses' warnings about meaningful change rung in his ears. He spoke with locals; an aboriginal elder suggested BP come up with a fuel that won't make kids high. Fuel companies had already infused gasoline with a rotten egg smell to deter sniffers. But the stanching agent evaporated in open air, so it didn't last long. Glazebrook challenged his company's engineers to design a fuel without the sweet-smelling additives that produce a high. After six months of research, they succeeded.

Typically, unleaded petrol contains higher concentrations of chemicals with hallucinogenic properties. The team at BP managed to limit aromatics to 5 percent, well below the amount typically used, in their new "low aromatic" concoction, with fewer intoxicating solvents for sniffers.

In 106 towns where BP Australia's new "Opal" fuel was introduced, gas-sniffing dropped between 70 and 90 percent. And when the government passed a law in 2013 that all gas sold in rural Australia had to be "low aromatic fuel," BP cornered the market. Solving a social problem gave the company a sales monopoly throughout much of rural Australia, boosting its brand halo. Government subsidies ensure that customers pay the same for Opal as they would for regular unleaded fuel, encouraging use.

"The good news is
you don't have to quit your day job
to find meaning at work."

REINVENTING YOUR WORK LIFE

By Holly Branson

YOU can be a Pioneer of Purpose

Everyone wants to derive meaning from work. Meaning for some will be the sense of personal achievement they get from a job well done. For others it will be that they feel valued, included, and respected by a company that sees the human being behind the payroll number. And for an increasing number of people—across all age groups and industry sectors—it is the desire to work for a purpose-driven company. Being part of an organization that embeds its purpose, by including all of its staff and stakeholders in the amplification and execution of that purpose, has rapidly become the number-one driver to achieve meaning at work. Survey after survey, in the past couple of years, has seen a sea change from a desire for happiness at work to the desire for meaning at work.

If you don't work for an organization that has started its journey to achieving profit with purpose yet, you may be thinking: this purpose stuff sounds great, and I'm glad some other people are doing it. But I'm not about to leave my job, start a charity, or move to Kenya to find fulfillment. So how does the average employee bring about social change at a company?

ANYONE CAN ACHIEVE PURPOSE AT WORK, AND EVERYONE SHOULD TRY, SINCE IT BENEFITS AN EAGER EMPLOYEE AS MUCH AS IT DOES THE BUSINESS.

The good news is you don't have to quit your day job to find meaning at work. The better news is that by injecting purpose into your work life, you can advance your career, too. Building social impact into your job description can be as simple as welcoming new hires with a coffee break, or volunteering to be part of the office environmental team or charity task force. Your first step could be rewriting your job description to include social intrapreneur skills. After all, the boss rarely complains if you add valuable skills to your job role!

Definition of a Social Intrapreneur: "People within a large corporation who take direct initiative for innovations that address social or environmental challenges while also creating commercial value for the company."[1]

By using purpose as your icebreaker, you'll meet people you might not have met otherwise.

So, What's a Social Intrapreneur Anyway?

Encounters with colleagues from departments outside your own are a huge workplace advantage. There's even a book dedicated to the subject. Wayne Baker, author of *Achieving Success through Social Capital*, writes: "If you bridge disparate parts of the organization, you can link a problem in one group with a solution for another."[2] That kind of perspective could be invaluable to your business. Buying a round at the happy hour post charity event is an excuse to mingle with colleagues you don't normally work with, and could really pay off.

Purpose is not a singular task reserved for the higher-ups. Anyone can achieve purpose at work, and everyone should try, since it benefits an eager employee as much as it does the business.

If your day job doesn't give you the chance to take on leadership positions, stepping up to lead a cause at work will inevitably attract the attention of other leaders. Running the company's volunteer day, you'll likely bump into a few executives, while you budget and seek approvals—at the very least, earning you a thank-you note and name recognition.

Always remember—as we said in the chapter "Purpose 101"—whatever role you have in the business, you make decisions every day and you, as an individual, have the power to use purpose to drive those decisions.

By using purpose as your guide, not only in your work life but in your community and your home life as well, you will be striving to continuously improve and better your environment. A job well done, I'd say!

Want to reinvent your job with purpose? Build these traits[3]

A learning mindset: Learn as much as possible as quickly as possible, and see everything you do as an opportunity to learn. Remove the stigma from mistakes and errors; they are learning opportunities.

Trust in yourself: Have a quiet confidence that you can take on whatever may come. Instead of fearing the unknown, develop trust that you can handle whatever challenge might be next.

Humility: Be open to other opinions, admit your mistakes, spend time in self-reflection, and recognize you can't do everything yourself. Accept blame and share praise. Trust others instead of micromanaging.

I'd also like to add a few useful traits to the list above: be resilient, be tenacious, and be creative.

Not only will these projects help you find meaning at work, they just might help you move up the ladder. Social capital, the value of gaining influence and respect among peers, is more than just office gossip. In his book, Baker cites studies demonstrating that most people get jobs through existing contacts. Once hired, people with higher social capital are paid more and promoted faster and at younger ages.[4] Seeking purpose at work will build your skill set, fill out your résumé, and increase your value as an employee.

During the past year, we went in search of such success stories, and we've drawn lessons from some of the best to show you how to succeed at putting purpose into your job. Sometimes that's all it takes—a few good examples to inspire and motivate, or successful case studies that you can use to convince your boss that it's worth permitting you (and your team) to develop an idea or run with a purpose-project. Reminding them that it will help the bottom line doesn't hurt either.

To help you along, here are the journeys of two intrapreneurs, Nicola and Tania.

Railway Town: Platform for Social Good

When Nicola Griffiths, an employee of Virgin Trains, came up with the idea of adding pop-up shops to the platform at Crewe Railway Station in Cheshire, England, she had no idea of the impact it would ultimately have. Her idea resulted in a retail hub supporting small local businesses in a country still suffering the aftermath of a triple-dip recession just a few years earlier.

Here is Nicola's story—mostly in her own words:

Crewe Alexandra is the local football team, nicknamed "The Railwaymen." They made it to Wembley Stadium for the first time in 2012 in the League Two playoff final, where they went on to beat Cheltenham 2-0.

"Apart from being a great railway town, Crewe is also really behind their football team, so in the buildup to the big match, they were really excited," she says. "We had a big banner up at the station supporting the team, and there were also lots of people along the road with shopping trolleys selling souvenirs, football flags, and scarves."

On the day of the match, Nicola was working an early shift. During her usual security checks, she found an interloper—one of the merchants who usually set up a cart down the road was trying to sell scarves right on the doorstep of the station.

"I had a couple of thoughts," she says. "First: should he be there? And secondly: what a shame we didn't have him on the platform. The shopping trolleys [outside the station] brought such a fantastic atmosphere," she says, to the otherwise drab commuter journey. "I was left thinking: why couldn't we support this in a different way?"

Nicola adds that it had always frustrated her that there was so much space at Virgin Train stations, yet "we don't do anything with it." She adds: "I thought it would be good for local businesses to do pop-up shops on the station platform to promote their businesses and showcase what's going on in the local area."

She wanted commuters to be more than passersby, and to get a feel for the town—perhaps giving it an economic boost on their way through the station.

Small business suffered greatly when the global recession hit in 2008; in the UK, an estimated 200,000 businesses were forced to close their doors and as many as 1.3 million people lost their jobs.[5] Along many high streets throughout Britain, boarded-up windows became the norm. And so Nicola's brainchild, sparked by an enterprising soccer fanatic, could not have been more timely—not only for local businesses, but also because it brought back a sense of community to areas devastated by the recession.

Getting Local Businesses on Board

As the development manager at Crewe Station, Nicola persuaded local businesses to get on board, pardon the pun. Virgin Trains' station managers have lots of

No matter where you are in a company, if you're passionate, persistent, and gutsy, you can make waves.

autonomy, so Nicola didn't need to start with a big pitch to the higher-ups. Instead, she was up and running with community buy-in, getting locals involved. The rejuvenated town of Crewe would be all the proof she needed to grow the idea further down the road. And grow it, she would.

58%

of Managers

58 percent of managers are either very willing or extremely willing to support employees who want to capitalize on a new business opportunity within their company.[6]

Hitting the phones hard, she convinced area businesses that Crewe Station Platform was the town's next big outdoor market.

"It's a unique way of showcasing their products and getting a wider audience," Nicola says. "We also started taster days on board our trains. So we get lots of things going on around customer engagement, and there might be samples of a food product or beverage or a service that customers can try and then buy. We've even had a business going through the train offering people hand massages." Since the inaugural pop-up in 2014, Virgin Trains now runs pop-up shops every year for five consecutive days at 17 West Coast stations across the UK and ad hoc at East Coast stations. For one week, local businesses get massive foot traffic and a new storefront. Virgin Trains even hosted a pop-up for Richard Branson's 65th birthday in 2015. Now, that is buy-in and recognition from the big boss—hosting his birthday party around your business idea.

Nicola and Virgin Trains make sure to foster a larger commitment to local business. Once those five days of pop-up shops are over, "we find ways within our own business to support the small businesses," Nicola says, pointing to a ceramic designer who recently won a contract with Virgin Trains. "She's redesigned our sugar bowls for our first-class carriages to go with our new crockery."

A true win-win. And customers love it, too. When the hand masseuse came on board to offer hand massages, Nicola says Virgin Trains "saw Twitter go crazy."

Even more important than the social media frenzy?

Nicola solved a social problem and rallied a community. Naturally, Virgin Trains supported the plan.

Thanks to the company having faith in Nicola's lightbulb moment, and her persistence to make it a reality, Virgin Trains pop-up shop events along the West Coast Main Line have supported more than 200 businesses in the communities. Business case studies on SMEs who take part in regular pop-up events show that they have enjoyed a 33 percent rise in revenue growth and a 50 percent rise in becoming regular suppliers to other businesses in their region.

You may not be the CEO, but you have your own resources and a sphere of influence that includes your community—not to mention your local football supporters.

Nicola's story shows that no matter where you are in a company, if you're passionate, persistent, and gutsy, you can make waves. You'll find lots of hints and tips in this chapter to make sure you swim—not sink!

Don't Change Companies— Change the Company You're In

And now on to a socially conscious accountant. Tania Carnegie is the senior manager in the Toronto office of the global accounting firm KPMG. Before heading to rural Kenya to volunteer with WE Charity, Tania steeled herself to confront hopelessness and despair, but her emotional armor proved useless.

Daily life in the remote, marginalized community was undeniably hard, but she witnessed none of the resentment or self-pity she had anticipated. Instead, the locals were filled with the mirth of family and the joy of community. "This caused me to reflect on my values, my definition of success," she told us.

On a flat red rock overlooking the Great Rift Valley, the very "Cradle of Civilization," Tania came to ask herself some fundamental questions: What did these people have that she didn't fully understand? What does success really mean? What did she want her legacy to be? Her soul-searching led to a life-changing conclusion: she should quit her job and take up development work full-time. She and her husband, Christopher, discussed moving to Africa to apply their skills to the many challenges they'd seen on their trip. Back home on the verge of quitting her career and uprooting her life, Tania had many

Add purpose to your career and reap the rewards

Volunteering your time at work—or outside of it—can only boost your career. Here are some of the big reasons why:

 Get noticed by upper management: Maybe you'll end up briefing senior managers on your volunteer initiative or sit on the Board of Directors as the Volunteer representative.

 Training and development: The volunteer space is a great way to explore areas that you might never encounter in your day job. You can learn leadership skills, hone your writing abilities, or practice giving presentations.

 People look at you more positively when you volunteer your time: It will help you network and arm you with icebreakers for meeting colleagues outside your normal sphere.

 Résumé builder: All of the above will pad your résumé and make it easier for you to find a new job or advance in your current workplace.

difficult conversations with friends and family as her suppressed fears surfaced. It's one thing to fantasize about running away to Africa as a single, recent graduate looking for perspective before real life sets in, it's another to leap when you have so much to lose. Craig offered valuable, and perhaps surprising, perspective. He told Carnegie: "You can uproot your life to switch careers and find a nonprofit. Or you can use the credibility, the resources, and the expertise of a massive company like KPMG."

Back home, with a new perspective, Tania began to imagine a different future for herself at KPMG, one that would also transform the company. At the time, her idea seemed as absurd as it was revolutionary. Simply put, she hoped to tie salaries and advancement at one of the largest accounting firms in the world to an employee's volunteer efforts outside the company.

KPMG is certainly a progressive company—the international accounting firm is committed to environmental sustainability and was among the first professional service organizations in Canada to sponsor a volunteer day. But Tania's plan envisioned an even more engaged form of corporate social responsibility. Bill Thomas, the firm's incoming Canadian CEO at the time and now KPMG's Global Chairman, asked many tough questions, but Tania had accounted for that (because she's an accountant . . . get it?). She told him it would not require more money. An investment of strategy and leadership alone would produce more engaged employees with deeper connections to their communities. And Tania agreed to run the program. The CEO was supportive, and named Tania KPMG's first National Executive Director of Community Leadership (which means she basically invented, pitched, and won her title). She gave herself a promotion!

> *"Social intrapreneurs are quickly becoming the most valuable employees at many companies because they are good for the bottom line, good for the brand, and good for staff morale."*
>
> —Ashoka editorial in *Forbes* magazine. (Ashoka is the largest network of social entrepreneurs worldwide, with nearly 3,000 Fellows in 70 countries)

Key traits of the social intrapreneur[7]

- More ambitious for social change than for personal wealth and advancement
- Willing and able to take risks
- Has an understanding of business process and priorities as well as sustainability imperatives
- Adept at fighting and surviving cynicism, caution, and the status quo
- Never stops learning, innovating, and simplifying

Tania's plan, rolled out in the fall of 2009, made community involvement one of the four pillars of KPMG's business strategy in Canada. Volunteering became part of every job description; employees would be accountable in their annual performance reviews for what they had done in their communities, alongside client satisfaction ratings and income generation numbers. As Tania told us, with typical understatement: "This was not what was traditionally associated with a job at an accounting firm."

The program is mutually beneficial for both the community and the company. Nonprofit groups have gained budgeting, tax, and governance expertise provided by KPMG volunteers. Volunteers gain professional development opportunities and new contacts (oh, and the satisfaction of helping others). Accounting firms are nothing without their reputations—KPMG's employees are also acting as do-good brand ambassadors. Meanwhile, employee surveys show the program has boosted staff morale. More than 90 percent of KPMG employees regard the firm as a responsible corporate citizen. The program is also used to lure talent, an enticing part of the recruitment process. Tania has since taken the program global as Chief Impact Officer and Leader.

In the WEconomy, employees can help invent new products, break into new markets, and even get promoted, while bringing about social change, all within the safety net of their current employer.

You can even change the rules of how one gets promoted, like Tania did in the stodgy accounting industry at an established firm. She effectively created her own position to marry her passions with her business ambitions.

So there you have it—you can do good by changing your industry from within, and at the same time help your company differentiate its offerings. These are just two examples of the many thousands of intrapreneurs changing their companies from within (just put intrapreneur in your search engine and you'll find many, many more). Read their stories, and apply the lessons learned to your own companies—their successes are hard to ignore.

"Unless you're Kanye West, no one believes that your plain white T-shirt is fundamentally different from any other."

DIFFERENTIATE PRODUCTS

By Craig Kielburger

Add two scoops of purpose, stir, and stand out

PacSun is an uber-cool retail clothing brand marketed to teens, with headquarters in Anaheim, California. It's a destination for style that is effortlessly L.A., offering maxi skirts, floppy hats, and billowy dresses, as if the only occasions worth dressing for are beach parties and music festivals. It also carries a number of licensed product lines, including ME to WE Artisans, as well as designs by Kendall and Kylie Jenner. This is the most Marc and I will ever have in common with the Kardashian clan.

A few years back, Marc spoke at a Santa Monica conference for PacSun's general managers. It was like a fashion trend convention, with everyone clad in skinny jeans, Hawaiian shirts, and Buddy Holly glasses. They eyed Marc with detached looks. He walked in wearing his cross-country flight uniform of ergonomic sneakers, Dad jeans, and sport-coat-over-tee. Marc was there to help these fashion industry insiders solve a clothing problem: How to elevate the plain white T-shirt?

Marc and the PacSun team discussed a co-branded fashion line called The ME to WE Essentials that would consist of women's basics like white tees, tank tops, and other staples. This was an audacious venture. In this space, we would be competing with every other retailer peddling

White T-shirts by the Numbers

Amazon Hits

1,072,700: Hits on Amazon.com for "white T-shirt."

Saint Laurent

US$340: Price of Saint Laurent's slub cotton-jersey T-shirt.

Costco

US$2.45: Price of a Costco's Kirkland Signature 100 percent Pima Cotton T-Shirt (sold in packs of four).

Stain Prone

100 percent: Chance of spilling coffee or mustard on a brand-new white T-shirt.

a tee. And unless you're Kanye West, no one believes that your plain white T-shirt is fundamentally different from any other. These products are too similar to distinguish beyond price point.

Marc had a hunch that we could differentiate our basics line from all others on the market, with a revolutionary tracking system our team had developed that could identify the purpose in any product.

The idea had come to me a while back, standing in line at a grocery store. The cashier asked, "Would you like to donate $2 to charity?" Um, maybe. Charity? Any charity in particular? Can you tell me anything about the social impact? After a puzzling exchange, it was clear that she had no idea where the money would go; no one bothered to offer even a basic explanation to this person on the frontline, responsible for engaging customers in the company's cause. She sighed, probably thinking to herself, *I work here part-time, why would I have this information?*

The old cash-register charity offensive is a guilt-driven ask that drives most customers crazy. Built on superficial corporate-charity partnerships, there's little information available to consumers about the cause, and no information about how the collected money is being spent. Most often, the point of purchase is the first time that consumers encounter the cause. It preys on a person's guilt, incurs public shaming as those behind you in line are watching, and provokes that inner monologue: Is the company also supporting the charity, or just asking for my money? If I give, how is my donation going to be used?

Pressuring people to make insta-donations doesn't inform donors or create long-term supporters of the charity. Companies don't fare much better because this model often negatively affects the consumer experience. This last-minute request model has existed unchanged for decades, despite massive innovations in every other part of the consumer experience. Just think about the transformations within the past few years for payment options alone: smartphone wallets, self-service check-outs, and so much more.

Donors want transparency; they want proof and a connection to the cause. If we can track the status of a package in the mail, why can't we track a charitable donation? If I can see my accounts via online banking, why can't I see where my charitable funds go?

In an age when you can track everything on your smartphone—caloric intake, daily steps, coffee purchases, stock portfolios—you should be able to track your social impact.

The team at WE has often thought about how this could be done better. We wanted to deliver real-time proof of impact.

It was a challenge that brought together our corporate partners, our social enterprise, and our charity. We sought a solution that would benefit the charity by raising more dollars for social impact, as well as improve business outcomes for partners by enhancing the customer experience, engaging retail employees, and differentiating the product and/or the retailer to increase sales.

Our team created something unprecedented called Track Your Impact (TYI). It's an inventory tracking system, but it's so much more than that. The system leverages a product's existing Universal Product Code (UPC), those black-and-white bars unique to each product that are scanned at checkout to reveal more information. To the existing system, the manufacturer or seller can add a sticker with an eight-digit TYI code. When customers input the UPC or TYI code online, they can find out exactly what charitable impact their purchase will make. Each TYI product unlocks a unique charitable impact—whether in developing countries, delivering five gallons of clean water to a family or a package of lentil seeds for a farmer; or in developed countries, providing a curriculum resource for a local school or leadership training for at-risk youth.

Consumers can see information about their specific charitable impact, and pinpoint on a map the region, village, or city where their impact is being delivered to change a life. Consumers can even opt-in to receive ongoing updates about their impact via email.

WE launched the TYI pilot with codes on Artisans products and donations to our WE Village charity projects. So the sales of Artisans goods not only provided a fair wage to the mamas who made them, but also

Track Your Impact

A Game Changer

82%
Users

82 percent of TYI consumers talk to friends and family about their purchases.

76%
Users

76 percent of TYI consumers strongly agree that offering products with transparent social impact proves retailers care about the community.

68%
Users

68 percent of TYI consumers chose TYI over similar products, even if they cost a little bit more.

—Mission Measurement Survey commissioned by ME to WE

supported development initiatives in the villages where the women lived. And customers could track it all, typing codes into the website to pinpoint the specific village on a map, with photos and stories about the people in that community, telling why and how the impacts change lives.

We quickly realized these impact codes didn't have to be confined to our own Artisans line. Track Your Impact makes any product stand out. It brings an online edge to the in-store shopping experience, and fuses the transparency of technology with the selling power of purpose. So often companies try to sell what their products don't do: No animals were harmed, no rainforests were cut down.

The beauty of TYI is that it shows you what your purchase will do. And with sharable content that customers can take to social media. Shoppers buy the product, make an impact, meet the community affected, and share the story, like pictures of clean-water projects or facts about drought and small-hold farmers. The social media halo amplifies the brand, and invites other consumers to join. And when consumers opt-in to receive information about their impacts, at the bottom of the message they see additional products and services that deliver more impacts to change the world. All of this amplifies the cause, inspiring others to shop with impact.

If you want a real-time example, flip to the back cover of this book and enter the TYI code online.

Back to sunny Santa Monica and to PacSun, where Marc cracked the veneer of the hipster fashion crowd with these stories of impact. We gave our co-branded white tees a distinguishing feature no other retailer could offer—purpose, so transparent that customers could discover how their white tee would make a difference while they shopped. The ME to WE Essential line started with T-shirts, but quickly expanded across multiple product categories to become one of PacSun's top four apparel labels, a big feat considering the hundreds of brands carried include Nike, Adidas, and Calvin Klein.

Tracking proved that purpose could prop up the white T-shirt. It also proved an important aspect of customer behavior—shoppers will go out of their way to make socially conscious choices. Initially,

Consumers today are informed, empowered, and not easily manipulated. They want to buy the change they wish to see in the world, and so they want companies to be able to prove purpose.

PacSun assumed that customers would make a purchase, then take the product home to trace the impact. Instead, shoppers dug through piles of merchandise, brandishing their phones, inputting the codes online from the tags on a pile of identical T-shirts to find the one that gave vitamins to a child in India, or a chicken to provide eggs for a mother in Ecuador. Decisions weren't random, and not just relegated to a choice between making a difference or not. Shoppers craved a personal connection to their impact, choosing Latin America because of a family connection or school supplies because their parents are teachers.

Product differentiation has always been a challenge. Add the fact that the consumer landscape is shifting constantly—spending preferences, technology, ethics, retail models—and the problem increases tenfold. Product options in most categories are endless. And, as much as we worship the concept of choice and variety in our culture, science tells us that too many options diminish the motivation to buy.[1] Choice and oversupply are major and growing challenges for business today. "Competition is infinite. A flat world and low barriers to entry, thanks especially to the Internet, have neutered the biggest product differentiators: price, quality, and convenience," writes Jason Saul, CEO of the social impact consulting firm Mission Measurement.[2]

What if purpose is the game-changing differentiator that gives products an edge? Purpose can be the inspiration for a new venture, but it can also be used to retrofit an existing product, all the while providing a tangible social impact that consumers can see.

Carol Cone, global practice chair for international public relations giant Edelman, suggests adding "purpose" as the fifth "P" in the traditional marketing mix of product, pricing, place, and promotion. "Beyond CSR, cause marketing, or altruism," writes Cone, "purpose is a core strategy for profit and growth based on linking an organization's reason for being to improving lives and impacting society."[4]

In other words: purpose sells. Purpose is a differentiator.

Shoppers report that they are willing to pay more for products that do good. In the largest study of its kind, researchers at New York University examined a raft of consumer surveys and found that 60 percent of shoppers are willing to pay

of Shoppers

60 percent of shoppers are willing to pay a premium for socially conscious products.

a premium for socially conscious products. Granted, it's easy to seem righteous in a survey, and many respondents likely overestimated their commitment to responsible shopping to boost their own self-esteem. Maybe only a percentage of these respondents are willing to buy the change they seek in the world. Even still, don't you want in on that? Five or ten percent of customers in the consumer packaged goods industry, for instance, adds up to billions of dollars for the brand on the right side of the premium. That's a lot of money for being on the cutting edge of recycled packaging or environmentally friendly home cleaners.[5] On average, consumers would spend 17 percent more for products that came with social or environmental benefits.[6] Research suggests that consumers value and prefer the promise of transparent impact.

There's mounting evidence of both consumer fatigue and cynicism with traditional cause marketing. A 2015 survey by social research firm Mission Measurement found that 58 percent of respondents want to understand the impact they're having when they buy a product linked to a social cause, as opposed to simply noting the colored ribbon on the wrapper.[7] Where is the money going? Who benefits? We had to make the customer understand how shampoo (or a white T-shirt) relates to international development. As consumers track their impact online, they can access further information about the cause. We find that the initial purchase of a Rafiki or co-branded T-shirt is what we call a "gateway engagement" that spurs additional interest in making a difference through service, philanthropy, or further purchases. This is why TYI works. It's not a commercial; it's a connection.

If the thought of adding a social mission to your already established brand feels daunting, know that you don't have to do purpose, or even find the cause, all on your own. Working with partners for brand credibility is nothing new. Think back to the golden age of celebrity endorsement, which, for me, peaked somewhere between Pepsi and Britney Spears and Fabio and I Can't Believe It's Not Butter. Today, it might be a nonprofit partner that boosts your business instead of a pop star.

In fact, when the quality and price of two items are similar, a brand's social purpose has become the most powerful trigger for consumer purchasing decisions. Think about that for a moment. What compels shoppers to buy isn't Britney with a sweaty can of soda. Since 2008, social purpose has consistently outpaced other considerations, even design and brand loyalty, according to a study by Edelman.[8] I have witnessed this phenomenon with our corporate partners.

All else being equal, purpose is the tiebreaker.

Later on, we'll help you find your cause, plan your purpose, and reap all the benefits, with a step-by-step plan that can be used by business leaders and individuals, in the workplace or at home. (Take a peek at the chapter titled Find Your Cause if you're curious).

Changing the World, One Shower at a Time

The challenge in our PacSun partnership was to distinguish a product, the white T-shirt, that was very similar to its competitors from a consumer perspective. With the naked eye, it would be hard to tell the difference between 10 white T-shirts from 10 different companies.

On the other end of product choice spectrum was what I called the shampoo-and-conditioner conundrum.

I admit that my hair-care products consist mostly of miniature hotel freebies. On the rare occasion that I run out, I dread the endless corridor of bottles at the drugstore. This one promises to give your hair 10 percent more volume (10 percent more than what?); that one claims to repair damaged ends (are my ends damaged?). There is too much perceived difference between brands, and an excess of information. It

A Step-by-Step Plan

Step 1

Make a purchase

Step 2

Enter your code

Step 3

See exactly what you gave and where—pinpoint on the map

Step 4

Follow your community for updates

becomes white noise. Why should I grab your bottle when I can leave the decision to the hospitality industry?

The answer begins on a freezing Minneapolis night in 2014, when Johnathan Atwood, Unilever's VP of Sustainable Living for North America, bumped into a group of Walgreens executives. All were waiting at the curb outside their hotel for a ride to an evening party, which happened to be for WE Day Minnesota. What started as small talk to distract from the blistering cold breaching their coats turned into a partnership that would drive both brands, jump profits, get the praise of each guy's CEO as well as the press, and do a massive amount of good. It was a chance encounter that would lead to a beautiful business relationship.

Unilever had already made a name for itself in the area of corporate social responsibility, having led the Food Producers sector in the Dow Jones Sustainability World Indexes for over a decade.[9] It was a good-on-paper partner, the kind you could bring home to your parents. Walgreens is a drugstore partnered with the UK's Boots chain; with its 8,000 stores nationwide, it's a distribution giant. As a basis of comparison, for those readers outside the U.S., there are thousands more Walgreens stores than Walmart locations in America. It is a massive—and popular—chain, found in almost every community across America.

Over the next several months, teams from our three organizations put their heads together to come up with a campaign that would infuse Unilever products, sold at Walgreens, with a social value proposition that included Track Your Impact. The campaign would involve three of Unilever's flagship products: its TRESemmé, Suave, and Caress brands of shampoos and body washes. Andrea Farris, VP of Inventory Management and Supply Chain at Walgreens, reflected on the process: "Those brands aligned with the goal we were trying to achieve: while you're taking care of yourself with these products, you can also do good."

It was a natural progression to choose clean water as the social impact these products would deliver, since personal care products are often used with and linked to water.

In other words, if you own a restaurant, you probably want to consider hunger or food waste as a cause, over, say, animal rescue. Pick something with an intuitive connection to what you do, making

Customers tend to respond better to cause marketing that makes an authentic connection to the core business.

it easier for consumers to link it to your brand. Again, we'll talk more about you creating your own purpose plan in Part Three.

So it was settled: Every purchase of one of these shampoos would provide five gallons of clean water to a child in a developing country through our charitable programs. The cause was meaningful and a logical extension of the core business.

Unilever's "GiveH2OPE" campaign ran from July 26 to September 30, 2015. It was, by all measures, a glowing success. Our estimate that 15 million gallons of water would be delivered through purchases was exceeded by 2.5 million gallons. This program literally saves lives. The United Nations cites unclean water and poor sanitation as a leading cause of child mortality. Childhood diarrhea, which is closely associated with insufficient water supply in the developing world, is estimated to cause 1.5 million child deaths per year, mostly among children under five living in developing countries.[10]

Walgreens told us that the products saw double-digit sales lifts. We aren't authorized to reveal the exact numbers, but I can tell you that consumer goods companies fight hard for even a small percentage increase, and so "double digits" is basically code for kicking butt. These were already popular brands, but purpose gave them an unprecedented boost. We all expected that the campaign would lift sales, but what our partners really loved about the project was the social media halo. Working from a benchmark based on previous campaigns, Walgreen's set a social media goal of 94,000 engagements on Facebook. That would have been terrific as their stretch goal. But after eight weeks, GiveH2OPE had garnered 1.7 million engagements. A Twitter engagement goal of 66,000 engagements was surpassed by almost 400,000. It would take a lot to generate more buzz on social media about personal care products than we did here. David Beckham himself would have to publicly reveal his body wash preferences to beat those numbers.

"We aspire to be a standout global CSR company. By remaining dedicated to causes, we have made a substantial impact."

—Ornella Barra, Co-Chief Operating Officer, Walgreens Boots Alliance, Inc.

In retrospect, there were many reasons for the campaign's success. Among them, a well-aligned partnership between the manufacturer and the retailer was based on a common purpose. Because of the partnership, Unilever products got prime placement in Walgreens stores for the duration, in the coveted end-cap that juts out of every aisle and attracts foot traffic. Those with retail experience know that it's a constant battle among manufacturers to occupy that space, but adding purpose to the products convinced both companies that prime placement would move additional quantities, driving both purpose and profit. Each partner was invested in the outcome, and therefore deployed resources and strategies to ensure its success. Both Unilever and Walgreens CEOs spoke publicly about a cause that made sense for their business goals. The *Chicago Tribune* newspaper and other press covered the story about consumer transparency, resulting in a boost in free advertising. A partnership without purpose would have been more white noise.

If you're looking to differentiate from the competitors, look to purpose. Savvy customers are looking to help causes, so help them look to yours. In the age of product parity, use purpose to make your brand pop and make the world a better place while you're at it.

"Companies don't operate in isolation: customers, suppliers, policymakers, investors, and an entire industry of competitors act as an ecosystem that will adapt to new standards."

SWEAT THE BIG AND SMALL STUFF

By Holly Branson

It's rare to find me, Marc, and Craig in the same room. So what better time to tell the two of them about Virgin Atlantic's sustainability initiatives than on our flight to visit a WE Villages community in rural India? If we couldn't be in the same office, at least we were in the same cabin.

People often tell me: "I'd love for our company to be more sustainable—but it's just too expensive." So while starting dinner at 35,000 feet, I wanted to explain the significant and sizable challenges faced by the airline industry, as it has been an intensive but fascinating journey for our airline Virgin Atlantic and one that I am asked about a lot. But I also wanted to show that sustainability doesn't always have to be costly or for that matter complicated to achieve. In fact, investing in purpose-spurred initiatives, the small ones just as much as the grander ones, can save you money—which you can reinvest in other sustainability projects.

If you're interested in aviation (yes, all you plane spotters out there!) or want to learn more about sustainability within large industries (you may be part of one), I hope you'll discover something new from the massive steps that have taken place across the airline industry and at Virgin Atlantic in order to cut carbon. For the individual, there are also some hints and tips for small changes you can make at home and while traveling that collectively can have huge positive impact.

So sit back and relax, Marc and Craig, and welcome to Virgin Atlantic's nonstop service to Delhi, complete with my sales pitch on sweating the small—and the big—stuff.

First, a bit of background. In the first decade of this century, the airline industry was suffering a serious image problem in Britain. Climate change was finally starting to get the attention it deserved among UK politicians. In 2006, the Bishop of London described flying as a "symptom of sin" while British newspapers debated the morality of holiday air travel. Aviation, indeed, was fast becoming a dirty word.

All that bad press might have sent a company scrambling for short-term solutions to boost quarterly profits, or a superficial marketing facelift to lure customers. In fact, at Virgin Atlantic, we'd made a start on making our operations greener, but we lacked a comprehensive strategy to reduce our emissions, or to tell the public the story of our efforts. So in 2007, we set up our brand-new Change Is in the Air sustainability program to get focused on what we needed to do.

We knew we had a responsibility to make changes that would have real, positive impact on the planet—after all, we're all dependent on it for our survival. Establishing Change Is in the Air meant we started to look at what our biggest issues were and how we could do better. We wanted to be part of setting the standard for sustainability initiatives instead of playing catch-up as the problem worsened. We also knew this would have a number of benefits, and we could build on our Virgin values. Enhance our reputation. Increase efficiencies. Run a successful business. And help to be a leader in our industry.

Sweating the BIG Stuff: Where Do You Even Begin?

We recognized early on that, as an airline, our biggest issue would be our carbon emissions. In fact, our carbon footprint measurements have confirmed that Virgin Atlantic's carbon emissions from aircraft operations dwarf everything else we do, with more than 99.9 percent of our direct emissions coming from aircraft fuel use. Even when we factor in our supply chains, aircraft fuel consumption still accounts for around two-thirds of our emissions, with only a fraction of a percent from ground energy and ground fuel use. The remaining third—that's across both our airline and holiday operations—come from the upstream carbon associated with our supply chains, that is, all the products and services we buy, anything from aircraft to hotel rooms. You'll hear a lot about how important it is to manage your supply chains later in the book.

All this confirms that, first and foremost, we need to prioritize our efforts on improving our aircraft fuel and carbon efficiency.

Celebrities who sweat the small and the big stuff[1]

Gisele Bundchen

The supermodel raises funds for conservation efforts in the Amazon and Atlantic Rainforests through her eco-friendly flip-flop line (Ipanema Gisele Bundchen), and she is a Goodwill Ambassador for the United Nations Environment Program.

Jamie Oliver

The celebrity chef is a long-time advocate of healthy eating and sustainable farming. Proceeds from his "American Road Trip" (the first fully carbon-neutral TV show) were distributed to environmental initiatives including solar energy projects in India and wind power schemes in China. Oliver's London restaurants are partially powered by wind turbines he installed.

Cate Blanchett

The actress was a key proponent of Greening the Wharf, a project that oversaw 1,900 solar panels being installed in The Wharf Theatre at Sydney's Walsh Bay. This now provides 70 percent of the theater's electricity requirements.

So What Are We Doing about Carbon?

By far the biggest single thing an airline can do to reduce its carbon emissions right now is to invest in new, more efficient fleet—swapping out older planes for much more fuel efficient ones. And that's precisely what we've been doing for a number of years. As a result, over the last nine years, we've reduced our total aircraft CO_2 emissions by a very encouraging 22 percent.

In terms of new fleet, first to come into service were 10 lovely new A330s in 2010. This was followed by the first of our 17 shiny new 787s in 2014—we expect to take our last in 2018. It's these 787s that have made the biggest difference to our latest results, with an 8 percent drop in CO_2 emissions from aircraft operations in 2016 alone. It doesn't end there. In 2019 we'll start bringing 12 new A350s into our fleet to replace the last of our older, less efficient aircraft. Each of these aircraft gives us about 30 percent carbon savings per trip compared to the older aircraft they're replacing. That's a combination of the massive improvements in airframe and engine design, as well as making sure we're using the right aircraft on the right routes, maximizing passenger numbers per trip and getting the best efficiencies we can. Now I sound like a plane spotter, and proud to be one! Once this multi-billion-dollar fleet renewal program is complete, we'll have one of the most efficient long-haul fleets in the sky.

That brings me neatly back on board our flight to India and my goal to convince Marc and Craig that the smallest changes can also make the biggest impact.

Because using aircraft fuel is such a big part of what an airline does, shaving fractions of a percent off fuel use can add up to significant CO_2 reductions, and for this, we need all our teams to get involved.

Green Rockers

Dave Matthews Band

The Grammy-winning band founded Green Music Group, a large-scale coalition of musicians, fans, and music industry leaders seeking to bring about lasting change in the industry. Members include Linkin Park, Sheryl Crow, and Willie Nelson.

Jack Johnson

The surfer-turned-singer/songwriter popularized EnviroRiders (riders are the contractors bands use for specific functions while on tour), which require venues and tour operators to purchase renewable 100 percent renewable energy at shows, recycle at least 50 percent of the total waste generated, and change all lighting to efficient compact fluorescents.

Maroon 5

Since 2008, the Grammy-winning band has been committed to green touring by using biodiesel-powered tour buses, promoting recycling at its concert venues, and donating a portion of ticket sales to Global Cool, an environmental charity that works with entertainers.

First, think of our pilots up there on the flight deck, getting you safely from A to B. Much like driving a car, how they operate our aircraft makes a noticeable difference to carbon emissions. In 2016, we published the results of a study in which we reminded our Captains about some of the routine things they could do—those things already mentioned in their operating manuals—that would affect aircraft fuel use. Even we were surprised to find that in eight months of simply sending them reminders, we saved 6,828 tons of fuel, 21,507 tons of

> *"Integrity may be about little things as much or more than big ones."*
>
> —Tom Peters, author of *The Little Big Things: 163 Ways to Pursue Excellence*

CO_2, and a very welcome £3,309,489 for the business (about £1 million at current fuel prices)—a double win for us.

And then look out the window, guys. You'll notice that the red-tipped wing of this Boeing 787—we call her *Birthday Girl*—is sparkling. During regular maintenance, our fastidious engineers clean the aircraft's wings by hand to make sure they're as squeaky clean as possible. Clean aircraft are more aerodynamic, whereas dirt causes friction, which uses more fuel, which in turn produces more greenhouse gases. Who knew a lowly cleaning cloth and some elbow grease could help to save the planet?

Just as you would never leave your car idling—really . . . never, right? Or drive around town with a full trunk (boot for our UK readers!), or a roof rack full of camping gear long after the trail's end, so airlines are working to lighten the load.

Here our in-flight services team has had a huge role to play. Our dining carts are now nine kilograms lighter than our old ones. During the course of just one year, that's the equivalent of eliminating 500 London buses worth of weight, saving about 8,000 tons of CO_2 a year. Heavier aircraft use more fuel, which means more emissions, so every ounce on board counts. We've also trimmed the weight of our trays, meal containers, china, glassware, and cutlery—even the humble teaspoon doesn't escape attention!

Hopefully, this has given you a good idea about how we've been getting our carbon reductions so far, but aviation is still undoubtedly carbon intensive, so what else can be done?

A New Global Carbon Agreement for International Aviation—It's a Massive Deal, in More Ways Than One

Back in 2008, Virgin Atlantic was one of a handful of airlines that set up a small, pioneering industry group called Aviation Global Deal (AGD), to campaign for an international carbon deal for our sector. At the time it was seen as kind of weird by our competitors—airlines operate in a very challenging economic environment, so why would we suggest voluntarily adding to costs by paying for some of our carbon emissions?

But AGD members knew that, after doing all the things already described, it would be the best, most effective, and efficient way to secure carbon reductions. And if we all acted together, it would also be fair. Fairness is a key UN principle. In international law, airlines operating on the same routes need to be treated equally in terms of financial incentives or penalties. It's why an international aviation deal has been forged alongside the 2015 Paris climate agreement (which includes domestic aviation)—we needed our own agreement to deal with the equality principle, while also achieving measurable environmental results. It's why AGD set about coming up with some ideas that might work for everyone. Thankfully our airline industry body IATA later got involved and did a fantastic job of bringing airlines from around the world into the fold, supporting the intense negotiations between the UN and nation states.

Fast-forward eight years—and a *huge* amount of hard work later—and the world's first global, sectoral deal was achieved—a massive breakthrough. It's called the Carbon Offsetting and Reduction Scheme for International Aviation (CORSIA) and means that from 2020 onward, international airlines from all over the globe will collectively be spending billions of dollars in new, meaningful, carbon-reduction projects around the world—like renewable energy projects to reduce our reliance on fossil fuels and conservation projects that keep CO_2 out of the atmosphere. And naturally, we're pleased.

Low-Carbon Jet Fuels: Pipe Dream or Reality?

We're not stopping there. The next biggest change for airlines is likely to come in the form of low carbon fuels. Unlike ground energy and ground transport, it's pretty clear that airlines have no alternatives and are going to need liquid fuels for a long time yet. Which is why, in 2011, we partnered with exciting new cleantech company LanzaTech. Their ground-breaking approach makes fuels out of waste industrial gases. Did you know, for example, that many steel mills around the world produce carbon monoxide (CO) as a waste gas—and this is often flared (burned) off as CO_2, directly into the atmosphere? LanzaTech captures and recycles the carbon in the waste CO, converting it into fuels via fermentation and other processes. Clever, huh? And so far they're making great progress.

In 2016, they produced their first significant batch of jet fuel (4,000 U.S. gallons) and also won a U.S. government grant to design their first

Top tips from the team at Virgin Atlantic for traveling more sustainably:

Choose an airline with independently verified carbon reduction measures and results.

Choose a sustainably certified hotel when possible: *Lots of hotels are now doing more to be green.*

Pack lighter: *By packing only what you need, you'll reduce your traveling weight and that means fuel use and your carbon emissions. The smaller things help, too, like removing the outer packaging from items before you travel. This reduces weight and reduces the burden of waste in other countries, too, which is extra important if they don't have the same recycling opportunities as back home.*

Be prepared: *Always carry a lightweight, reusable water bottle and refill it before you travel instead of relying on bottled water.*

Buy and carry a lightweight, pack away, reusable bag for your souvenirs and beach gear. You can use it for your shopping when you get home too.

Offset your own flight: *Virgin Atlantic has partnered with award-winning Natural Capital Partners to support communities around the world by providing them with cleaner, cheaper, safer renewable energy, for example. If you offset your flight with us, you'll reduce carbon emissions and make a real difference to people around the world. Visit www .virginatlantic.com/changeisintheair for details.*

Go explore: *When you're away, grab a map and walk or cycle instead of taking a taxi. You'll be amazed what you'll discover!*

Live like a local: *Eat, drink, and shop locally. Use local forms of public transport, too. You'll reduce your carbon footprint, help support the local economy, and learn more about the country you're visiting.*

low carbon jet fuel demonstration scale plant. We're working with them to develop plans for the world's first commercial jet fuel plant using this exciting new technology. With a bit of government support, we could see the fuels used in our aircraft in the not too distant future.

It's Not ALL about Carbon . . .

Anyone working in sustainable business will know that one of the other big things a company can do is to work with suppliers on making the products and services it buys more sustainable, particularly in terms of improving their people, animal, and environmental credentials.

Reaching thousands of suppliers is a massive challenge, but here, too, we've made a start, and not only in terms of our low carbon fuels work. For example, as you ponder your onboard menu offerings, you can rest assured our onboard food and drink have been rigorously assessed by our in-flight services team for their impact on people, the planet, and animals. In fact, we were the first airline to partner with the Sustainable Restaurant Association, setting new industry-leading standards for our caterers around the world on factory and farm workers' rights, humanely sourced meat and dairy, sustainably sourced fish, and the removal or replacement of high-deforestation products, like palm oil and soy.

To spot another supply chain example on a Virgin Atlantic flight, check out the striking red uniforms on the cabin crew who direct you to your seat. Designed by Dame Vivienne Westwood—the Sex Pistols used to wear her clothes—the men's and pilots' uniforms are made, in part, from recycled yarn that comes from used plastic bottles. All suit fabrics have a nano-coating designed to make them last longer, reducing waste. And all of the uniforms are fully recycled when they finally wear out. Even the buttons are snipped off and used as spares.

And finally, a recent initiative comes from the holiday side of our business. In 2016, our Virgin Holidays team updated our stance on working with tourist attractions featuring captive whales and dolphins. There's no doubt it's a tricky and controversial area to stray into, but we're pleased to have made a number of new commitments, including: working with existing facilities to improve the welfare of animals currently in captivity; not selling any new attractions that feature captive whales and dolphins; supporting the development of sanctuaries for animals currently in captivity; and providing more choice for our customers in the form of responsible wild whale and dolphin watching experiences.

Manage Your Supply Chain

Becoming a WEconomy company is challenging for any business. Why not start by asking the following questions about your supply chains. These are also questions you can ask as a consumer, by the way!

- *Do you need it (all/at all)?*
- *Who made it? And how?*
- *What is it wrapped in?*
- *How will it be transported?*
- *How will it perform throughout its life?*
- *What does it say to our customers?*
- *Where does it come from?*
- *What is it made of?*
- *Where will it end up?*

We don't invest in sustainability initiatives just because it's the right thing to do, although it certainly is. We also see it as smart business.

This kind of impact will pay financial dividends. Customers recognize when you're working for the good of their community, and the loyalty and respect it garners is invaluable. Giving people the warm and fuzzies is quantifiable. Loads of market research suggests consumers are going green, including a McKinsey survey in which 87 percent of participants ranked environmental and people issues of utmost importance to their purchasing decisions. Green consumers also tend to be less price-sensitive and more loyal.[2]

Companies don't operate in isolation: customers, suppliers, policymakers, investors, and an entire industry of competitors act as an ecosystem that will adapt to new standards. Customers expect products and services that minimize the impact on people, animals, and the environment. Once the hard work is done building awareness and capacity in the supply chain, it's easier for others to follow.

In the WEconomy, a company's survival and prosperity depend on its ethics.

I hope this has given you a flavor of some of the things we've been doing. There are lots of hints and tips below to help you personally make a difference too.

Thank you for flying Virgin Atlantic. I finally think it's time to let Marc and Craig get some shut-eye!

Sweat the small stuff at work and at home to save big

Switch to renewable electricity at home, either by installing solar panels or a wind turbine. Just not possible? Why not switch to a renewable energy supplier such as Good Energy or Ecotricity. Make sure you ask them how they source their energy, because not all green tariffs are what they seem.

Remember to switch everything off that's not in use: TVs, computers, lights. Small changes like this really add up, and will save you money, too.

Switch off or adjust your heat or cooling system to closer to the ambient temperature. You'll save money and emissions if you do.

Even the smallest stuff like **reducing your computer monitor brightness to 70 percent** can save 20 percent of the energy it uses. And remember to program that same monitor to go to sleep after 10 minutes, rather than 30 minutes.

Buy less stuff, create less waste

If you need to buy, support the most **sustainably sourced products** you can find.

Always carry a lightweight, foldaway reusable bag and save on those plastic carrier bags when you're out and about.

Ditch the straw. It's a single-use, throwaway item we can all manage without. Remember to remind your bartender.

And of course, **always recycle** when you have the option.

Carry a refillable water bottle. Tap water is often fresher, better quality, and, of course, it's free! You'll help save emissions on all that unnecessary transport moving water around, as well as help reduce the millions of tons of waste plastic bottles generated every year.

Before you buy, always ask yourself if you really need more stuff. Spend your money on fun experiences instead!

Transport

For short journeys, walk, run, or cycle. This will get you fit while reducing your carbon footprint. Too exhausting? Use public transport whenever you can, and if you're shopping for a new car, choose the lowest fuel consumption/ CO_2 emissions car possible and look up car sharing schemes. These measures will save you money, too.

And remember those little things that add up. Stop idling your car—just ten minutes less per day can save you 8.9 gallons of fuel each year.

Food

You may love your meat, but the livestock industry is a huge source of emissions. **Consider eating less meat (especially beef):** even if you can only manage this one or two days a week, to begin with. Widespread vegetarianism could cut food-related carbon emissions by 63 percent.

Remember to shop for more sustainably sourced food, too. Purchase local, seasonal, sustainably sourced fish, and watch out for hidden high-deforestation-risk products like soy and palm oil.

"Use purpose to prove to young consumers
that your values align with theirs."

UNLOCK NEW CUSTOMERS

By Marc Kielburger

Millennials, Gen Z, and Gen WE, oh my!

It was the end of an era in Canada. The Royal Canadian Mint was phasing out the one-cent coin. A single penny is a rounding error, the reason lone coppers are found abandoned on sidewalks or loose in junk drawers. But what about all of the pennies still in circulation? Our 2013 WE Create Change campaign encouraged Canadian kids to collect endangered pennies for clean water projects in WE Villages overseas. Who wouldn't offer their last few pennies to dig boreholes and build wells in developing communities? The coins were about to become extinct. But there was a small snag in our plan. We envisioned millions of pennies pouring into our offices. Who would count them? Who would roll them into those finicky little paper tubes for processing? For that matter, who would process them? And finally, who would accept pennies as payment and turn them into real money? The coins were about to become worthless.

Enter the Royal Bank of Canada (RBC), the country's largest bank for much of modern history, and among the top fifteen banks in the world. Like any business, it couldn't be guaranteed that plum position in the future. Competition for banking customers is intense. More than four million Canadians swapped their financial partner between 2010 and 2015 and 70 percent said switching was simple.[1]

Customers today are less loyal to brands and services, and they have very high expectations. They want everything on their smartphones, instant digital transactions, longer branch hours, and they don't want to pay for their accounts. What's more, convincing the junior wedge of the demographic pie to choose a particular bank is incredibly tough. Young people are especially cynical about financial institutions, thanks to a global recession that, in the U.S., was largely blamed on Wall Street and big banks. (Canadian banks fared far better than most anywhere in the world, but that was a minor matter in the news during the Occupy movement.) This is why new checking accounts often come with free TVs or other electronic toys as enticements. What's more, technology has opened the fiercely competitive financial sector to new, nimble players like pay services from Apple and Google. Some big banks fear these are Trojan horses that will bring interference from more tech giants. When you can walk into a grocery store and walk out with a credit card and a car loan from its financial services partner, then, suffice it to say, the market is crowded. It's a tough time to be a bank.

And critics are harsh. Canadian banks are not meeting the expectations of 75 percent of their customers, according to a survey by financial technology firm, FIS. In fact, Canadian consumers are among the most likely to shop around for financial services.[2]

RBC was well aware of these challenges when they partnered with us. They also knew that gaining access to future investors from a notoriously skeptical and well-educated generation would mean transparency and authenticity in these efforts. Customer engagement was a big bonus that year when the bank processed CND$1.4 million in donated pennies for WE Create Change. Allow me to move the decimal. That's 140,000,000

Teen participants in our RBC programs were surveyed, and are twice as likely to believe that RBC positively impacts their communities compared to other adolescents. They are also 1.3 times more likely to recommend the bank to friends and family.

pennies, enough to outweigh five Boeing 747s—passenger jets always make numbers easier to digest. The feat is made even more incredible when you consider that kids ran the show, excavating couches at home and holding coin drives at school.

But there is one thing kids can't do—drive. And pennies are heavy. Across the country, proud parents walked into RBC branches with their kids, who hoisted bags of coins onto bank counters. Children and teens, rarely seen inside brick-and-mortar financial institutions, were welcomed like activist rock stars.

"We have made a long-standing commitment to invest in and support youth—not only for their own benefit, but for the collective benefit of our local communities and the world."

—Dave McKay, President and CEO of RBC

Because of WE Create Change alone, RBC had a boost of 55,000 unique customer walk-ins. That's 55,000 interactions with customer service reps, 55,000 pairs of eyes locked on in-branch advertising for the duration of their visit. More importantly, the cause of clean drinking water was aligned with RBC's Blue Water Project, which supports organizations that protect fresh watersheds, reduce water usage, and facilitate clean drinking water. Because RBC helped us with a logistical hurdle that we couldn't possibly have done in-house—processing millions of loose coins—more than 56,000 people received a sustainable source of clean drinking water, with wells dug and pump systems installed, community members trained in maintenance and repairs, and small businesses established to generate funds for any future repairs and expansion. Clean water scarcity still affects almost 40 percent of the global population, creating a host of sanitary and disease concerns. But clean water also has an economic benefit. The United Nations estimates that every US$1 invested in clean water translates into an average return of US$9, with those benefits being experienced specifically by poor children in disadvantaged communities.[3] Canadian kids rolled up their sleeves to help impoverished children they'd likely never meet.

All of that social impact delivered, and scores of beaming parents watched their children give back while standing in line at the bank, not queuing for mortgage advice or currency exchange, but for purpose. In fact, they did more than just watch. One in four parents whose children participated in WE programming used an RBC banking service as a result of the partnership.[4]

You can almost see RBC's brand halo glowing, its customer base swelling. RBC has also supported financial literacy education in our WE Schools curriculum. The bank's "It All Adds Up" program encourages youth to save, spend, and donate, demonstrating that smart money management and giving back go hand in hand. This commitment to financial literacy for students—in other words, an investment in purpose—has nabbed attention from youth. In a focus group, WE Schools educators said the program has kids and teens thinking smarter about spending. One high school math teacher said, "Students are now starting to save for college. A group who were fundraising were able to better understand the impact of dollars raised."

> *"Philanthropy can often be the most cost-effective way for a company to improve its competitive context."*
>
> —Michael E. Porter, Professor at Harvard Business School

Marketing experts suggest that brand consciousness, the ability to recognize a product as distinct from others, starts when children are about 24 months old.

If you don't know much about industry marketing, it might seem pointless to win over teens who lack stable paychecks or stock portfolios.

But today's teen is tomorrow's investor and easily becomes a lifelong customer.

As early as 36 months, children are aware that brands are meant to reflect personal attributes (cool, smart, sporty), learning most of their brand associations from mom and dad.[5] Any parent walking through a grocery store can attest to the consequences of this research. It's no accident that cereal and cookies are stocked at a toddler's eye level. My daughters will reach out for a box from inside the confines of the shopping cart as if they are about to be reunited with a long-lost love, the aluminum chariot a cruel cage. What's actually in the box is of no consequence, as SpongeBob SquarePants stares out at them expectantly.

Purpose unlocks new customers.

"There is a spiritual aspect to our lives—when we give, we receive—when a business does something good for somebody, that somebody feels good about them!"

—Ben Cohen, Co-founder, Ben & Jerry's

The under-25s spend about £5 billion annually in the UK, with an increasing amount of disposable income. Pocket money for youth has reached an average of £6.84 per week, an increase of 500 percent compared to rates in 1987.[6]

In America, teens earn an annual income of $91 billion collectively, but are responsible for approximately $259 billion in spending. Clearly, they are living beyond their means, with a discrepancy covered by the Bank of Mom and Dad, making teens persuasive influencers in household buying habits overall.[7] Figuring out what they want is quite lucrative.

This is not a generation lured by marketing gimmicks or confined by brand loyalty over the long term, says our friend David Stillman, co-author (with his teenage son Jonah) of *Gen Z @ Work: How the Next Generation Is Transforming the Workplace*. He tells us that for this cohort, the oldest of whom are now entering their twenties, purpose has become a given. "Just like we saw with millennials, Gen Z loves to make purchases that have an impact. However, where millennials accepted this as common practice, Gen Z expects it," says Stillman.[8]

If this trend continues, future generations will be shopping for world change and scrutinizing corporate causes more thoroughly. Use purpose to prove to young consumers that your values align with theirs; that you care about the world they live in and issues that concern them. Purpose can grab this demographic and their disposable spending habits, and channel its buying power into bettering the world, while creating lifelong consumers for socially conscious companies.

Believe it or not, millennials are worth billions

73%
Millennials

73 percent are willing to pay more for brands that are sustainable, more than any other age group.[9]

$30
Trillion

Within a few decades, $30 trillion in assets is set to pass from boomers to their heirs, including millennials.[10]

A $12 trillion market is opening: Are you ready to unlock the customers?

In 2015, more than 150 world leaders adopted the United Nations Sustainable Development Goals, 17 concrete steps to change the world over the next 15 years. The ambitious plan includes actions to end poverty, hunger, and inequality, and to improve global access to health care and education. Delivering this social impact will also be quite lucrative.

One report estimates that sustainable business models related to the goals will create US$12 trillion in economic opportunities, and add 380 million jobs by 2030.[11] That adds up to a whole lot of potential new customers.

ME to WE Greeting Cards

When people think of the market as a driving force for social innovation, they conjure up headline-grabbing examples: solar panels, electric cars, and cutting-edge recycling technology. These are exciting areas. Still, fewer people see the opportunities that come with disrupting more traditional industries. The next wave of purpose and profit will upend our daily routines with subtle changes that deliver big impact in unexpected places. For instance, WE attached purpose to paper.

In the era of Snapchat and Instagram, greeting cards are about as relevant to young people as landlines. There's only so much technology the industry can add to a folded piece of paper. So ME to WE did a trial partnership with American Greetings, the world's largest card company, to inject a social conscience into cards with Track Your Impact. Adding purpose connected the cards to causes overseas, delivering life-changing impacts to those in need. And, since shoppers could share the impact on social media, it also connected paper cards to the digital world. Did it work? ME to WE cards achieved the near-impossible: sales rose in the age 17 to 30 demographic, a group that didn't even have greeting cards on its radar. And because of the partnership, over 300,000 positive impacts were made, including the provision of clean water to 97,000 people, education for almost 150,000, and healthy meals for over 30,000. The partnership changed perceptions in a tired industry.

Even if cards aren't your business, there's a larger lesson here. Many other industries are ripe for destruction. As you make appeals to the generation about to come into peak spending years, those willing to research consumption footprints and who very much want to do good, think about your own game-changing ideas. By disrupting with purpose, you could turn new heads.

Source: Partnership Impact Quantitative Survey (November 2015); Mission Measurement and WE

Want to prove your purpose to the socially responsible shopper? Get certified

For Jay Coen Gilbert, it was like watching someone take a wrecking ball to his dream. In 1993, Gilbert and two college friends launched AND1, an ethical basketball footwear and apparel company outside Philadelphia. They'd built an above-board supply chain and a business that gave back to the community, donating 5 percent of the company's annual profits to youth organizations. When they sold the business in 2005, AND1, was worth US$250 million. But the new owner moved production to low-wage Chinese factories; the only charity he supported was his own pocketbook.

Frustrated by this experience, Gilbert wanted to help other entrepreneurs build socially responsible businesses with a public legacy that would be preserved, even if the reins were passed on. Equally important, Gilbert wanted to help consumers make informed choices, to invent a way to check the authenticity of a company's purpose.

Enter the benefit corporation, or B Corp, a nonprofit that assesses for-profit companies against rigorous standards of social and environmental performance, accountability, and transparency.

The assessments are done at the B Lab, based in Pennsylvania, which evaluates and grades any organization that wants B Corp certification. Gilbert created a system to measure the veracity of corporate causes, and certification to offer transparency to shoppers—ideally, unlocking new socially conscious customers and encouraging more businesses to take up sustainable practices. To uphold standards, B Lab puts a series of questions to companies about packaging, employment practices, energy and water use, sourcing and recycling programs, and other processes. Candidates are given a score (a minimum score of 80 out of 200 is required for certification) and every two years, the purpose audit is repeated. As of 2017, more than 2,100 businesses in 50 countries are certified B Corps.[12]

"We're at a tipping point in the evolution of capitalism."

—Jay Coen Gilbert, Founder of the B Lab

Whether it's a home-based mom-and-pop craft business or a large multinational corporation, B Corp certification can help you build a better business and attract the ever-growing number of consumers who want to know their dollars are helping more than just a company's bottom line.

Other certification processes also are gaining traction, a great way to tap into a new customer base by proving that your company cares. The Rainforest Alliance certifies farming, forest, and tourist businesses against rigorous environmental standards.

To gain the customers of today and tomorrow, you need to be transparent and authentic. Independent certification brings credibility and entices responsible customers.

"Impact Investment: at its core is the insistence that any money invested must generate tangible social or environmental impacts, as well as financial returns."

THE NEW WORLD OF IMPACT INVESTING

By Holly Branson

Invest your cash and be the change

I'm lucky to work at a company that approaches every market as a champion of the consumer.

Two decades ago, joining a gym was not an option for many people because of extremely expensive fixed yearlong contracts. So what did Virgin Active do when it launched? It eliminated contracts.

Mobile phone rates and handsets were costly due to market domination from telecom owners. So what did Virgin Mobile do? It launched the world's first Mobile Virtual Network Operator—with the cost savings going directly back to our consumers.

Airline passengers in economy clamored for in-flight entertainment. So what did Virgin Atlantic do? It introduced seat-back TVs in every class on our aircraft.

The list goes on and on, I'm proud to say. It's a genuine commitment to put the customer first that's allowed Virgin to enter established markets and vigorously shake them up. Our competitors then followed suit all to the benefit of the consumer.

Virgin's approach has always been entrepreneurial. We've taken countless calculated risks in untried markets—not by throwing huge amounts of money at them, but by disrupting the market with innovative products and services and giving it a damn good go.

Everyone at Virgin knows of the need to continue to disrupt and evolve. When I started at the company in 2008, we knew we had to build on the market shake-ups of the previous decades to move into the 21st century with a radical approach to our new and existing businesses. And that "business as a force for good" had to become *the* most important part of Virgin's DNA going forward.

During the past few years, the phrase "impact investing" began to creep into conversations with friends and colleagues at Virgin.

So What Is It?

While traditional investing generally focuses solely on maximizing financial profitability and returns, impact investing takes a more two-dimensional view when evaluating investments. At its core is the insistence that any money invested must generate tangible social or environmental impacts, as well as financial returns. This means that consideration of both impact potential and financial viability are crucial in the investment process, and indeed both must continue to be monitored as the business grows post investment.

> The Global Impact Investment Network defines impact investing as "investments into companies, organizations, and funds with the intention to generate social and environmental impact alongside a financial return and provide capital to support solutions to the world's most pressing challenges."

While this may seem simple in theory, in practice measuring social and environmental impact is hard. As I found out more about the sector,

I realized just how difficult it could be. There are more than a few complicated questions that an impact investor must consider: What's an acceptable social or environmental return? How do you quantify it relative to your business and your investment? Each investment will have its own areas of impact, which need to be measured, but ideally, each will be put into context and measured against other impact investments. Can we find a set of common measures to help gauge the quality of the impact?

These are questions that need to be addressed during the due diligence of the business, in addition to the typical questions that should be asked for any investment—including reputational risks, which cannot be ignored, even with impact investments.

And finally, the biggy: as an investor, you will also need to decide whether you accept lower financial returns to support higher impact returns. If so, what is the trade-off you are ready to accept?

Given these hurdles, impact investing is sometimes still viewed with cynicism in boardrooms. So I was feeling slightly nervous when I went to the Virgin board to argue that we should approach many of our future businesses with a focus on investing in targeted social and environmental initiatives with measurable impacts. I sold it by appealing to what Virgin has always done.

We have always entered markets from the point of view of positive impact and the value we would bring to our consumers. This was simply a more formalized way of approaching future business investments. If our initial impact investments proved successful, there is no reason we couldn't move all of our interests to impact investments in the future. Thankfully, I wasn't met with blank stares or shaking heads, but rather with real interest and a sensible desire to find out more. A steering group was immediately formed to consider how impact investing might be adopted by Virgin Management.

> *"I've been a long-term proponent of the view that any of society's problems that can be solved with market-based solutions must be solved that way."*
>
> —Bill Gates, in a statement announcing his investment in Capria Accelerator, an impact investing fund.

I was inspired by the board's enthusiasm, by my dad, and by the team that researched impact investing—a sector in which, it appeared, smart people had been increasingly putting their money and, more important, making those investments deliver the intended financial and social-environmental impact in a sustainable way.

In a World Economic Forum study, 5,000 millennials surveyed in 18 different countries indicated that the overall top priority for any business should be "to improve society."[1]

The team identified that we already had businesses that, in hindsight, could have been marked as impact investments. For instance, Virgin Pulse, our U.S.-based health and wellness company designs and develops technology to promote good lifestyle habits for employees. There is also Virgin StartUp, a not-for-profit company for entrepreneurs that provides government-backed loans and one-to-one business advice to those launching or growing businesses in England or Scotland. So these companies already met the criteria of generating social and financial returns, but we hadn't established at the outset that they would be delivering on both fronts and that we would measure the impact they were driving. Hindsight is a wonderful thing.

In other words, we were already running businesses that met much of the criteria; we'd just never considered it that way.

Given our history, we knew that Virgin was well-positioned to explore this growing sector further. Now we're working to ensure new investments align with the goals and objectives around impact investing, but also that our existing companies incorporate social and environmental goals through our Purpose work. That way we learn from each other and bring everyone into the conversation.

We are truly just getting started. We have decided to focus on investing in businesses that carry impact and financial opportunities in areas we believe address the most pressing social and environmental issues. Organizations that could really benefit from the expertise and public profile that a Virgin investment brings to the table. We've dedicated funds and a team to finding investment opportunities, starting in the UK, to help budding entrepreneurs create jobs and develop new businesses with a social conscience. We hope to source these opportunities through Virgin StartUp but also through entrepreneurs and investors we meet elsewhere. We're particularly thrilled to be working with young entrepreneurs as they develop new companies. After all, they're the leaders of tomorrow.

As we work with young entrepreneurs, we know the rest of our investment teams will begin to look at our larger investment strategy with the same impact lens. The investment teams are already excited and have been great advocates for this initiative.

Let me introduce you to our impact investment team: **Edouard Muuls**, **George Howard**, and **Bruno Igreja**, who are better placed to take you through our first deal, one that was particularly close to my heart. Not only because of my medical training, but also having had my babies six and a half weeks early, I experienced firsthand these wonderful life-saving machines . . .

mOm Incubators: Virgin's First Official Impact Investment
Edouard Muuls, George Howard, and Bruno Igreja

The first challenge was to find investment opportunities that met our criteria. In short, and in true WEconomy style, our selection needed to link purpose with profit. To build a pipeline of opportunities, we started meeting entrepreneurs and like-minded investors, joined impact aggregator networks, engaged with external advisors, attended conferences, but also picked up the phone to call management teams of businesses that struck us as great impact businesses.

When we discovered mOm Incubators (mOm), it was immediately clear they were unique and had the potential to be an ideal first investment for us. We had discussed with Holly, a trained doctor, our potential to do something game-changing in the area of infant mortality, particularly given the migrant crisis across Europe. At first glance, mOm seemed to bring a solution to a dire problem along with the market and product potential to grow into a significant and profitable venture.

mOm is a collapsible, portable infant incubator—much lighter and cheaper than traditional models—that provides a regulated environment to keep babies warm every bit as effectively as the incubators in well-equipped neonatal intensive care wards.

James Roberts created mOm after watching a documentary on Syria in which he learned that the stress of war has caused infant mortality rates to soar. He saw this as an opportunity to make a difference and invented mOm in a Design Engineering course at Loughborough University, where he went on to win the Sir James Dyson Global Prize for Innovation in 2014. The genius of mOm is that it's designed to be used anywhere, from rugged, harsh environments in rural Africa to time-sensitive neonatal transport in the developed world—and everywhere in between. mOm provides high quality, durable infant care conditions to service the most challenging settings.

First steps at Virgin were to meet the team behind mOm. James and his partner Matt Khoory jumped at the chance to show off their product and to talk about seed funding. It took only a single introductory meeting, in which James demonstrated the functionality of a prototype unit, to get us jumping straight into our due diligence process.

Emotionally, we were sold. But we needed to create more rigorous parameters for it to be a true impact investment. If we didn't define our returns, it would just be a donation. We concentrated on the following key areas:

- Nature and measurability of impact, and how this might evolve
- Achievability of the go-to-market strategy, particularly across developed and developing markets
- Intentions and motivations of our co-investors, particularly the lead investor in this seed funding round

It is the final point that's worth dwelling on. "Intentions and motivations of our co-investors" is very close to the fundamental principles we use to invest under at Virgin in the broader sense. As a multifaceted family office with investments in sectors ranging from financial services to space tourism, we have always been very keen

Infant mortality in the developing world: A tragedy in numbers

Million

According to a World Health Organization (WHO) analysis, an estimated 15 million babies are born prematurely each year (less than 37 completed weeks of gestation), and the number is rising.

Million

Premature birth complications are the leading cause of death among children under five years of age, responsible for nearly one million deaths in 2013.

Million

In 2015, 4.5 million (75 percent of all under-five) deaths occurred within the first year of life.

The risk of a child dying before completing the first year of age was highest in the African Region with 55 deaths per 1,000 live births. That is over five times higher than in Europe, where the rate is 10 per 1,000 live births.

75%

Three-quarters of them could be saved with simple interventions, but are prevented often through lack of funds and/or equipment (access and availability of incubators, for example, or vaccinations and antibiotics).

to bring in co-investors who align with our goals, but who also bring sector-specific expertise.

We also had to get up to speed with mOm's business and impact model. To do so, we spent time with James and Matt to go through some of our key due diligence questions, notably how they planned to bring the product to market, who they would sell to, what the pricing would be, and how they would plan to scale the business over the medium to long-term—at the end of the day, we needed to make sure they had a strong plan to scale and therefore achieve the impact that we all desired. With comprehensive responses to these questions from mOm, we then worked to review the information, including market analyses and financial models, with the goal of assessing the financial forecasts that mOm had shared and working out what our returns would be.

We focused on determining the financial viability of mOm, just as we would any other Virgin Group investment. But what set our impact investing process apart is the time we spent researching the extent of the problem that mOm was looking to solve. We wanted to truly understand the level of impact mOm could have. What we uncovered was eye-opening.

mOm had invented a lightweight and compact incubator for 5 percent of the cost of a conventional model, which was 100 percent as effective at regulating the thermal environment.

To underscore our commercial due diligence, we needed more firsthand intel on mOm and its product. We consulted an industry expert in pediatrics, an expert who had experience developing commercial medical products. We learned that a critical problem in the developing world was that existing technology, if it was even available, was not understood, maintained, or used. Simply put, the market was crying out for a simple piece of technology that would meet this growing need at an affordable price—seemingly a perfect backdrop for mOm to make a difference.

The final piece of the puzzle was to speak with our co-investors, and in particular MaSa Partners, the lead investor. Crucial for us was gaining an understanding of MaSa's intentions, particularly around mOm's potential humanitarian impact. We were encouraged by MaSa's

UNICEF involvement, and certainly saw the strategic opportunity and connections they could bring to mOm at board level.

Importantly, we agreed to embed a statement on impact objectives in MaSa's Articles of Association, thus establishing a degree of "mission-lock" for the company and ensuring impact would always be front and center in its goals.

Reassured by MaSa's commitment, and alongside our other due diligence efforts, we sought formal Virgin approval to proceed, and met with Holly to get her views.

The rest is history! As a co-investor (as opposed to a lead investor) in this round, our role was to insert our purpose into the various terms of the investment, particularly what we could and could not accept. All the hard work of aligning these views fell to MaSa and its lawyers.

With one investment under our belt, we're looking for other impact investment opportunities. It's true the first is often the hardest. Even though there were scant doubts about the virtues of mOm, it was certainly difficult at times to reach full agreement among all investors on the exact terms of the deal. We've learned lessons we'll bring to our next venture. mOm is a very early stage investment, and carries with it all the risk typical of seed companies. For mOm, the journey is just starting. Like any other company, it will undoubtedly encounter hurdles along its development path. Our role, as a key shareholder and investor, is to support management as the company matures, lend a hand when needed, but above all to allow James and Matt to get on and build a great business that could lower infant mortality rates.

Virgin StartUp: A prime example of measuring return on investment in terms of social and economic impact

Just as Richard Branson launched his first venture, Student magazine, with a £300 loan from his mother, he is now using StartUp as a way to pay it forward. Virgin StartUp funds businesses like Mini Nom Nom's, which makes healthy, ready-made meals for kids inspired by international cuisine and launched with seed capital from StartUp. Each Mini Nom Nom's purchase also sponsors a meal for a child in India. Founder Lisa Sohanpal says "If it wasn't for the loan, I wouldn't have started."

That's just one of more than 2,000 loans approved to date, boosting Britain's economy and sustaining a culture of entrepreneurship, encouraging young people to pursue their business ideas in a poor economic climate where youth unemployment is high. But StartUp doesn't just provide access to early capital; it offers dedicated mentorship, pairing loan recipients and Virgin mentors with the same devotion to compatibility as a high-end matchmaking service, identifying shared values and knowledge gaps. Virgin StartUp also offers a wide range of programs to help startups to grow and be sustained. These include: workshops (Doing Business with Big Business; Crowdfunding Boost), Masterclasses, networking events, competitions (Virgin StartUp Foodpreneurs), and accelerator programs. Virgin StartUp has supported some of the country's most innovative new ventures, especially in the food and beverage sector.

Virgin StartUp is set up as the nonprofit Virgin company for entrepreneurs. The primary measure for its success is based on the contribution it makes to the UK economy at large. Fostering small business growth is, of course, good for the economy, which is also good for Virgin's business. Entrepreneurship is the economic engine of the UK, driving job creation and regional regeneration after a triple-dip recession. StartUp has funded projects from Cornwall to Northumbria with more than £20 million loaned out since 2014.

Impact Investing: The Future Is Now

Impact investing isn't the next big thing—it's the current big thing. Here are three groups heavily investing in creating global impact:

Bridges Ventures

Founded in 2002, Bridges Ventures is an investment fund that focuses on providing capital to businesses that tackle the world's pressing social and environmental challenges.

Bridges has pioneered and developed a proven model that invests in four key areas: Education and Skills, Health and Well-Being, Sustainable Living, and Underserved Markets.

As one of the first institutions to develop the field of impact investing, Bridges built a platform to measure and optimize the impact of each of their investments, and provide regular reporting on progress.

Omidyar Network

Established in 2004 by eBay founder Pierre Omidyar, the Omidyar Network is both a charitable foundation and an impact investor.

The Network supports a range of enterprises, from for-profit businesses to nonprofit organizations, across five key areas: Education, Emerging Tech, Financial Inclusion, Governance and Citizen Engagement, and Property Rights.

The Rise Fund

A global impact fund led by private equity firm TPG in collaboration with renowned stakeholders, including Bono, Richard Branson, and Pierre Omidyar. The $2 billion fund was announced in September 2016 and made its first investment in April 2017.[2]

The Rise Fund will partner with creative entrepreneurs and build successful businesses that drive meaningful, measurable, positive change in seven key sectors: education, energy, food, and agriculture, financial services, growth infrastructure, healthcare, and technology, media, and telecommunications.

"Business-based solutions are
more sustainable and empowering
than aid or a handout."

OPEN NEW MARKETS

By Craig Kielburger

Think outside the box store

Many great athletes are restless and unhappy in retirement, unable to replace the thrill and adulation they knew as stars. Earvin "Magic" Johnson had a national collegiate title, five NBA championship rings, and an Olympic gold medal on his résumé when he quit pro sports. Regular life seemed destined to be dull by comparison. But unlike so many of his contemporaries, Johnson had a social mission, which drove him to find his footing off the court after he retired in 1996. Diagnosed with HIV in 1991, he launched The Magic Johnson Foundation to finance HIV/AIDS awareness campaigns, prevention, testing, and treatment. By announcing his positive status at a time when few understood HIV/AIDS, Johnson likely did more to combat the stigma surrounding the disease than any public awareness campaign at the time. His foundation also tackled the education gap in America, offering Internet access, computer training, and college scholarships to underprivileged students. It was Johnson's involvement with the urban poor—his understanding of inner-city America—that led him straight to a business opportunity that everyone else had strolled right past. Having grown up in a poor but hardworking family in the economically depressed city of Lansing, Michigan, Johnson knew there was opportunity where others would never bother to look.

In the early 1990s, entertainment businesses like theaters and restaurants were less than plentiful in U.S. inner-city neighborhoods, a general term for impoverished areas populated largely by minorities. In most cases, the inner city lies at the urban center of major cities. Los Angeles had South Central, Chicago had the South Side, and New York had Harlem. At the time, urban and mostly minority residents seeking dinner and a movie had to head for the suburbs. "African Americans had no retail opportunities, nowhere to take their families to have a sit-down meal, to socialize, and to have a good time," Johnson once told me. There was an economic side effect: skills training, jobs, and economic growth accrued in other, wealthier neighborhoods. And so the inner cities stayed poor. But Magic saw an opportunity to make money and do good at the same time.

Johnson courted Loews Cineplex Entertainment to partner on a multiplex in South Central L.A., romancing them with research. He told them that a quarter of U.S. moviegoers were African American, even though few of their neighborhoods had theaters.[1] What's more, he said, theaters in the inner city would be cheaper to run since the cost per square foot would be about half of what it was in the well-heeled suburbs.[2] And African American and Hispanic communities could easily drive future business expansion, since they accounted for more than two-thirds of the country's population growth.[3] In hindsight, Johnson was far ahead of his time. A more recent Nielsen study found that America's African American population is an economic force, with a buying power of $1 trillion that is forecast to increase. As a demographic, black shoppers are also bigger consumers of media, on average, than the general population.[4]

Loews had the foresight to heed Johnson. The partnership opened two theaters, first in the Crenshaw district in south L.A., then Harlem, New York. For a time, they were among the chain's most profitable venues, with concession sales soaring higher than in other regions. Johnson pointed out, anecdotally, that suburban moviegoers were more likely to grab a bite at a restaurant before the show, while inner-city populations, partly from lack of options, preferred to grab a hot dog from the concession stand (good for the theater, since that hot dog has a high-profit margin).

Magic Johnson's postseason stats

"When you talk about disposable income, minorities have it. Don't look at it like you did 20 years ago. Things have changed a lot. A lot of you were scared off before, but today it has changed. You will make money in urban America."

— Magic Johnson

Net worth: US$500 million
Even though he was an NBA legend, he was new to business. Johnson started at the bottom, cold-calling L.A. Lakers' season ticket holders to share news of his new ambitions.

Ka-ching: In 2010, Starbucks acquired Johnson's shares in his inner-city coffee shops, ending a 12-year partnership. The same year, he sold his stake in the LA Lakers; he made a combined US$100 million on both deals.

What now: *The Magic Johnson Enterprises portfolio includes stakes in the Los Angeles Dodgers, Hero Ventures, and Vibe Holdings. Johnson also launched a billion-dollar infrastructure fund in 2015 aimed at tackling the lack of diversity in tech, and in February 2017 was named President of Basketball Operations for a team he knows a bit about: the L.A. Lakers.*

Sources: *Business Insider, L.A. Times, Wall Street Journal*

Heads started to turn in corporate America, including that of Starbucks CEO Howard Schultz. Magic Johnson Enterprises helped facilitate the launch of seven Starbucks coffee shops in new neighborhoods, where the twin-tailed sirens drew big business. Magic proudly recalled that he suggested a few tweaks to the menu, and to the atmosphere, for these inner-city coffee shops. Scones were replaced with pound cake and peach cobbler. Melodic jazz was switched out for R&B. The partnership grew to include 105 locations, and the expansion lured other brands to the area. Johnson launched a similar partnership with the restaurant chain T.G.I. Friday's[5] and the electronics retailer, Best Buy. It was the business equivalent of a slam-dunk. These ventures didn't just bring entertainment to inner city areas, but jobs and opportunity. Urban dollars were no longer seeping out to the suburbs. Magic Johnson kept funds circulating in areas where they were desperately needed.

In recent years, Magic Johnson Enterprises has divested from many of its early entertainment-based ventures. However, the impact on communities has been significant. Johnson's Starbucks franchises alone created more than 2,100 jobs and paid an estimated $29.8 million in wages and benefits from 1998 until they were sold in 2010.[6] Johnson estimates that among all his current businesses, he employs over 30,000 workers from minority communities.[7]

Therein lies his magic: Johnson filled both a social void and a market void in one fell swoop. He solved a social issue with a business plan and tapped into an underserved market, flawlessly blending purpose and profit. Johnson's genius, in part, was recognizing the pent-up demand in disadvantaged neighbourhoods and adapting to the market accordingly, partnering with established franchises but offering his intimate local knowledge. He also nurtured his new market, taking into account its unique challenges. Charitable work and other community programs were organized in conjunction with his businesses.

Johnson tells me that all his companies offer more comprehensive training programs for staff than franchises in other areas, which enhances loyalty and retention in places where the lure of gang culture and street crime is rife. And it creates "the best brand ambassadors," he says. "They'll go out and tell a hundred people, 'I work for Magic. You better come see me, man.'" Employees know Johnson isn't just their boss; he's a pillar of their community. By investing in the region that's keeping him in business, Johnson is perpetuating his own success. He achieved his purpose, and banked a sizeable profit. With $18 million in earnings in 2015, Johnson continues to hold a place among the 10 richest former professional athletes in the world.[8]

He continues to give back. The Magic Johnson Foundation has now celebrated its 20th anniversary. Among the foundation's achievements is a mobile HIV testing van, which has clocked over 100,000 miles and provided free HIV tests to more than 60,000 people in communities with limited access to medical care. The Foundation also hosts health fairs to help educate people about HIV prevention and to provide testing. It hosts job fairs and offers a scholarship program targeted at minority college prospects coming from urban environments.

Put the Cult in Culture

Sharmadean Reid moved from her hometown of Wolverhampton to study fashion and communications at Central Saint Martins design school in London. She started blogging during the advent of social media, back in 2006, chronicling all things pop culture. When she was coveting a Dior double French manicure, she went to her local salon to try and replicate it. But the salon staff was either too disinterested or too uncool to pull it off. So she took matters into her own hands.

With her savings, Reid opened WAH Nails (named for the acronym "We Ain't Hos") in 2009. She leased a building in London's East End, but soon realized she hadn't planned for a few important details, like lawyers' fees. And she'd acquired more floor space than she could afford. With little money and too many square feet, Reid didn't panic. She finished renovations on her own, and leased out half of the cavernous space to another business, a now uber-trendy salon called Bleach.

Reid didn't have any business training. She had intuition and a good corporate conscience. WAH Nails aims to employ mainly single moms because Reid, as a single mom herself, knows the conflict between career and family. She hosts power lunches and mentorship programs, and hopes to open a more formal business academy for women. WAH polishes are vegan and chemical free, and the salon space itself is a cultural hub for the community, hosting art exhibits, record launch parties, and movie nights.

Reid now has her fingerprints all over the beauty industry with a line of polishes for UK drugstore chain Boots. She's collaborated with the mega-chain Topshop and written two books.

Put the Cult in Culture continued

The *Independent* named her one of 15 people who will shape the future of arts in Britain.[9] Reid proves that the very blueprint for becoming an entrepreneur has changed. You don't need an Ivy League degree to launch a business. "You need a URL, Instagram, £15 and 15 minutes on Companies House to register it," Reid told one reporter.[10] But she's being modest. Reid also had something that money and formal degrees can't buy—a strong brand identity built atop a strong sense of purpose. Not bad for an entrepreneur who shirked all traditional business strategies. Reid did nothing by the book, and still carved out a niche market in her neighborhood. Purpose doesn't have to be a far-fetched goal like saving the rainforest. Creating jobs in your community can be a powerful cause. This could mean jobs for veterans returning home or factory workers whose plants closed. If you're a small business, consider serving your community first.

Selling to disadvantaged communities can often be a means of social and economic empowerment. Poor communities can be uplifted by the sale of productive or healthy options that are otherwise unavailable. In inner-city America, it was family-friendly entertainment. In other regions across North America, there are food deserts with scant fresh fruits and vegetables due to a lack of grocery stores or farmers' markets, contributing to an obesity epidemic and other health concerns. Done right, an entry into these markets brings increased choice, opportunity, competition, and a chance to increase quality of life in those communities. Business-based solutions are more sustainable and empowering than aid or a handout, which is finite and can create dependency.

Hidden market prospects exist globally. In his landmark book, *The Fortune at the Bottom of the Pyramid: Eradicating Poverty through Profits*, business professor C.K. Prahalad laid out the money-making opportunities that come with appealing to the world's four billion poorest people. The world's poorest socioeconomic group is also the largest, and the most neglected by the market.

The emerging markets[11]

The future is here

In 2014, the OECD estimated that the population in emerging markets made up 85 percent of the world's population.

Billion

The OECD estimates that the global population will increase by an additional 1.6 billion by 2034, and about 95 percent of growth will occur in developing countries.

Some multinationals heeded this advice, including Unilever and Procter & Gamble (P&G); both companies reach out to customers living on less than $4 a day. For the bottom billion demographic, the cost of a single tube of toothpaste might eat up an entire day's wages; many basic hygiene products are unattainable. Reducing the size of the product can slash its price, making smaller doses more affordable, so Unilever and P&G downsized package sizes for detergent, toothpaste, soap bars and shampoo, all priced under the equivalent of 10 cents USD.[12,13]

Selling packets means the communities aren't dependent on aid. Awareness campaigns convince consumers that the products have value. For example, enabling better handwashing habits saves millions of lives every year and is especially important in preventing illness in children in the developing world. The U.S. Centers for Disease Control and Prevention (CDC) estimates that 1.8 million children under the age of five die each year from diarrhea and pneumonia diseases. Handwashing reduces those numbers by 25 to 35 percent.[14]

Making the small packets of soap available quite simply saved lives, and increased sales along the way. In Vietnam, Unilever's Lifebuoy's handwashing campaign increased domestic soap sales by 29 percent.[15] In the village of Thesgora, India, the handwashing program reduced incidents of diarrhea among children, from 36 percent to just 5 percent. Before the program, the village had one of the highest rates of the disease in the country.[16]

Social Entrepreneur Seeks Investors[17]

Have an idea? Need funding or an investment? Connect with the following groups:

Investors' Circle is an early-stage impact investment network that favors startups with an American presence

Put Your Money Where Your Mouth/Meaning Is Company (PYMWYMIC) is a European community of funders

Go Beyond is a traditional network of angel investors that lists social impact among its five priorities

Toniic is a global community of impact investors

Impact Assets showcases 50 impact investment fund managers each year

Cause Capitalism lists 15 social venture capital firms worth knowing about

Impact Space is a database of more than 2,000 impact investors, searchable by objective and location

The **GIIN**'s Investors' Council lists 50 leading impact investors

Where Would You Invest?[18]

5%

Rate of Gross Domestic Product (GDP)
growth by 2020: In emerging markets,
5 percent.

2%

Rate of Gross Domestic Product (GDP)
growth by 2020: In developed markets,
2 percent.

37%

by 2020

Projected percentage of global GDP in
emerging markets: 37 percent by 2020.

66%

by 2050

Projected percentage of global GDP in
emerging markets: 66 percent by 2050.

50%

by 2050

Biggest players: India and China will
represent 50 percent of that global GDP
by 2050.

⁺ONE

Billion

The middle class: By 2050, India and China
will add more than one billion people to
the middle class, representing 41 percent
of global middle-class consumption.

These companies created inroads into poor, rural areas, creating customers by establishing partnerships and building up local capacity. In Unilever's case, local female entrepreneurs act as partners, training with the company to become beauty consultants and product experts—from Vietnam to Pakistan to Egypt, and all over the world. Even impoverished communities can be revenue generating for companies willing to make the right investments.

Don't neglect underserved markets, at home or abroad. Somewhere, potential customers are being ignored.

A Market-Based Response to a Life or Death Crisis

It's not just basketball legends and big multinationals who can use social innovation to break into new markets. Aspiring entrepreneurs and startups can find a launch pad by rethinking their target markets, narrowing their focus on underserved communities.

In the mid-2000s, Ashifi Gogo, a Ghanian-born electrical engineer living and studying in New Hampshire, developed a labeling system to help consumers identify the origin of their purchases. When a shopper picked up a product with his label, they could scratch the tag to reveal an ID number. Entering that number online would reveal where and how the product was made, and whether or not it was a fraudulent knock-off.

"As a company founded in 1857, we remain steadfast to our guiding principles of embracing change, evolving to meet the needs of our customers and giving back to the communities in which we operate. These core values are essential to our firm's longevity, especially in today's highly competitive global marketplace."

—Hartley Richardson, President and CEO of James Richardson & Sons

Gogo launched a startup called Sproxil, and began to pitch to various sectors, including the organic food industry. He was certain he'd found a niche with middle-class shoppers who were worried about whether their bananas had been sprayed with pesticides, or their tomato was genetically modified. He was sure high-end shoppers would want to know about the origin of their produce. But he found no takers in specialty foods.

The idea didn't gain traction until 2008, when Gogo read about a health crisis in Nigeria. Eighty-four babies had died after ingesting what their mothers thought was brand-name teething syrup. Investigations found the syrup laced with diethylene glycol, an industrial solvent commonly used in antifreeze and brake fluid; counterfeiters use it instead of harmless glycerin because it's a cheap substitute with a similar consistency. And to a baby, the toxic chemical tastes just as sweet. Parents hoping to ease their babies' pain gave them a medicine that instead caused fever, vomiting, and kidney and liver damage and attacked the central nervous system, causing paralysis, labored breathing, then death.[19] The tragedy in Nigeria was only one incident, symptomatic of a widespread problem.

Across the developing world, people afflicted with malaria, tuberculosis, HIV/AIDS, and many other less-serious health problems, face a terrible game of roulette every time they walk into a local pharmacy. Counterfeiters have descended on the lucrative pharmaceuticals market, hawking medicine that is ineffective, diluted, and even toxic. As many as 700,000 people die each year from phoney tuberculosis and malaria drugs alone.[20]

Gogo abandoned his produce plan and approached Merck and GlaxoSmithKline with an idea to help expose fraudulent medicine. In 2010, the two pharmaceutical giants began attaching Sproxil's label to their products in Nigeria. Consumers could scratch the label and text the revealed number to Sproxil, which would instantly verify whether the product was real medicine. Pharmaceutical companies readily paid for the service; it promised to squeeze fraudsters out of the market, which would naturally increase their own share of it, build brand credibility, and save lives. The service has since expanded across Africa and India. Just three years after its launch, consumers had requested more than five million drug verifications.[21]

There's a tendency to view activities like improving hygiene, reducing poverty, and saving lives as solely the jurisdiction of governments and charities. But a market-based solution has the power to be self-sustaining. It's worth remembering that some of the most innovative global antipoverty measures today, like Muhammad Yunus' Grameen Bank, are built on business models that bring enterprise to regions that typically receive only aid, not business propositions. The best form of charity is safe, sustainable employment. The observation that every crisis is an opportunity has become something of a cliché. But that doesn't mean it's not true. Problems facing communities—be it inner-city Los Angeles or remote rural Bangladesh—can present a business opportunity to crack open lucrative new markets that your competitors are avoiding, provide profit with purpose, and better the world in the process.

"Why should your relationship with
your place of work be different from
any other relationship in your life?
The best and most rewarding are always
based on mutual trust and respect."

PEOPLE ARE YOUR PURPOSE

By Holly Branson

Teambuilding 2.0: engaging your people in the WEconomy

It was like an episode of the *The Twilight Zone* and *The Stepford Wives* rolled into one.

Suits and ties as far as the eye could see. Every desk occupied by 9 a.m. sharp but the presence of 130 people produced only deafening silence. No music, no shouting across desks over the sound of the cappuccino machine or the crunching of toast. Glum faces abounded as curt emails were sent to any staff member caught checking Facebook or not wearing the appropriate office attire. Lunch kept to a strict 30 minutes. Teabags rationed to 1.4 per member of staff.

At 5 p.m. the office emptied and only the deafening silence remained.

I cringe writing the above because I'm aware that for some of you this is a typical day at the office . . . welcome to your world, right?

For Virgin Management Limited (VML), our "Corporate Day" was a novel experiment to raise money for charity and give us all a new appreciation for how "uncorporate" we usually are at the office. It also resulted in a telling-off for my brother Sam, who forgot and turned up in jeans and trainers. The following morning, we returned to normal (well, our standard of normal) with flexible working, unlimited leave, an endless supply of tea and coffee, lunches, and snacks. We were back in full force, with a soundtrack of sporadic singalongs, usually led by my wonderful E.A. Louise, to whatever music was on shuffle.

After my first few weeks at Virgin I quickly learned to keep my mouth shut when a couple of my unluckier friends were talking about their working conditions. They were expected to leave their personalities at the door and not to call on them again until they clocked out at the end of the day. Simply put, their employers didn't trust them to be themselves and still do a great day's work. As a result, my friends didn't trust that their employers valued them at all. So apart from putting in the bare minimum, what was the point?

A lot has been written in the past few years about beanbags and ping-pong tables, bring your dog to work days, sleep pods, in-office massages, and yoga being the only ways to keep millennials happy at work. That's all very well in Silicon Valley, or for the hipsters in Shoreditch, London. But for the majority of professions, these toys and perks just won't fly. A colorful bean bag and free tea are great added benefits, if you are in a position to provide them. None of these things need to eat up your yearly budget or turn your place of business into an unruly party.

But even the mighty teabag means nothing if your company is not built on a culture of mutual respect. Build a people-first culture. Your business will be better off for it.

Employees today value trust, transparency, and a sense of purpose above all over things when choosing and, most important, staying with a company.

Who Are Your People? The Biggest Workforce in the World

By 2025, millennials will make up 75 percent of the global workforce. Of course, these are not your only employees. But in less than 10 years, the vast majority of the workforce will be made up of a single age grouping for the first time in history. To enable our companies and our economies to thrive,

The bottom line on employee engagement[1]

50%
Employees

Employees who feel enthusiastic about their work are 50 percent more likely to exceed their bosses' expectations than those who are less engaged.

60%
Customers

According to Target Training International, more than 60 percent of all customers stop dealing with a company because of perceived indifference on the part of an employee.

Employee engagement can be improved by aligning the goals of the business with the goals of the individual, including pay and compensation, but also by ensuring they see opportunities for personal growth and that they're working for a common cause.

Companies with highly engaged workers out-perform those with unengaged employees by 54 percent in retention, 89 percent in customer satisfaction, and by 400 percent in revenue growth.

we need to understand and nurture this unique and diverse generation. There are hundreds (perhaps thousands) of research reports, consumer surveys, and work audits available to explain what makes millennials tick, but I'll draw from two in particular in this chapter: Gallup's 2016 report "How Millennials Want to Work and Live" and our own research through an initiative called 100% Human at Work.

Dispelling the Millennial Myths

From the outside, the millennial generation—or the selfie generation, as we've all heard it called—has been labeled shallow, apathetic, coddled, discontent, always distracted, and permanently attached to their technology. Sounds a bit harsh, doesn't it? I'm a millennial, but even I find these criticisms hardly surprising. We were the first generation to truly grow up in the age of the Internet, and many of us do spend a lot of time attached to our smart devices. Remember though, this cohort was also severely affected by the global recession that started in 2007—with the oldest among us entering the job market when the full force of it hit.

In reality, this craving for connectivity and information has resulted in a workforce who want to be involved in all aspects of the company. Millennials are Participators. They want to shape the organizations they work for. Yes, they can be opinionated, self-confident, and questioning, but that also means they seek and offer input in order to be a meaningful part of growing your business.

Frighteningly, for the biggest workforce in history, polls and surveys put millennials' workplace engagement scores (on average) as low as 23 percent in 2016. Companies must be getting something very wrong. It might be that too many businesses are living in the past (stuck in a permanent "Corporate Day"). Millennials are the business leaders of the future, and it is in our best interest to get it right and engage

The Job Hunt
Seeking purpose[2]

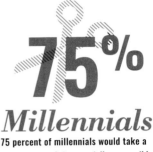

75%
Millennials
75 percent of millennials would take a pay cut to work for a socially responsible company.

76%
Millennials
76 percent consider a company's social and environmental commitments when deciding where to work.

88%
Millennials
88 percent say their job is more fulfilling when they're provided opportunities to make a positive impact on social and environmental issues.

them at work. (Feels strange writing about millennials in the third person—as I said, I am one!)

Virgin has always believed in the value of happy people first and foremost. The business was founded on the belief that our people should be valued; our team has always been considered family, not just staff. We have always believed that above all else in any business your workforce should be number 1. If your people are happy and engaged, customers will follow.

To be the best employer we can be, we have pledged to be 100% Human at Work, an initiative developed by an organization called the B Team.

In 2013, the team at Virgin Unite called together some of the most forward-thinking businesses in the world, with the hope that these responsible companies would help drive the same value systems in thousands of businesses worldwide. After a series of workshops and many meetings, the B Team was born.

B Team Purpose Statement

"Founded in the belief that the private sector can, and must, redefine both its responsibilities and its own terms of success, we are developing a Plan B—for concerted, positive action that will ensure business becomes a driving force for social, environmental, and economic benefit.

Plan A—where business has been motivated primarily by profit—is no longer an option.

We are focused on driving action to meet a set of challenges that underpin Plan B—by starting "at home" in our own companies, taking collective action to scale systemic solutions, and using our voice where we can make a difference."

Co-chaired by my dad and Jochen Zeitz, former CEO of Puma, this global group of 24 leaders are working together to accelerate Plan B.

What millennials want[3]

 Millennials want a purpose, they don't just work for a paycheck. Of course they want fair compensation but beyond that, they want to work for a company that has purpose baked into its culture.

 Millennials are pursuing development, they are not simply pursuing job satisfaction. They want to be involved in decision making. They want to learn what makes a business tick and not be treated as cogs in the wheel.

 **Millennials want coaches,** they don't want bosses. Without doubt, if you don't provide mentorship programs, you should. It's also worth exploring the idea of reverse mentoring: pair the CEO with a more junior employee, who will have much to teach about day-to-day work on the frontlines.

 **Millennials want ongoing conversations,** they don't want annual reviews. They enjoy giving feedback as much as receiving it.

 Millennials want to flex their strengths, not fixate on their weaknesses. Look at your training and development programs. Millennials don't want to be force-fed workshops or seminars that expose their weaknesses, and they're less likely to engage in learning a skill that's foreign to them. They'd much rather use resources to maximize their strengths.

 It's my life, not just my job. They want to know: Do you value me as a person and not view me as a payroll number? Can I bring my personality to work with me to prove that my company values me and my contributions?

They have pledged to achieve a number of goals during the next decade, including getting more businesses on board. For now, I'll deal with one goal in particular: 100% Human at Work, based on the premise that the time has come for businesses to start thinking of people as human beings and not as resources.

The 100% Human initiative uses five elements to achieve this goal: respect, equality, growth, belonging, and purpose.

But what do these words actually mean in the workplace? What does it mean to be 100% Human at Work? Here's a look at how Virgin implements these ideas—some are groupwide, some are individual company examples. We have embraced these elements, as we believe every company needs to create a truly "human" organization. Feel free to adapt, use them to open a debate with your colleagues, or blatantly copy them.

Respect

We believe work is a place where different values and beliefs are respected, where there is respect for privacy, and where all workers are treated with dignity.

Across the Virgin Group, we have actively encouraged our people to be part of this discussion. Through workshops, surveys, and inter-departmental debates, we brought thousands of our people together to help define what respect means to them.

Together we determined that combining two concepts—diversity and inclusion—would provide the most powerful building bricks for a respectful people culture.

To our people, diversity means understanding that everyone is unique, and that we're all made up of multiple dimensions that create our personal identity. We refer to this as BE YOURSELF.

To our people, inclusion means being welcomed, valued, respected, and supported. It's about focusing on the needs of every individual, and ensuring the right conditions are in place for each person to thrive. We refer to this as GO TOGETHER.

We determined that combining two concepts — diversity and inclusion — would provide the most powerful building bricks for a respectful people culture.

Growth

We believe that through individual growth, workers can contribute to business growth.

The coming workforce is looking to build on their strengths in their professional lives and to continue to learn and develop in their personal lives. Take advantage of the wealth of development options available online; consider facilitating a portal and allowing your people to access courses as they choose.

Virgin has had great success with our Learning Lounge and Online Hub, a virtual space for both personal and professional development. Our team can choose from a wide range of online, self-taught courses—including An Introduction to Particle Physics! We believe that development isn't just related to your daily tasks at work. Allowing your people to satisfy their curiosity and interests proves that you value them as whole persons, not just employee numbers.

If your company doesn't have resources for a portal, seek more specific feedback from your team about what they're looking for. It may be a matter of allowing time off for your team to attend seminars or volunteer to use their professional skills for a good cause.

Equality

We believe that only through fairness and equality of opportunity can a business realize the true potential of the talent within it. We also believe that diversity is good for business.

At Virgin Management Limited (VML), we are very proud of two particular policies that foster and promote equality, parental leave and flexible working. As with many of you reading this, a few of the Virgin Group companies are unable to offer such policies, due to the nature of their industries. But we firmly believe that any industry can test and implement better people policies within the constraints of delivering core business objectives. Find out what "best in class" means for you.

In April 2015, shared parental leave launched across the UK. Available to eligible working parents in the first year following the birth or adoption of a child, it offers more flexibility to share statutory childcare and pay. Many UK companies chose to offer the minimum statutory pay (a small percentage of normal earnings) for anyone taking advantage of this legislation. We saw this as the perfect opportunity to take a more genderless, inclusive approach and add to our continually developing suite of family-friendly policies. At VML, all eligible parents who qualify for shared parental leave are entitled to an enhanced payment of up to 52 weeks' full pay. We believe we were one of the first, if not the first company in the UK to implement such a policy, supporting parents financially while they are away from their desks doing the most important job in the world.

When parents do return, they (and everyone who works within the company) benefit from our "flexible working for all" and our unlimited holiday leave.

Unlimited Leave is one policy, among many, you can adopt to help foster and promote a healthy work-life balance for your workforce (more on that later in the chapter). If you feel that for your business this is a step too far, why not give more paid time off? Why not start with one or two days extra a year? Encourage your staff to use it to do something fun, spend valuable time with family or friends, or explore a new hobby. The list is endless and so will the sense of being valued that it instills in your people. I can assure you there is a solid business case for going above and beyond the basic and setting yourself on the path to becoming an exceptional employer. You'll learn more about that later in the chapter.

Over decades, the British press has caught my dad on camera—first with his notebooks and more recently with his iPad—working away while swinging in his hammock at home. I am proud to say that his unconventional work style has changed the face of business and set an example for entrepreneurs the world over. Dad has never used (or believed in) a conventional office or nine-to-five rules. He has always believed that flexible working is smart working.

In 2014, we introduced flexible working for all our people at VML. Given my dad's philosophy, it would have been rude not to! Our people can work from anywhere—at home, at the coffee shop 'round the corner, or from a sofa in our office. The only exceptions are team meetings as they are invaluable bonding and creative sessions and are always held in the office and face to face. We have seen a marked increase in morale since this policy, and no downside at all in productivity. All we did was prove to our wonderful staff that we trust them to be the capable adults that they are.

Belonging

We believe that workers achieve more through partnership and teamwork than through competition and politics.

Working in industries as diverse as travel, telecoms, music, media, financial services, and health and wellness, you can imagine that promoting a sense of belonging can be logistically challenging for us. Still, we always strive to promote a sense of belonging and family.

In the early days, we had annual staff parties in our backyard in Oxford, but when we reached 30,000 staff they got a little tricky to accommodate! Now, dad and I host my favorite Virgin event of the year, our annual Stars event. One winner and a guest, from every Virgin company, join my family and Virgin CEOs from across the world, at our home, to celebrate their work and meet their extended, global Virgin family. This is a chance to not only celebrate our incredible people, but to have them break out of their silos and to meet team members from other companies.

Josh Bayliss, CEO at Virgin Management, explains the influence that better people policies have on the business:

- Attracts and retains talent, creating an environment where people can have a career and a family, giving them the opportunity to thrive in both areas of their life

- Pioneers the diversity and inclusion work already taking place in the business, increasing engagement and productivity

Studies by McKinsey and *The Economist* have identified a strong link between profitability and a company's approach to diversity and inclusion. Companies that have family-friendly policies in place tend to perform better than their peers

Here Are a Few More Things We Do to Make Sure Our Team Is Part of a Community

Town halls

First, you'd be amazed at the amount of positive support, loyalty, and personal investment that comes with simply keeping your people informed. Every three months, our wonderful Virgin Management CEO Josh Bayliss does an in-person update for all of our people at VML. He not only gives them a comprehensive (and honest!) overview of what is happening in the businesses across the Virgin Group, but also of the state of markets and the global economy. When I say "all our people," I do mean every member of staff—not just middle management and up.

Roger

Our internal magazine, *Roger*, is available to our staff globally, in print, and online. It celebrates our people and their achievements, both professional and personal, as well as introduces new companies and team members. It's an opportunity to showcase companies and individuals and share their day jobs with their 70,000 colleagues. *Roger* also features articles on well-being in the workplace and new ways of working, to ensure we

Netflix: Where Everyone Gets Time Off for Good Behavior

Reed Hastings does not have to work overtime to set a good example for the thousands of employees who work at his $60 billion firm—just the opposite.

The CEO of Netflix takes six weeks of vacation every year—to set an example.[4]

The father of two explained this at a conference. "You often do your best thinking when you're off hiking in some mountain or something. You get a different perspective on things."

It started with a PowerPoint that went viral—seriously! The deck "Netflix Culture: Freedom & Responsibility" was created by the video-streaming company's former chief talent officer, Patty McCord, and was shared over 13 million times on Slideshare. Sheryl Sandberg called the presentation "the most important document ever to come out of the Valley." McCord started a revolution for work-life balance.

In it, the company explained its policy on holidays: "We should focus on what people get done, not how many hours or days worked. Just as we don't have a nine-to-five day policy, we don't need a vacation policy." [5]

Hastings says work must also be about play. Not only that, he believes if the company cares for its employees, its employees will care for the company.

So no one keeps track of vacation days.

"What we're trying to do is earn loyalty and trust that they'll really care about Netflix in addition to caring about their families, and they'll find successful ways to integrate it."

keep the discussion going. It shouts loud and proud about the fantastic purpose and charitable causes our people are passionate about. I'm proud to boast that in 2017 Roger Magazine won GOLD at the Global CMAs (Content Marketing Awards) beating off IKEA and British Airways as a leader in the internal communications sector.

Work should not be an end in itself. We believe that working for a company with purpose is more fulfilling and productive.

The Virgin Way

The Virgin Way is our comprehensive online portal for all the People, Purpose, and Development departments across the Group to share ideas and learnings.

In our "Purpose 101" chapter, we offered examples to help you embed purpose into the DNA of your business, and we told you that purpose is profitable. In this chapter, I hope I've given you some incentive to involve your people in the process. Your purpose, like your business, is only as good as your people. Get them engaged and committed for a more successful purpose project. Here's one example of how Virgin did it.

A while back, Virgin Mobile Australia (VMAU) joined forces with R U OK?, a charity that encourages people to have regular conversations as a way of assisting in suicide prevention. As part of a multilayered campaign, VMAU offered incentives to customers who participated, but they also worked hard to ensure staff were actively involved. All staff got a voucher entitling them to a free coffee in a local café, with the proviso that they took the time to catch up with colleagues and have a chinwag, rather than dropping the usual two-line email. The company also facilitated staff volunteering at R U OK? events, and hosted a Conversation Zone in the office, with comfy seats and free coffee, inviting people to sit down and have a chat. The campaign was hugely successful—internally and externally—because everyone on the team felt a sense of pride in what they were achieving. Everyone bought into the Purpose of partnering with R U OK? and participated in the mission.

Daydreaming about a Holiday at Your Desk? Get Up and Go . . .

As you can probably tell, we at Virgin Management Ltd. spend a lot of time thinking about our people and culture. Within the Virgin Group, VML is in a very unique position: we're not a retailer, we don't require shift work, and we don't build or manufacture products that require assembly lines. We don't have to assist millions of travelers on the rails and in the sky every day. This allows us to test forward-thinking "people policies" with more flexibility than do teams with more rigid work requirements. One such policy that grabbed headlines here in Britain when we introduced it was unlimited leave. I had read about Patty McCord, former Chief Talent Officer at Netflix, causing a stir with a radical new approach to culture at her company. I excitedly proposed to our senior team that we follow suit and introduce unlimited leave. (I did tell you that blatantly copying purpose leaders was an option.)

Dad jumped on the idea from the get-go, but it took a little while for some of the team to get to grips with what unlimited leave actually entailed and what effect it would have on the company's productivity. As it turned out, they had some time. In the UK, unlike the U.S., workers are entitled to a statutory 21 days of annual leave. We hadn't anticipated the legal issues we'd encounter while trying to give our people more freedom. Our policy left it completely up to each individual member of staff to determine their leave, for an unlimited number of days. Still, legally, we had to ensure that 21 statutory days were protected! It took 18 months to implement the scheme in Britain.

In a nutshell, unlimited leave permits all salaried staff to take off whenever they want for as long as they want. All of our staff can request holiday leave, in addition to the 21 days, without restriction.

It is left to the employee to decide if and when he or she feels like taking off a few hours, a day, a week, or longer. The assumption here is that staff are only going to leave work when they feel comfortable that their absence will not in any way damage the business. We are proud of our culture, and trust our people and their ability to make empowered decisions.

I'm delighted to say the company didn't collapse because everyone rushed out the door with their suitcases. Instead, we saw a spike in morale, creativity, and productivity. Our people are proud to work for a company that assumes they want to do a good job and therefore should be trusted to do just that. Unlimited leave will not work for all companies for many, many logistical reasons, but the principle it is based on, trusting your employees, absolutely will.

Since he's my boss (and to earn myself a couple of brownie points), I'll leave the final words on how to foster that trust to our CEO, Josh: "Why should your relationship with your place of work be different from any other relationship in your life? The best and most rewarding are always based on mutual trust and respect. If you want people to be themselves, be 100 percent human, and bring all of themselves to what they do, you've got to respect them. You've got to include them in the conversation, be transparent about challenges you are facing, and celebrate the highs with them.

"Remember the phrase 'talk is cheap' can also be seen as a positive: your bottom line is never going to suffer because you took time out to talk, converse, and interact with the people who work for (and with) you."

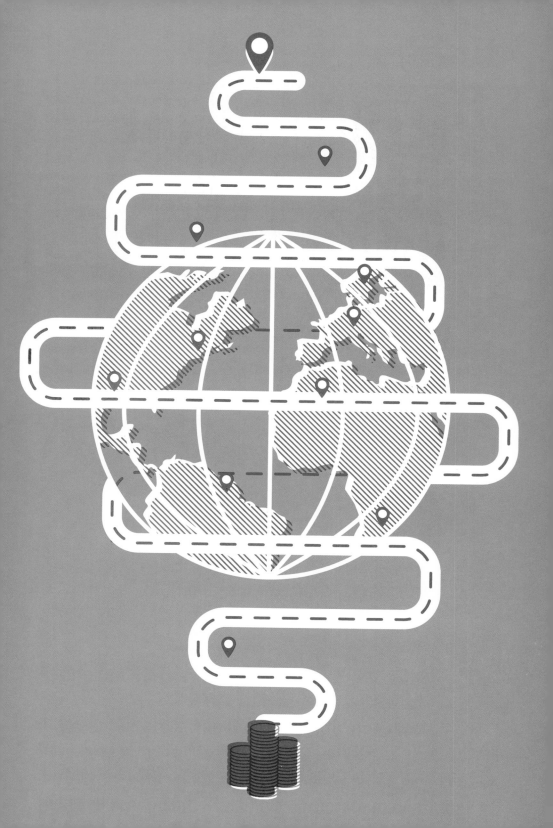

IF YOU BUILD IT, THEY MAY NOT COME: HOW TO GET PURPOSE RIGHT

By Craig Kielburger, Holly Branson, and Marc Kielburger

Our caravan plane descends onto the remote edge of the Maasai Mara grasslands. It's nothing but lush green carpet for miles. The only sign is a handpainted rock, propped up like a monument stone, that reads "Bogani Heimark Airstrip." We disembark and are greeted by Wilson Meikuaya, a Maasai warrior and our guide. He's outfitted in the tribe's traditional plaid shuka and armed with a machete to fend off black mambas—lethally poisonous snakes native to sub-Saharan Africa. We pile into a lorry to visit Kishon, a local medical clinic.

The building had stood empty for two years, abandoned by a corporate development project. The clinic's first benefactor had covered the cost of a structure and the great fanfare of an opening ceremony. Representatives cut a ribbon, snapped a photo, and left. They neglected to hire doctors or partner with local governments to ensure that the clinic was actually operational. The result was a shiny new building, still with plastic coverings on the door handles—and zero medical care for the community. Still, the villagers were hopeful; they pooled money to pay a gardener to maintain the grounds. For two years he

Registered nonprofits in the United States[1]

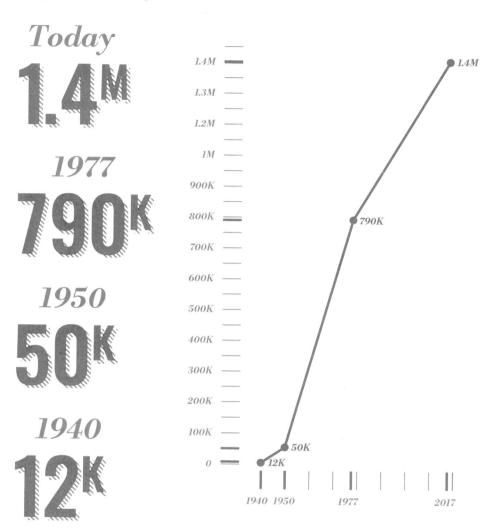

Today
1.4ᴹ

1977
790ᴷ

1950
50ᴷ

1940
12ᴷ

1.4M —
1.3M —
1.2M —
1M —
900K —
800K —
700K —
600K —
500K —
400K —
300K —
200K —
100K —
0 —

● 1.4M

● 790K

● 50K
● 12K

1940 1950   1977   2017

50ᴷ
New Charities
The IRS approves 50,000 new charities each year.

kept it up, fighting the unruly grass with a machete (lawnmowers aren't easy to come by in rural Kenya). The community reasoned that if the grounds and the building looked nice, the company would come back to resume the project. They never did.

No doubt there is a framed photo of the clinic in the lobby of a corporate headquarters somewhere.

A plan was laid with the best intentions, but without foresight, consultation with the community, or even short-term maintenance structures in place. Granted, this was a for-profit company and not a charity that specialized in delivering medical infrastructure to remote regions. But even putting aside the bad development model, the failed clinic was just bad business. Even the most ardent capitalist, one who reduces charity projects to media impressions or brand reach, should see the flaw in the plan here. The clinic was a PR disaster waiting to happen.

The bad news is that purpose is often done poorly. No one assumes: "I'm going to wake up tomorrow and start a highly specialized multimillion dollar company" without proper training and experience. And yet everyone assumes they can run a charity; they don't consider that they will need to oversee development projects and manage contractors and foreign government relations. This mentality could explain the large number of charities popping up.

Over in England and Wales, one estimate puts the number of new charitable organizations at 6,661 in 2013, a 16 percent increase over the previous year.[2] In Craig and Marc's homeland of Canada, there are more than 170,000 nonprofit organizations.[3]

Businesses must find a unique role in the marketplace, or risk failure. The same rule should apply to charities, but often doesn't. As we'll discuss later, not every new charity adds value.

Everyone thinks they can run a charity because everyone cares about a cause—and that's admirable. But here's the truth: good intentions do not always result in good work. It's not easy to do purpose well. As with Kishon: It's one thing to build a clinic, but filling it with doctors, nurses, and patients and delivering quality care is another thing entirely.

We're not suggesting that companies stop funding development

*GOOD
INTENTIONS
DO NOT ALWAYS
RESULT IN
GOOD WORK.
IT'S NOT
EASY TO DO
PURPOSE WELL.*

work—in fact, we're really, really not suggesting that. On the contrary, WE Villages adopted the hollow building and turned Kishon into a functioning clinic with support from corporate and family donors (and youth fundraisers, of course). One of those donors was Midmark, a multi-generational family medical equipment business based in Dayton, Ohio. The family helped revive the project, hire local medical staff with support from the regional government, and build wells and other infrastructure. If anyone has the knowledge and reason to start a clinic, it's the people running a medical supply company. Even with this experience, they still recognized the need to partner with an established organization.

The WE Villages model depends on these smart investments and mutual partnerships, both with benefactors and with locals. All development models should build in sustainability from the outset by partnering with local elders and governments. You'd be surprised how often developing communities are not actually consulted about what they need. The first WE College is currently being built, an adjoining medical college next to our first permanent clinic, Baraka, at the community's request, in order to train the next generation of nurses and technicians. Volunteers can also visit the projects and stay invested. Medical trips run regularly to Kishon; specialists come from all over the world to share knowledge with local staff. When Holly visited, she spent a very rewarding day consulting with local physicians and visiting patients.

A business alone doesn't have the resources to do any of this—integrate

Here's what's inside:

- *A step-by-step guide to find a social cause that fits you or your core business*

- *Tangible tips to achieve both charitable and career or corporate goals*

- *A how-to guide to define success, measure outcomes, and maximize the efficiency of your cause program or personal donation*

- *A team engagement plan to amplify your social mission within your workplace*

- *Creative, cost-effective tips to help charities without writing checks*

- *Tips to refine your pitch for a social mission and present the best business case to your boss*

into overseas communities, ensure long-term success, and plan an exit strategy so that locals can take over. And yet so many companies spearhead development projects and other complex charitable programs.

The same strategy and discipline that goes into a business plan should go into making a purpose plan, but often doesn't. None of us are afraid to admit that we learned this lesson the hard way. We know why the corporate clinic failed because we've experienced all of the same warning signs in our early work, with WE Charity. In fact, our advice for people who often ask us about starting a charity is: "don't!" (unless, of course, you've identified a serious need that isn't being addressed). But there is good news. When purpose is done well, the social impact is sustainable, scalable, and effective.

Let's be clear: when we say "don't start a charity," we are talking about a legally registered organization, with a special tax status and reporting structure. As a business or employee, you should absolutely start a charitable partnership or a purpose project that benefits an existing cause. Why be just another digit to add to the 1.4 million charities in the United States alone? Your passion, energy, and drive will be better served agitating for positive change within your current organization, or volunteering your skills and time to an established charity you admire.

In Part Two, you read about the benefits of the WEconomy for companies and individuals—case studies like Magic Johnson's takeover of a new market in urban America and Tania Carnegie's self-driven promotion after she took responsibility for KPMG's social mission. You already know why you should get into the WEconomy. It's now time to take a closer look at how.

We've mapped out a plan to help you or your company design a purpose strategy. For individuals, the plan will not only help you pick the right cause, but also help you give back in a way that's rewarding, both for the cause and for you. And on a corporate level, we'll take you through everything from finding a cause and forming the perfect cross-sector partnership, to linking internal performance reviews and rewards to the company's larger purpose plan.

Part Three is your how-to guide for achieving purpose and profit.

We should warn you that it isn't one-size-fits-all. It's possible, and sometimes necessary, to pick out just one or two stages of the process and go from there. Goals will differ depending on the size of the company and its current status as a corporate citizen. In other words, you don't have to do all of this all at once.

However, you certainly can't ignore all of it, either. The WEconomy isn't going anywhere. Companies that get on board early will reap early benefits, setting precedents for what customers expect from a well-run corporate purpose mission. Left in their wake will be the companies struggling to catch up.

These are the nuts and bolts to help you and your company profit with purpose.

"To really shift things we needed to shake up the way we approach charity for (and with) the next generation— equipping young people with the tools and motivation to lead their own change."

BE A PURPOSE-LED "LEARNING ORGANIZATION"

By Holly Branson

Listen, Learn, Lead

In 2010, Virgin Money had just taken on the title sponsorship of the world's largest fundraising event: the London Marathon. To support them, and join the other 37,493 runners taking part, Sam and I tied ourselves to 32 tutu-wearing mates, to form one giant caterpillar.

Never a group of friends to do things by halves, over several beers (we weren't in training yet!) we decided, why just run, why not set a Guinness World Record while we're at it? The next morning, with slightly woozy heads, 34 of us woke to the realization we'd committed ourselves to setting the World Record for the largest number of people tied together to run a marathon.

It was one of the most inspiring, affirming years of our lives, from the training through to coming up with the plan of how to safely tie 34 people together for 26.2 miles, while wearing green tutus and keeping our antenna bobbing. Each of us believed we were part of something special. We were.

When we set the World Record on April 25th—a cold, crisp, sunny London day—we'd raised £250,000 for 12 very worthy charities.

As the blisters healed and the nipples "uncracked" (any of you who have run a marathon, know what I mean), we all felt pretty empty and a bit deflated. While sitting around my kitchen table, six of the original caterpillars admitted that it wasn't simply because of the absence of training or the constant email trails that we felt this way, but the fact that

In 2007, £46.5 million was raised for good causes by runners, making the London Marathon a Guinness world record breaker as the largest single annual fundraising event in the world. That record has been broken every year since, with more than £59 million raised in 2016. Following the 2016 race, more than £830 million had been raised for charity by London Marathon runners since 1981.

we had raised all of that money and then simply handed it over. We had no influence, or in fact knowledge, of what that money was being used for, apart from the broad brushstrokes of twelve great charities' websites. Our role was over. Our job was done.

Those six caterpillars (yours truly, my brother Sam, my wonderful sister-in-law Isabella, and our dear friends Princess Beatrice of York, Sam Richardson, and Philip Nevin) knew that we had the passion, energy, and, importantly, the ambition to do so much more together. We had come to the realization that, although many charities were doing great work, the vast majority exist to treat the symptoms of a broken system. We wanted to look at how charitable funds could be a catalyst for positive change. As we've said before in the book, more charities is not always the answer. But how do we improve the system so that over time there would be less need and dependence on traditional charities? We decided our charity would invest its funds to affect change. Big change, if you will.

Set against the sense of despair, and the resulting violence, that fueled the inner city riots across England in 2011, we witnessed how much need there was on our own doorstep. The seed that would become

Big Change germinated and grew. We formed Big Change with the founding principle: **to really shift things, we need to shake up the way we approach charity for (and with) the next generation—equipping young people with the tools and motivation to lead their own change.**

In that first year, we climbed Mont Blanc in France in our epic Big Climb for Big Change to raise £250,000 to support great organizations that were aligned to our values of empowering young people and driving positive change. We hired our first employee (again, never forget the importance of the investing in top talent when it comes to being a true purpose-driven organization) and recruited a young, earnest managing director (M.D.): Alex Walters.

We outlined our core values with a website, marketing materials, and our initial manifesto for positive change. We were well on our way to being the change-makers we dreamed of being. Or were we?

Even though we were still a young organization, we decided to take a step back and honestly appraise Big Change and our achievements. With a little bit of soul-searching, it became apparent that we were still doing relatively traditional philanthropy (giving to great projects to scale their activity and reach more people). We had much to learn. If we are going to create BIG CHANGE, we need to think BIG.

We admitted there was an issue. We needed to get back to the core of our Big Change purpose. We wanted to bring about positive, long-term system change. We had to start our learning journey.

By simply admitting we didn't know it all, that day we became a Learning Organization. Today, we work with a wonderful organization called Generation Change and have funded an Impact Accelerator to turbo charge the learning process that takes place when delivering youth social action opportunities. More on that at the end of the chapter.

True to our entrepreneurial DNA, we started to explore funding early-stage ideas and pioneers, to get new projects with bold ambition, off the ground with our support. They could then go on and change the way things are done.

> *"Education is what remains after one has forgotten what one has learned in school."*
>
> —Albert Einstein

Alex (our M.D.) summed it up brilliantly at the time. He believed that we needed to embrace both patience and impatience equally on this journey: the patience to say that we are not quite there yet and that we need to learn more by reaching outside of ourselves to gain that knowledge, and the impatience to say that we must act quickly and just do it!

Big Change's Journey to Becoming a Learning Organization

The Big Change learning curve was steep at times, but always rewarding. As you now know, the WEconomy works best when businesses, social enterprises, and charities not only effectively collaborate and partner with each other, but also when they share knowledge, experience, and learnings. At this early stage in Big Change's journey, we reached out and started learning from brilliant people—including a young card shark named Jake Hayman.

Jake was still in his 20s when he co-founded his firm Ten Years' Time, with seed money earned playing poker in backrooms across London. Ten Years' Time helps philanthropists to become experts in the areas they care about, making us work hard to understand the communities we wish to serve and the systems we want to support or transform (for tips, see Lesson 3 below). It helps people to listen and to develop their expertise so that they can make better and bolder decisions.

Some of the points below we explored and developed with Jake—others came later in our journey as a Big Change team. I hope you find them not only useful, but also encouraging. It's okay to admit you have more to learn.

Big Lessons Learned

 : FIND YOUR UNIQUE STRENGTHS

Find the place where you can add unique value—be more than a checkbook and you can make a difference above and beyond your financial contribution. You will achieve much more by focusing on those things you truly understand and that play to your skill set as an organization and the passion of your teams. We realized, luckily early on, that we wanted to back early-stage ideas and help them prove their impact—the natural follow-on to this lightbulb moment was repositioning Big Change as a "social impact accelerator." Defining the type of organization we had become, and giving it a name, fueled our confidence.

Before investing a "charitable" dollar (pound or Euro), explore how you can add the most value: leveraging your profile, your networks, your time, your people, and/or your skill for innovation. Map out everything you have to offer that could be of value. Your first instinct may be to simply get out the checkbook while working on your end-of-year accounts, but it's not until you analyze the impact of each dollar you invest that you will realize you may well be missing a trick. It may not be a financial contribution that brings you (and the charitable partner) the greatest impact or purpose return. It could be mentoring, staff volunteering, or sharing your distribution networks or your retail space. Marc gives more examples in the chapter "Change without Cash," which may help while you have your thinking caps on.

I strongly recommend you do this exercise whether you work for a business, charity, or social enterprise. I promise you, you'll be surprised by what you have to offer that is outside of the norm and highly valuable to the purpose projects you wish to back or launch. Hopefully, we've given you some ideas and inspiration from the WEconomy.

 : DON'T BE AFRAID TO BREAK THE MOLD

Bold statement time: Most philanthropic capital is spent addressing failure

Think about the charity campaigns that pull at your heartstrings: they call out for support when young people, old people, vulnerable people have already been failed by the system. This can be quite an attractive, romantic notion of charity, but in reality, you will achieve much more if you treat the root cause and not only the symptom.

> *You will achieve much more if you treat the root cause and not only the symptom.*

As a social impact accelerator, it became clear that supporting projects that were already proven to work meant we weren't learning anything or contributing to change. Not only was there other funding available for these organizations, we were also seeing incremental change rather than the exponential change we wished to see.

We began to search out those big ideas that could create a lasting system change—ideas that address a gap or an opportunity that could change the way things are done. I don't want to frighten you off with phrases like "system change"—the monetary sums involved do not need to be huge. By exploring the positive impact the project you wish to back will have on the whole system—for example a $5,000 investment could result in $25,000 of positive impact and a $25,000 investment could result in a $1 million of positive impact and go on to attract ongoing funding from other interested partners.

Just like a typical business investment, there is nothing wrong with expecting a strong return on investment (ROI) on your purpose investments.

Ask yourself these simple questions

"If this project was a startup business coming to us for seed funding, would we see enough growth potential in their idea to back it?"
"Will our investment bring us the returns we seek?"
"By backing this project is my/our investment going to change something meaningfully?"

Fun little aside: We were all immensely proud when Prince William and Catherine visited some of the projects we had worked to bring to scale in our first year as Big Change. Their visits brought much-needed publicity and awareness to these projects and the issues that we were hoping to address. When we moved to a social impact accelerator model to help us determine those very early stage "big idea" projects to invest in, we relied on what we called the "Will and Kate" test. This test was one based on absolute love and respect (Prince William's cousin is one of our Founders, after all) and was on the principle: Is this project one that William and Catherine would be seen visiting and supporting within the next 12 months? If "yes," then we knew others would also support them and therefore they didn't really NEED us. The big idea was simply not risky and disruptive enough to benefit from the support and skill set Big Change had to offer. Simply put, if it was worthy of a "Will and Kate" visit, it didn't need our help.

That being said, naturally, there is an open Big Change invitation to the Duke and Duchess of Cambridge to pop down and visit any of our projects either now or in the future. Yes, we know we've just contradicted ourselves!

 **: LISTEN AND LEARN**

If you don't understand the people that you want to help, you can waste a lot of money by giving big donations to new ideas. Given that our focus was the system around young people in the UK, we spent a lot of time listening to experts in the sector and on the frontline. We reached out to teachers, social workers, youth workers, psychologists, influencers, and young people, as well as policy and research experts, data experts, MPs, and charity experts. We wanted to identify the root causes of the issues. We listened. We learned. We then approached the whole sector from a position of strength in the form of knowledge.

If you are reading this as a businessperson (rather than a charity or a social enterprise), the same advice applies: seek advice and learn from the widest group of people possible.

Learn what worked well (and badly) on their purpose journeys and with their project—in turn, you can use that knowledge to get your projects to their next stage.

Seek advice and learn from the widest group of people possible.

In a nutshell, know enough to make good decisions. Surround yourself with good advisors. It's that simple. Would you simply hand over an investment check to a business working with a product, in a sector, in a country that you know absolutely nothing about? Unlikely. Why should investing in your purpose project be any different?

 : TAKE BIG BETS—BE BOLD IN YOUR CONVICTIONS

This learning may not apply to everyone working within the WEconomy—not everyone may be in a position to take big financial bets. Remember, however, that you can agitate your bosses and colleagues—those who hold the purse strings. At Big Change our biggest and most nerve-wracking change came when we decided to BET BIG and BE BOLD. We had been averaging around £20,000 into organizations of £1 million and more turnover. Our major shift was to turn that into an average gift of around £150,000 directed to much, much smaller organizations. I'm not going to lie—we were more than a little nervous.

That is until we met Josh MacAlister. Josh was an inner-city teacher who grew increasingly frustrated that he was simply handing troubled kids over to social workers, who, for a variety of funding, political, and logistical reasons, were not providing the level of care those youngsters deserved. Josh knew that social work in Britain was facing a major challenge. But rather than holding his hands up and saying that's someone else's problem, he decided to try and change the system for the better.

Josh worked hard to get the funding to do research in the social care sector. On the back of that research, he developed a business plan and approached the British government.

He managed to secure support from the government to test a 3-year pilot project called Frontline, but only if the program also attracted independent money. They had a minimal amount of

"Frontline is an amazing example that if you invest boldly at the right moment you can have extraordinary impact."

grant funding, but they needed financial support to raise awareness of the organization. In particular, he wanted to promote social work as a rewarding career for outstanding leaders and top graduates. Frontline's mission was to transform the lives of vulnerable children by recruiting and developing outstanding individuals to be the leaders in social work and broader society. (For our North American readers, think of Frontline as the equivalent of the Teach for America of social care.)

We were blown away by Josh's drive, ambition, and his belief that it was the system (in this case social work) surrounding young people that needed to be changed, in order for those kids to thrive. It was our biggest grant to date and we felt strongly that it could not be just about giving the money. We wanted to get involved. We worked with them on their marketing, videos, and public launch, even pulling in Virgin people as a valuable resource for them. Our collaboration was rewarding on so many levels.

In 2012, we invested £215,000 (a massive amount to us at Big Change) to fund their pilot project. In 2016, they secured multi-million-pound investment from the government to roll out their program across the UK. Frontline is an amazing example that if you invest boldly at the right moment, you can have extraordinary impact.

Essie North, current Big Change M.D., sums up exactly how elated we felt when we heard the news:

> "Today, the most satisfying feedback we get from our project partners is that by supporting them, when and how we did, we've influenced other organizations to do the same. An example of a similar model, but in the high-tech sector, would be the Y Combinator in Silicon Valley, which takes some of the best tech ideas and incubates them in those early stages with mentors. They can then access funding because they've proved their impact. Taking bold bets does mean you have to roll your sleeves up and get down and dirty sometimes."

You'll experience some trepidation because you are leading the way and approaching charity from a different angle—but you will encourage others to follow and therefore bring about real change. So why not "Go Big or Go Home!"

👓 : HAVE A CLEAR VISION

By early 2014, we were pretty proud of our work at Big Change—we were focusing our efforts in the system around "life skills" for young people in the UK and making real headway with our incredible partners. We had found our niche and approach. We were building our knowledge and confidence through supporting and learning from great projects. Virgin Unite had agreed to incubate us (just as we incubated our partners). We pitched our strategy, focus, and long-term plans. In turn, they agreed to support our overheads for 3 years, which provided us with the resources to be more proactive and continue to grow.

Our next opportunity (a.k.a. challenge) was to build a wider community outside our core group, not only to fundraise, but, just as important, to promote the change, we were fostering.

Around this time, a simultaneous brainwave of my brother Sam and cousin Noah provided the solution to not only our fundraising challenges, but also to helping to build a community around Big Change: the STRIVE CHALLENGE.

Strive is a multidisciplined, series of mass participation endurance events that pushed a group of Big Changers (yours truly included) to the limit both mentally and physically. Over the two major events so far we Strivers have: run 150km, cycled 3100km, hiked 350km, and swam 6km against some of the strongest currents in the world. A grand total of 3,606km—not for the faint-hearted.

To promote the Strive Challenge to a wide audience, we had to be really clear on our messaging. After all, we were asking our participants to fundraise. But while drafting the website, it became apparent

> *"Strive is a 'moment in time' that brings together a community of change-makers, who are passionate about breaking the negative cycle so prevalent around young people today. Strive epitomizes the Big Change philosophy: 'growth happens when you step out of your comfort zone to achieve bold ambitions. Magic happens when you do it with others.'"*
>
> —Sam Branson

that what Big Change did could be confusing to others. Explaining the thread that tied together our Projects (each with its own brand), Big Change, and now Strive had become increasingly difficult. I'm sure many of you have experienced this issue whether you work for a charity, social enterprise, or business. Big Change needed to more clearly define its purpose.

The exercise was both necessary and rewarding. We followed all the tips you learned about in "Purpose 101" (we weren't joking when we said you would need to revisit your purpose several times as you grow and evolve!) and developed Big Change's purpose statement: "To help young people thrive in life, not just exams."

When you get to a certain point—and you realize you are no longer embracing your core values the way you once did—take the time to revisit what you stand for. Your purpose statement will continue to evolve as your business does, but at its heart, it should be enduring. To quote myself: it is important to revisit your statement often to ensure you are still living up to it.

 : SCALE YOUR IMPACT

Easier said than done, right?

By our fifth year, helped by funds secured through Strive and support from Virgin Unite, we had nailed our approach, areas of focus, and our messaging. Finally, we were ready to SCALE-UP.

To aid our growth and gain invaluable advice from people smarter than ourselves, we formed our "Advisory Board": made up of amazing people from our key audience (entrepreneurs, venture capital, progressive philanthropists) who had experience scaling businesses, charities, and impact. They brought perspectives from different sectors that really helped to push our thinking in terms of how we set ourselves up now and how to scale in the future.

I may sound like a broken record, but reaching out and asking your networks, your partners, and your people how they think you are doing (as an individual, a business, or a charity) can have the biggest impact on what you go on to achieve. In our case, feedback helped to make us a more focused and effective partner, which directly impacted the amount of outside funding we have attracted.

On the eve of our fifth birthday, we had the confidence and belief that we knew what we were doing. We knew our focus. We had nailed our purpose. We had built an incredible community through Strive and our project partners. We were scaling and bringing on more people, and facing a whole new set of challenges.

We have always been keen to remain a small team punching above its weight, being smart about how we leverage the power of our network, rather than growing too big. A lot of our initial work and growth was organic and the result of a few passionate people who were living our values to their core. This worked well to a point, but created a bottleneck as we started to grow. As we scaled, we needed to enable others to think and act like Big Changers. We had to grow up and get the knowledge out of our heads and into systems (eek!).

Words such as process, templates, impact measurement tools, Scorecards, Theory of Change, and CRM/Salesforce tracking of our community became the norm in our office. You'll read more about Theory of Change later, and I talk about Scorecards and project finding and managing in "It's Time to Get Your Pitch On"—in essence, we set processes and structures in place that capture our ways of working so anyone could make changes "the Big Change way."

RED FLAG alert: this is the point at which you can lose your culture. Make sure your process has *your* culture at the heart of it. Yes, learn from others, ask to use/copy their tools and systems, and even borrow an operations person for a day or two from a local company (remember it doesn't always have to be a cash donation that you ask for). But make sure they capture your own way of doing things, and leave room for creativity and adapting to context. Just don't forget to involve your team in designing these systems. Your people are your culture, after all. What is the point in introducing templates that do not reflect the language they use or their personalities? Always remember these tools are useful aids to achieving scale and growth: they should enhance your magic, not dampen it.

Having more structure in our day-to-day work by introducing these templates and tools has meant our larger team no longer needs to rely on one or two individuals to get the job done. They get on and do it brilliantly and with Big Change flair (even if they are new members). This, in turn, has freed up our Founders so they can explore the next layer of opportunity to create *really big change* in the future. For us, that next frontier is starting to unite brilliant people and organizations to work together around Reimagining Education. No rest for the wicked.

The learning journey should never stop as an individual, a business, a charity, or a social enterprise. After all, the Strive Challenge purpose statement sums it up rather nicely at this point:

"Growth happens when you step out of your comfort zone, magic happens when you do it with others."

About Generation Change

Generation Change is a movement of organizations that are committed to helping young people change the world through social action. Together, our organizations support over 600,000 young people every year to take action on the causes they care about and to serve others. Our mission is to transform the role of social action in our society. We do this by empowering youth programs to evaluate and improve the impact that they and their young volunteers have on the causes they address.

Generation Change was funded by Big Change to develop an Impact Accelerator to turbocharge the learning process that takes place when delivering youth social action opportunities. We have worked with Dartington Service Design Lab, a research agency with over 50 years experience in helping children's interventions, to apply and learn from evidence.

So, What Is a "Learning Organization"?

Organizations that are committed to impact and are willing to learn and change on the basis of new insights to achieve this.

Key traits of a Learning Organization

- *Can articulate a clear theory for why they do what they do*
- *Relies on feedback from data and evidence to inform decision making*
- *Results are shared openly and honestly whether positive or negative*
- *Focused on "improving" rather than "proving" their outcomes*
- *A culture of commitment to transparency and openness in order to improve is seen across the organization and often instigated by those in senior management positions*

Theory: "From innovation to impact"

Learning organizations are committed to improvement and are always interested in building up a clearer and more consistent picture of how good results might be achieved. By doing this, they will develop over time toward being confident about what impact they achieve.

Steps to becoming a Learning Organization:

- *Define your starter questions—why does what you do work? What happens, and why does it happen? How does it have to happen in order to work? Be open to these questions generating further questions*

- *Begin to explore any inconsistencies or ambiguities with your theory of change: these may indicate areas that need a bit more time and consideration—that is, learning*

- *Identify honestly what incentives are driving the way you collect and use information. There might be funding requirements, someone on your board with a driving interest, marketing purposes . . . Are these going to distort what you attempt to learn as an organization?*

- *Equip your internal culture for learning. Be open and honest about your results: what was unexpected, what went wrong? Embrace the possibility that your understanding might be wrong, and develop a design method that makes it easier to spot false positives quickly*

Benefits of becoming a learning organization:

- *You will be more able to focus on what can help you improve over time*

- *You will foster a culture of innovation and continuous improvement*

- *You will learn unexpected things about your organization and the things that you do that may help you to get better at what you do*

- *You may discover or improve upon what works*

- *Your team may feel more ready to contribute to the development of the organization, in an open and supporting atmosphere, where failure is not the end but the fuel for greater success*

GENERATION
CHANGE

"If you should ever find yourself
sitting next to me on an airplane,
have your purpose-related answers ready.
Also, I apologize in advance."

WECONOMY IMPACT ENGINEERING, STEP ONE: FIND YOUR CAUSE

By Craig Kielburger

If I could change one thing about the world, it would be _____

You know those awkward moments before takeoff when you suss out the person sitting next to you on the plane? You know that annoying guy who won't stop talking about his work? A friendly guy with a big grin who prevents you from pulling your sleep mask over your eyes on the overnight to Europe, the one who interrupts you when you're reading *US Weekly* or *The Economist*?

That's me.

Sometimes my frequent flier status gets me upgraded to business class, where I can determine if my seatmate will be subjected to my charity charm offensive by asking three questions: Are you traveling for business or pleasure? What do you do? Have you ever thought of starting a purpose project? Business class is full of business leaders, so many of WE's corporate partnerships are hatched at high altitudes.

A few years ago, I sat down beside a guy traveling from Toronto to New York. As he talked into his cell phone, I picked up snippets of his conversation about business dealings in Colombia. He was worried about a new enterprise, shipments getting through customs. I was sure he was either a Colombian drug dealer or a money launderer.

It turns out that he was moving a lot of green. It was kale.

Matthew Corrin had just started a company called Freshii that promised a healthy fast-food offering and an alternative to the greasy lunches he'd been eating in urban financial districts while working various office jobs. At the time, Corrin was in his late twenties, seeking both financial reward and positive impact from his work. He considered his business partly a social service to encourage healthy eating, but he still wanted to make money. He was very honest about his objectives: purpose and profit, with emphasis on the latter.

I asked if he'd thought about starting something charitable. We're too small, he said. His biggest issue during those startup days was getting tortilla wrappers consistently into his stores; he didn't have time to oversee a charitable program.

I pressed on. "What kind of impact do you want to make?"

He wasn't interested in short-term fixes, reasoning that he would rather do something to tackle root causes or nothing at all. He had admirably high expectations.

"I want to fundamentally solve the problem of hunger," he told me.

So, to sum up, Corrin hoped to tackle an endemic social problem, but had minimal time to personally oversee operations for the charitable cause. As a busy CEO, that's entirely fair. I looked at my watch. Gate to gate, we had about 90 minutes. It was more than enough time to walk through the steps we use for all of our corporate partnerships.

We will go over each of these in detail over the next few chapters, helping you answer those fundamental questions that seem straightforward, but can come with hidden challenges. All in, there are three steps to WEconomy Impact Engineering (WIE). (Even our acronyms sound like "we" when you say them out loud.)

I asked a bunch more questions at a high level (30,000 feet, in fact):

 What do your staff and customers care about?

 How will you leverage your business assets to make the most social impact?

 What does success mean for you?

 How will you ensure your entire team is aligned on the purpose plan?

 How will you measure your impact and report on it?

I should add that I have just as many conversations with families, youth, recent graduates—those outside the C-suite who feel compelled to make a difference, but don't know where to start. These people all have the same things in common: they care about an issue and feel overwhelmed. If you're among this group, and you're grappling with purpose on a personal level, think about how you might apply these steps to your own life. Impact Engineering was first designed for the workplace, corporate teams, and their families, though many of the tips we're about to share are easily adapted for use outside the office.

In this chapter, we'll review the first step: find your cause, using three key lenses—your why, your assets, and your stakeholders. In the following chapters, we'll build on that cause with an action plan, engagement strategy, amplification platform, and formula for social impact measurement.

If you should ever find yourself sitting next to me on an airplane, have your purpose-related answers ready. Also, I apologize in advance.

Charitable Mergers?

Not as crazy as it sounds

Chip Wilson is the billionaire founder of Lululemon, a Canadian athletic-wear retailer that's become a global brand. He applies the same business rigor to social causes.

After considerable research, Wilson launched a charity for education in Ethiopia called imagine1day. Ten years later, imagine1day had built 43 schools and trained 12,000 teachers and leaders. It had government connections, a strong curriculum, and a local staff of more than 30 people. Still, Wilson realized that overhead was burning cash, and he was devoting much of his time to overseeing the governance of the charity. His time was better spent on his core expertise of building his businesses, generating profits to support high-impact philanthropy.

Wilson asked WE Charity to establish a partnership, integrating imagine1day with our projects. WE had expertise in multiple East African countries, an existing fundraising structure, and social enterprise to scale impact—and a model that ensures project sustainability. Wilson had done 10 years of groundwork, developed a proof-of-concept model, and built a great local staff. Thanks to the merger, Ethiopia is now an official WE Villages partner country.

WEconomy Impact Engineering: An Overview

Section 1: Find Your Cause

Use your why, your assets, and your stakeholders

Section 2: Build Your 360 Action Plan

Fulfill personal and professional objectives and own an outcome

Section 3: Engage Your Network

Including your team, your customers, and your supply chain

Too Much of a Good Thing

Before we give you a blueprint for impact—as a company or an individual—let's be clear about the difference between starting a purpose project and starting a charity.

Earlier, we looked at how charities are popping up like coffee-shop franchises. With the amount of growth in the sector, you'd expect the world's problems would be solved by now. Sadly, this is not the case. Most nonprofits don't grow much beyond a mom-and-pop initiative. In the U.S., just 1 percent of the country's nonprofits have annual budgets that top $1 million, and since 1970, only 144 charities have surmounted the $50 million revenue mark.[1] In Canada, 40 percent of charities have no staff, while 37 percent have a team of five or fewer. Half of Canadian charities have revenues under CDN$50,000.[2]

I should mention that we have nothing against small charities. Grassroots initiatives can do meaningful work in their surrounding communities. But there is little opportunity to scale impact—and many of the most entrenched social problems need big solutions. In a world of scarce resources, there are inefficiencies with fundraising competition, mass redundancies in administration, and an inability to implement systemic change. In the private sector, redundancies are weeded out with mergers and acquisitions. Small players are scooped up by bigger, more efficient ones with more purchasing power, better supply-management systems, and bigger R&D budgets for innovation and product improvements. The market won't tolerate failure as customer preferences shift and technology speeds up change. Imagine something similar in the charitable world—nonprofits merging together, sharing learnings, and combining resources for savings on administration costs.

Let's be clear, I won't advocate for hostile takeover bids, but I would like to see more self-awareness on the part of charities, and more willingness to merge. Without it, too many charities duplicate the efforts of existing organizations. Jason Saul, one of the nation's leading experts on measuring social impact, writes: "Simple math tells us that, on average, there are over one thousand nonprofits for each type of problem." There are, for example, over 700 charities supporting breast cancer research and prevention in the United States.[3]

Canada's 170,000 nonprofits add up to one for every 210 people. Even in a country renowned for being nice, 210 people is not enough to sustain a charity.[4]

Each new venture spends on administration and fundraising, with money that could have helped the cause had the founders supported existing organizations. Even those who claim to be selfless can get trapped in their own ego and the desire to put their name on an organization.

It's easy to see the upside to devoting your very own project to helping others. Rarely, if ever, do I hear people acknowledge that the downsides of starting a charity are similar to those that occur when starting a business.

A 2013 survey found that more than two-thirds of people believe there are too many charities raising money for the same cause.[5]

No model is perfect at launch—that goes for charity, too. There is risk, a steep learning curve, and a huge initial investment of your own time and money. Running a charity means years devoted to intense learnings about the most effective intervention models, building networks among nonprofit partners, and understanding the governance and fiduciary responsibilities. The skill set is enormous.

Why reinvent the wheel when you can build on something with a proven track record? Why not bet on a sure thing?

The day after my wedding, I met Warren Buffett at the annual Forbes 400 Summit on Philanthropy in New York. I probably should have been on my honeymoon—luckily I married the world's most patient woman. Buffett is a venerable businessman, consistently topping indexes of wealth, influence, and prestige. Those of us who don't regularly make Forbes rankings might be surprised to learn that he doesn't build companies from nothing. Even his most well-known holding, Berkshire Hathaway, was initially an investment in textile manufacturing; he bought shares until he took over the company in 1965. Buffett made his fortune with skilled investment techniques, instinct, and timing, snapping up bargains on the stock market. Buffett's area of expertise is scale and efficiency. Someone else does the dirty work during the initial set-up, and he comes in with capital and strategic strikes to make it bigger and better.

Buffett is a hunter, not a founder.

He applies the same strategy to philanthropy. Buffett pledged the Gates Foundation $31 billion with a series of stipulations akin to that of an investment—at least one of the Gateses (Bill or Melinda) must remain actively involved for payments to continue, for instance.[6] Here's a guy entirely justified in starting his own foundation. At the

A Note to CSR Leaders

A few Corporate Social Responsibility directors have confessed to me that they're concerned that partnering with an established charity might make their job redundant. Starting a corporate philanthropy project from scratch proves that they're "earning their keep."

The most successful CSR leaders embrace partnership because they understand that a charity partner handles on-the-ground project execution, while they lead a corporate team in customization, oversight, brand alignment, amplification, staff engagement, and achieving business objectives. Being the head of CSR is like being the Chief Technology Officer. You don't build your database or e-security system from scratch; you hire an external group that specializes in that function while you oversee the strategy and implementation. As a CSR executive, it is not your job to build schools or distribute food to the homeless. It is your job to set the company up for the greatest success in social impact and business outcomes.

If you're determined to launch a company-branded initiative, consider "white labeling." Many charities are open to being the "silent partner" in the background implementing the project, while the company gets the public credit. Clearly express your intent when approaching a potential charity partner. Leave financial logistics and execution of the donation to them, and set terms to uniquely brand an event or campaign as your own.

time of the pledge in 2006, Buffett was worth $42 billion and named the second wealthiest man in the world.[7] But he didn't start another charity. Buffett is an expert at making money, which is not the same skill set as using money to create high-impact change.

It seems virtuous to start a charity; sometimes it takes more guts and humility to lend your funds and expertise to an existing organization.

So the first rule of cause-finding is: Be like Warren Buffett. If someone else is already doing it, partner or invest in them. (If you're an individual, that means volunteering or mentoring.) If no one else is doing it, and you really do have a game-changing idea, innovation is always welcome! Kiva was one of those game changers. Launched in 2005, on the crest of an upcoming social media wave, the global microfinance charity now has the average Internet user easily offering $25 loans to small business owners overseas. That technology platform was revolutionary. If you are the next Kiva, far be it from me to discourage you. Godspeed.

If you're going to pair up, you'll still need to determine which partner or cause to choose. Before you pick a cause, examine it through the same lenses you would use to launch a for-profit plan. These three lenses can be applied in any order, and might vary in relevance to your company needs, sector, and goals.

Lens One: Your Why

The first lens is by far the simplest, and can be the strongest cause-finding compass.

First, for companies: In *Start with Why*, Simon Sinek argues that all great leaders share this trait—they start with why. "People don't buy what you do, they buy why you do it," Sinek writes, meaning that customers are more attracted to your mission and culture than to product attributes.[8] He cites Apple's motto to "Think different" and challenge the status quo. People buy into aspirations and dreams that feel larger than themselves—not just what you sell, but what you believe. Think about your mission.

Why does your company exist? Or, from a needs perspective, what problems are you already solving and how can those be modified to fit a social cause?

Patagonia outfits hard-core outdoorsy types. Their mission? "Build the best product, cause no unnecessary harm, use business to inspire and implement solutions to the environmental crisis." It's clear that this can also serve as a purpose statement for an environmental cause, and it does, with the company donating partial profits to grassroots protection efforts.

One of the world's largest communications companies, AT&T operates with the mission, "Connect people with their world, everywhere they live, work and play . . . and do it better than anyone else." For the wireless provider, the cause is leveraging technology for good, including support for STEM education (science, technology, engineering, and math) in schools, and addressing bad habits, like distracted driving. The company started a huge campaign to keep eyes on the road, not on cell phones.

For individuals, take time for self-reflection and consider personal values, cultural traditions, faith-based beliefs, and life experience. Many are motivated to run or walk or dance or bake for the cure, after losing a loved one to cancer. If you received life-changing mentorship from a great coach or teacher, consider paying it forward by becoming a Big Brother or Big Sister.

Picking a cause can be this easy.

Lens Two: Your Assets

Look more logically at your skill set. Are you a contractor or an architect with expertise in building homes? Think homelessness or housing infrastructure, and give your staff paid time off to volunteer with Habitat for Humanity. If you are the staff, ask for it—with a well-thought-out pitch. I stress these obvious connections because I've met with countless corporate groups to assess strategy only to find that the causes they've adopted are seemingly random. For companies, the purpose should be a logical extension of the business, both for ease of execution and for better customer response. ME to WE has commissioned studies with Mission Measurement and found that business–charity partnerships are perceived to be more authentic by customers when the brand and social mission are compatible, when it makes sense for the company to care about its cause. And a purpose that relates to the core business more directly drives further exploration of a company's products and services.[9] One way to ensure compatibility is to make your business assets work for your purpose.

GoodLife Fitness, the largest health club chain in Canada, leverages facilities, equipment, and instructors. The GoodLife Kids Foundation funds free fitness classes for partnering schools through its Goodlife4Kids School Program. And their Jump! Child Minding keeps kids occupied and physically active, while their parents get in a workout. The purpose is focused; it fits the healthy lifestyle brand and core business model by adding value to the service, since parents without babysitters can still use Goodlife facilities.

Over in another industry, eBay "provides a global online marketplace where practically anyone can trade practically anything, enabling economic opportunity around the world." So eBay uses its unique technology platform to hold charitable auctions, selling celebrity memorabilia to support various organizations and allowing individual users to donate partial proceeds from their own sales.

General Mills is parent to popular brands Cheerios and Betty Crocker, among others. The company feeds people, and its charitable arm, the General Mills Foundation, operates with the mission "nourishing lives." Naturally, General Mills picked the cause of hunger.

In America, food security is concerning not only for the homeless, but also for the working poor, with many kids in low-income areas relying on government-run school

Finding Your Cause outside the Office

WE uses the equation: Gift + Issue = Change

Combine passions and skills—your personal assets—with an issue close to your heart—your why. Are you a graphic designer looking to raise money for breast cancer? Design a campaign website. A financial planner could offer workshops in women's shelters.

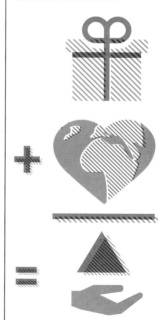

lunch programs. Those free meals stop when the school year ends. Outnumber Hunger launched in 2011, with General Mills donating partial proceeds from product sales to support food banks across the country, in partnership with nonprofit Feeding America. The annual campaign runs in April, close to the end of the academic year, when struggling families need it most. General Mills used product assets by donating partial proceeds.

Each of these companies thought smart about what they had to offer, making the process of picking a cause that much simpler. Look first to your corporate mission and core competencies to support the cause.

Lens Three: Your Stakeholders

It's possible that your mission or business assets don't lend themselves so easily to a cause. Maybe you work for a general consulting or investment firm. Of course, you have infrastructure and offer services, but those things can defy sectors, making the asset or brand lens more difficult to focus. Companies that fall under this category might be more concerned with stakeholder feedback. For these firms, human capital might be the most important lens.

Ideally, a good company looks at all three, and dials certain lenses up or down depending on the sector and goals.

Now we're going to look at your team, customers, and community groups, and how to enlist them to identify your cause.

In other words: the third lens is to simply ask your people.

Team and Customers

These people work for you and buy from you; they are the ones on the frontlines who will amplify your purpose even more if they have initial buy-in. What better way to help your team and customers form an attachment to your cause than to let them choose it? Deploy surveys. Ask: What causes would make sense for the business? What causes do you donate to personally?

In a bygone era, corporate philanthropy was a pet project. The CEO or their spouse loved opera or had a soft spot for endangered whales.

When the CEO retires, pet projects are dropped, without investment from any other level of management. These causes of old were typically disconnected from the rest of the staff.

A top-down cause platform won't be as effective as one that engages the whole team.

It is mid-level management who will drive a meaningful purpose strategy, integrate it within their teams, build incentives around it, and monitor the activities. Junior staff will organize volunteer days and turn up to mentorship programs if they're invested in the idea.

When companies consider the whole social ecosystem, interested parties include your team, your customers, and the community.

As an aside, individuals who are really keen to make the most impact can consult with grassroots charity groups to determine where their skills or time will be best put to use. Find out if your local animal shelter needs dog walkers, donations of kibble, or something unexpected like a new technology platform for tracking animal adoptions. So many people consider charitable causes, yet so few consider asking first about specific needs.

For Allstate, linking a cause to their core business wasn't immediately obvious. What social issue fits best with personal insurance? With 160,000 employees and an existing array of social investments, from financial literacy for domestic violence victims to disaster preparedness, the firm's charitable endeavors were scattered. "We were giving on an ad hoc basis," says Laura Freveletti, Allstate's Senior Manager of Corporate Social Responsibility. The firm hired social impact consultants Mission Measurement to probe customers about their cause preferences. Youth development emerged as one of the top concerns, more than any other cause the company had supported in the past. In retrospect, this made a lot of sense, since people tend to shop for more insurance coverage once they have kids. Many of Allstate's most invested customers were parents.

I met CEO Tom Wilson at the Aspen Ideas Festival soon after the firm was set on its cause, his team's feedback about youth empowerment fresh in his mind. Wilson was actively looking for programs to help reduce youth violence in Chicago, home of Allstate's headquarters, and promised me two minutes of his overly scheduled day. Over an hour later, we were swapping smartphones and watching our favorite charity campaign videos. Wilson showed me his photography collection, digitized on his phone, of images from civil rights struggles throughout history. The Burning Monk, shot in Vietnam. Police dogs attacking marchers in the Birmingham Campaign.

We bonded instantly as individuals who believe in massive social change. But Allstate is a big firm. Wilson introduced WE to his team; he wanted full engagement—total buy-in, so they vetted us in a process that took almost a year. We were part of multiple meetings with cross-sector departments to get all teams excited. Since then, Allstate has been instrumental in bringing our service learning and leadership curriculum to schools across America as title sponsor for WE Schools and WE Day, as well as coordinating thousands of Allstate team members in various cities to volunteer to support young leaders. It wouldn't be an overstatement to say that Allstate was instrumental in launching the WE Movement across America.

"We can't just depend on governments or nonprofits to fix the world. Businesses can and should help too. Companies are made up of people just like you. And they want to make a positive difference in the world. If we all use the resources around us, we can make the world a better place."

—Tom Wilson, Allstate CEO and 2017 Chairman, U.S. Chamber of Commerce

Wilson himself became deeply involved with WE Day, delivering a speech he titled "Rise Up" to encourage youth to get involved in service. As our national WE Day co-chair, he helped to secure a place for the event in stadiums across the country, including in Allstate's hometown of Chicago at WE Day Illinois. During the 2015–2016 academic year alone, 200,000 youth from 650 WE Schools across the state volunteered more than 385,000 hours and raised more than half a million dollars for hundreds of charities.

The company's involvement with the cause of youth empowerment goes back years, with support for multiple organizations. One of these initiatives includes financial literacy lessons, taught by their advisors. Allstate volunteers run weekly classes or half-day sessions for kindergarteners and middle school students, regularly interacting with the community to promote financial smarts, as well as volunteer-based learning, catered to youth. The program is also a job perk, since mentoring is a form of professional development and the volunteering takes place on company time.

In addition to offering an outlet to give back, the company's youth empowerment initiatives have also boosted brand awareness, measured by the advisory firm Reputation Institute. And, the company has received external accolades for its work in youth empowerment, including the 2017 Golden Halo Award from the Engage for Good Conference, organized by a cause marketing institute.[10]

What's the takeaway for Allstate's CSR leader Freveletti? "Research what is important to your stakeholders. A connection to the business is [also] really important. Allstate stands for safety and security, which is what we want for young people in the country. We believe that good starts young."

As a large company, Allstate went through a formal process with a third-party advisor. A small business could easily replicate this cause-finding experiment with an online survey. Many companies I've worked with use free online survey platforms to determine what cause their employees and customers care about most. Staff engagement can be quick or comprehensive, depending on your goals. If you're small enough, a casual poll of customer walk-ins might suffice. Running the coffee shop on the corner? Have customers write suggestions while they wait at the bar for lattes.

Here is where individuals can weigh in as customers. Remember, you are the most important stakeholder for businesses. If you're concerned about improper waste disposal at your favorite fast-food chain, say something to management. Better yet, Tweet at them. When companies solicit suggestions, make sure your voice is heard.

Community Groups

One of the most innovative workshops I've encountered was with City National Bank. The American finance institution convened about 50 guests in its Los Angeles office tower. Most of them were not bankers. I remember the construction workers' union and steel-toe boots. An

African American church group wore matching bowties and starched shirts. A Korean business association was there, along with local nonprofit representatives. The bank was hosting community interest groups to jumpstart an investment project focused on diversity and inclusion.

I assumed the big ask would be for more capital—and it was, although the requests were much more creative and nuanced. Groups wanted skills training and apprenticeship programs or guaranteed loans to minority businesses. City National was left with a long list after the two-hour session. With it, the bank devised an $11 billion community investment program to roll out over five years. Launched in 2015, it includes just over $4 billion in small business loans and $80 million earmarked for supplier expenditures with minority-owned vendors.[12]

Before any big charitable commitment, companies can reach out to local nonprofits and layers of government, from the chamber of commerce to the mayor, to state or federal departments. These groups can help advise you on the best intervention strategy for your cause.

Touchdown

As for Matthew Corrin, I like to think he didn't regret his decision to speak with me on the plane that day. Twelve months after our high-altitude encounter, he was in Kenya walking through the sustainable gardens that provide schoolchildren with hot lunches, partly through Freshii's partnership.

Having launched a company inspired by his own frustrations, Corrin had a pretty strong "why" that also served as his personal mission. For founder-led

Don't forget your extended corporate family

- *Retirees*
- *Alumni*
- *Employee families*
- *Shareholders*
- *Investors*

organizations like Freshii, or small startups with carefully cultivated culture, the "why" will probably be your focal point. The purpose of the company becomes the social cause.

Freshii is on a quest "to help citizens of the world live better by making healthy food convenient and affordable." Corrin wanted to solve the root cause of hunger and turn a profit. So we connected Freshii's cause to product sales, with every "warrior bowl" purchase providing a hot lunch for a student in WE Charity's partner communities in Kenya. The quinoa and chicken bowl was named after the Maasai warriors. Freshii also leveraged a product asset, adapting menu items for the purpose.

It was a truly sustainable initiative that provided nutrition for students, and also food security for the region, fulfilling Corrin's requirement that the change be systemic. Because the school lunches came from locally cultivated school farms, product sales supported agricultural development education. Our school gardens serve as classrooms for students who learn techniques from high-yield growers, taking the lessons home to their parents, many of whom are sustenance farmers. The long-term impact is a new generation of farmers empowered to grow the food to feed themselves and their families, and to uplift their communities.

And there you have it: why + assets + stakeholders = cause. Parts of the equation can be dialed up or down, depending on your business or your goals. After you pick a cause, you're ready to start your action plan.

"The cause always benefits more
from a purpose project that delivers
social value and financial returns."

WECONOMY IMPACT ENGINEERING, STEP TWO: BUILD A 360 ACTION PLAN

By Marc Kielburger

Changing the world starts with a whiteboard

In 2005, Hurricane Katrina ripped through the Atlantic coast leaving thousands of Americans homeless. Mandatory and voluntary evacuations in large swaths of the Gulf Coast displaced more than one million people. Many found themselves without basic amenities. In the aftermath, Tide, the detergent made by Procter & Gamble, launched Loads of Hope, a mobile laundry service for families affected by disaster. The company tricked out a truck, installing high-efficiency washers inside a flat-bed—a big-rig laundromat that they drove into relief areas. In a little more than a decade, 45,000 families in crisis have used the mobile laundry service.

Laundry soap can't rebuild infrastructure, but Tide's mobile program was able to fulfill an immediate need for clean clothing. One less thing for displaced families to worry about. Tide cleans the clothes, but leaves location scouting to the Federal Emergency Management Administration (FEMA), a government agency that bases decisions on population density in relief areas, groundwater, and electrical grids. Coordinating with other aid efforts allows Tide to dispatch its big rig to crisis areas without having to account for all the logistics. The company isn't known for disaster relief, so it relies on FEMA. Tide understands its limitations. In action, it owns what it knows and leaves the rest to experts. It all factors into action planning.

Devising an action plan can be trickier than determining what you care about. Once you land on hunger as a cause, for example, you'll still have to narrow it down. You might be interested in childhood malnutrition or access to healthy lunches in school cafeterias. Perhaps you want to support small-scale community farmers, or maybe your greatest concern is large-scale food security for a growing world population.

An action plan forces you to decide: What are you going to do about your cause, exactly?

When companies nail the execution, they have an unmatched ability to scale solutions to the world's biggest problems. WEconomy Impact Engineering is devoted to helping businesses get it right.

Welcome to the second step: "WEconomy Impact Engineering, Step Two: Build a 360 Action Plan." This chapter is meant to help corporate teams devise an execution strategy for their cause. Still, the advice can be easily adapted by individuals engaging in a personal purpose project.

We'll offer two lenses by which to develop a customized plan

- Fulfill corporate (or personal) objectives
- Own an outcome for your cause

Fulfill Corporate Objectives

Think about your reasons for getting into the purpose game. Of course you want to feed the hungry or preserve the rainforest, but you also have business targets and professional goals. In most cases, corporate donors are seeking a business return on their purpose investment in addition to positive social impact.

Before we go any further, allow me to add an important note on purpose and profit priorities. If you want to be in the business of making the world better, you'd better start with a real desire to better the world. Any malintent will be weeded out by savvy shoppers. Earlier, when we talked about inspiring brand fanatics, we touched on authenticity and cause washing, and how consumers have access to near limitless information to fact-check purpose claims. Charitable organizations will also vet potential partners to ensure the pairing will create real change.

As I hope is evident by now, we believe that profit and purpose can make the greatest positive impact in the world. Done right, cross-sector partnership is among the best ways to achieve this. Companies and social enterprises with the genuine intent to combine these two principles should be rewarded for making purpose-driven choices. This is the profit aspect of purpose and profit. When good companies thrive, they have an incentive to scale even more social good. It starts a flywheel of positive impact. (See the box in this chapter titled "The Compatibility of Companies and Charities" for a discussion about priorities and authentic intentions in our own charitable partnerships.)

Building a 360 Action Plan requires hyperawareness of the desired outcome, both in terms of the impact on the cause and the impact on key corporate outcomes. Knowing what you want to achieve will give you clear architectural scaffolding to build the ideal project. The cause always benefits more from a purpose project that delivers social value and financial returns. Corporate benefits mean more investment of funds and resources in the cause, attracting more attention across departments. Companies can reach beyond modest CSR budgets to leverage other funds earmarked to achieve specific outcomes. If purpose also serves an HR or marketing function, for instance, why not draw from those funding pools to support it? All of this adds up to even greater social change.

In the WEconomy, more and more corporate leaders understand that purpose and profit reinforce each other. Progressive leaders are baking purpose into the DNA of companies as core functions instead of as add-ons.

All of this is to say: vocalize your company's desired outcomes at the blueprint phase of a purpose plan or charity partnership. Take a look at the business and personal goals that will

91% of Customers

91 percent of customers value honesty in companies, well ahead of "Product Utility" (61 percent) and "Brand Popularity" (39 percent).[1]

96% of Companies

96 percent of companies believe partnering with charities enhances their reputation and credibility.[2]

ensure your cause becomes a priority, one that will unlock the necessary level of investment and cross-department engagement. If your sales team needs more face time with clients, this year's volunteer initiative could bring sales and customers together. If your company needs to reduce shipping costs, a packaging redesign can help minimize transport expenses while eliminating environmental waste.

To create a 360 Action Plan with our own partners, the WEconomy Impact Engineering Team meets with four internal stakeholder groups—HR, Marketing, Product, and CSR—to identify opportunities and pain points. Though it takes more time, we hold sessions separately to isolate and identify challenges unique to each team. We ask each department to hold nothing back as it discusses needs, challenges, and incentives. Our team compiles the answers to build a cause-activation solution to drive both business and charitable goals.

Individual employees can also reap benefits and job perks from the corporate cause. It would be great if your sales team drew in new leads with a purpose halo, or your recruitment team was flooded with resumes from candidates attracted to your culture. Or, if you could take time out from your workday to give back with your boss' support. Submit your departmental needs to a corporate CSR committee. Or, even better, volunteer to join the committee. I guarantee you'll get recognition, and likely some face time with senior leadership. You can use the questions listed below, even if you're doing your own professional assessment.

Through a series of open-ended questions, we hone in on each team's priority.

For companies, here's a list of sample questions by department:

Corporate Social Responsibility

- Can customers, employees, and other stakeholders articulate your company's social impact?
- How much closer are you to your social goal? Can you measure and track progress?
- Does accountability for CSR impact live outside your department? Have you created a system to engage the whole company?
- Do staff know whom to contact and how to engage with your purpose?
- How do you incentivize employee volunteerism, philanthropy, or other forms of service?

Human Resources

- Do you need a recruiting tool to attract new employees?
- Are you trying to bridge generations and get your socially conscious millennial employees more engaged, or retain baby boomers looking for purpose at work?

- Was there a recent merger or departmental reorganization, and you're seeking to build a stronger shared culture and bonding experiences?
- Is employee morale low after a rough quarter?

Marketing

- What is the reputation of the company? Are you trying to rebrand, rebuild, or redefine?
- Are you a parent company trying to grow your master brand by creating a cause that links together all of your subbrands?
- Is there a special stakeholder group (government officials, community leaders) you are trying to influence with a message, or to gain positive credentials from?
- Are you seeking a high-profile celebrity partner or cause ambassador?

Product Team/Customer Success

- Do you need to differentiate your product from the competitor? Is there a new challenger brand emerging that's trying to take you on?
- Are you trying to convince a retailer to carry your product and provide coveted shelf space in stores?
- Are you seeking to create unique bonding experiences between your sales team and customers?
- How can you make your customer-appreciation gifts, holiday parties, and special occasions stand out?

So, what might this process look like? What kind of challenge or objective would emerge from this series of questions?

The German company Henkel, makers of Purex and Dial among other products, is parent to a huge brand family spread across three product categories and around the globe. Their problem was one of geography. Henkel's U.S. branch had operated from headquarters in Scottsdale, Arizona, for years. When the company acquired Connecticut-based Sun Products, teams from old and new offices were consolidated in New England. Those based in Scottsdale moved across the country to offices in

Stamford, Connecticut— more than 2,000 miles away. Physically moving a large chunk of staff, nearly coast to coast, was a massive undertaking. Real estate agents and education consultants were brought on to help families find homes and pick schools. Offsite retreats were planned so teams could meet new coworkers in social settings, including the bowling alley. Gutter balls and rented shoes are a great outlet for team building and friendly competition, but the company was searching for a more profound solution.

Planning purpose outside of work? No problem

We've learned that volunteers and donors find the experience more rewarding when their support for a cause is also personally beneficial.

Volunteers might be working to develop a skill, such as playing music at a local seniors' residence. You may want to enhance your résumé by serving on a charity's board of directors, or expand your professional network by joining a service club like Rotary. Parents may be seeking to raise more compassionate kids, looking for family-focused service opportunities. Honesty about your own self-interests can help you stick with your cause.

Henkel realized it could do even more for its employees, bringing staff together through volunteer service. The action plan involved a partnership with various charity organizations, providing resources for Henkel staff and families to discover their cause and engage in local community service. Staff not only interacted with each other, but also with local organizations and leaders, establishing a network outside of work. Families got the chance to plant roots while giving back in their new hometown. Henkel solved an HR need, engaging and retaining staff during an important transition, breaking down silos between office sites.

Once you've identified the corporate or personal objectives that will help make your cause stick, it's time for the second lens: Define success in terms of a social outcome.

Own an Outcome: Find a KPI you can take credit for

You wouldn't launch a product without knowing in advance what success looks like: market penetration, sales, revenue. And you'd be sure to have systems in place to capture data and report against those goals. An action plan to support a cause should not be treated any differently. Set up correctly, it can yield quantifiable data that will guide you through tough decisions. Every high-performing charitable model betters people and planet, but if you're clear on your goals, you can make a strategic choice about how to invest your scarce time and resources. Numbers let you know when to pivot and regroup.

Within your action plan, define the success metrics for your social impact. We call this owning an outcome because it requires you to determine the change you are capable of creating and to take responsibility for it. It's more easily understood with an example. Let's say you've chosen to help the homeless in your community: that's your cause. Your team's corporate objective was staff engagement and professional development, so your action plan is regular mentorship opportunities at a local shelter. That's your program, but what are your social impact goals?

Consider carefully which outcomes are within your power to change, given your resources. As a general rule, the narrower the better. You might want to eradicate homelessness in Chicago, but unless you're the City of Chicago, that's probably not realistic. That said, you can work with a social services agency to promote life-skills development

How are the top CEOs putting purpose to work?

In 2016, the top brass from dozens of companies as diverse as Nielsen, Barclays, and designer brand Coach were asked about their strongest motivation for expanding social investment.[3] Here are the top corporate cause objectives from global CEOs:

63%

Strengthen human capital

21%

Enhance brand reputation

and workplace readiness for youth transitioning out of homelessness at one specific shelter. You can then track the rate at which program participants gain job offers, remain in stable housing for at least six months, or the rate at which they continue their education compared to their peers.

If the goal is focused, you can measure it to track progress. We all want to know whether or not our time, money, and efforts are making a difference. Measuring a targeted goal helps us answer those questions.

Measure the Outcome

Jason Saul once told me about an amusing exchange. His client, a pastor, was reluctant to submit to an assessment of his social work, saying, "God's work cannot be measured." This was worrisome news for Saul, CEO of a company dedicated to measuring social impact. A spiritual man himself, Saul thought for a moment. After a pause, he replied that in the Old Testament, God made the Earth in six days and rested on the seventh, meaning that even God benchmarked success at six days.

> One of the reasons charitable work is massively undervalued is because people are unwilling to attach metrics to it.

The truth is almost anything can be measured. Adding numbers to social impact can elevate it from a knee-jerk emotional act to a results-driven investment. Nonprofits and corporate purpose projects can use the same monitoring and evaluation (M&E) tools available to track business targets. Because each action plan is unique—with highly focused goals—I'll briefly review some general best practices.

Partner

67 percent of companies are involved in a partnership with a nonprofit or charity.[4]

Monitoring tools, or what you might call "business intelligence," track your program's vitals. How were resources spent? How many participants signed up? How many team members were involved? Did participants experience the intended outcome? If these questions seem like no-brainers, you'd be surprised to learn I've encountered many companies that forget how to be well-run companies when they pick a cause. They don't track action plans because they don't expect to gain anything from them.

As a business, think about what you might include in an annual or quarterly report, and use the same mindset for your cause. All of this data is easily obtained while running the program. Ideally, monitoring is ingrained in daily operations—at event registrations that consider numbers and demographics. Don't mail out a survey two weeks after a program when you can hand one out at the end of a session. Think of monitoring as the fitness tracker of social impact. Looking at day-to-day progress, like stairs climbed and calories burned, will help you adjust your actions and behavior toward achieving your goal.

Evaluation is more involved, with a study conducted to assess a program's performance and efficacy, to provide insight into bigger changes that might be required. This is a more time-consuming and expensive process, sometimes involving outside experts, but a formal evaluation is helpful every three to five years. Enlist an expert when the action plan fails or plateaus, or whenever your goals, resources, or commitments change. Keep track of your action plan to make sure it's working for you.

Finally, if you want to get really granular, look at the cost per life changed by your social impact. I realize the vast majority of people give because a family member has cancer, or photos of a smiling sponsor child make them happy. Those are valid reasons for picking a cause,

The Compatibility of Companies and Charities

Charities can benefit from corporate partnerships that will help scale social change. But they need to carefully avoid companies that will negatively impact their mission.

Each charity establishes its own protocol for vetting corporate-charity partnerships. As many will say, it's neither an art, nor a science. For example, some companies have steady track records of socially responsible action, but almost every company could be doing more. How much is enough? Other companies have failed in the past on ethics, but subsequently improved their practices. How long do charities keep them on the blacklist?

We certainly don't have all the answers for a kaleidoscope of charities, each with its own unique causes and stakeholder groups. But in case our methods are helpful to some, here's a look at the three lenses we applied to designing our partnership vetting system. Applying such lenses might help other charities develop their own criteria. Companies should also consider how their practices affect their chance at a beneficial purpose partnership.

First, we looked at charities that work with similar stakeholders, youth and families, to determine how they vet and establish partnerships with companies. Craig is a former member of the Scouts Canada Board of Directors, and we borrowed heavily from their vetting guidelines. For example, there's zero chance you'll see a tobacco sponsor anywhere near our WE Day stage.

Second, we looked to the best practices of socially responsible businesses. ME to WE, our social enterprise, went in the running to become a B Corp, a designation granted by the third-party certification system B Lab, which puts companies through rigorous testing on environmental impact, worker well-being, and ethical sourcing. ME to WE excelled in these standards and is now a certified B Corp. The insider insight and learnings gained through the certification process informed our own analysis of potential corporate partners.

Finally, we relied heavily on our WE Charity Board of Directors for their expertise. In fact, we still bring them case questions. Our Board has extensive experience in nonprofit governance, ethics, education, child and youth protection, and other related fields. Depending on your cause, you may want to seek specific topic experts. Our research systems and Board assist in weeding out inauthentic companies. We have declined many corporate offers in the past, and we know other charities have, too.

We believe in challenging the corporate sector to be better. In our early days we held our share of protest signs and wrote petitions and campaign letters, lobbying for higher standards in business. We strongly believe that there is still a role for this type of pressure.

Likewise, we should also reward companies and social enterprises seeking to do good: the ones that actively create well-paying jobs, promote social progress, and give back to communities. We believe that the best corporate–charity partnerships will help influence both the for-profit and nonprofit sectors to achieve greater social good.

but there's nothing wrong with also adding a bit of rigor when it comes to impact. Everyone wants to know if their money is making a difference. When you give your monthly donation, how much good is actually achieved and how much does it cost to deliver the social outcome? For those who are curious, it's possible to objectively review achievements in terms of input (donation dollars) and output (cost per life changed or impact delivered). This answers questions like, "Which charity will distribute the most food to shelters using the same amount of funding?" With some back-of-the-napkin math, any donor should be able to find this out after asking charities a few simple questions.

We're not advocating where to spend your donation dollars, only that you consider the investment carefully. Fair warning that there will be a little bit of math in the next section.

Buy an Outcome: Costing Out Social Change

Much like purchasing carbon offsets to mitigate the impact of company travel, you can purchase social outcomes. It's not as simple as ordering from a menu, but you can buy a better world—in increments of social change. Companies will have the infrastructure to be more rigorous about this process, but individual donors also should consider efficacy and impact.

A while back, Allstate approached us, wanting to buy election results. Hold on, it's not what you think. For the insurance firm, the cause is youth empowerment. One of their desired outcomes is for youth to be civically active, and to vote. Of course, the company didn't push any particular candidate or issue, but the civic duty of engaging with the system itself.

WE converted its service actions into metrics. Between donations and time invested, WE Schools volunteers generated approximately US$220 million in social impact in the 2016/2017 academic year.

With some research, we discovered young people are more likely to vote if they see themselves as agents of change. News consumption, self-confidence, and leadership skills all get young adults to the polls. This demographic is more likely to cast a ballot if, first, they believe their vote matters and, second, they care about a cause: tax rates, the environment, the armed forces—anything.

WE Schools is built to achieve these outcomes on a large scale. Our service learning program gets kids involved in causes for school credit. In 2016, the program expanded through a partnership with The College Board, the nonprofit association of colleges and universities that offers Advanced Placement (AP) courses, allowing high school students to take college-level classes. Together, we launched AP with WE Service. Certain AP courses are now taught within a framework of service learning. For instance, in AP Computer Science with WE Service, students learn to code by developing apps for nonprofits.

WE Schools alumni become good citizens

80 percent had volunteered time during the previous year—150 hours on average.

82 percent demonstrate increased leadership among their peers.

90 percent believe they are responsible for addressing social justice issues.

Independent studies found that WE Schools students are more actively engaged, self-confident, and aware of social issues because of these activities. The same studies also found that when they reach voting age, alumni are in fact more likely to cast a ballot. Surveys of our alumni in 2012 show that 79 percent had voted in the most recent Canadian federal election—double the turnout rate for their peers.[5]

WE Schools decided it could, in a sense, buy the youth vote (no felonies were committed, I promise). We could calculate the cost of our program, count participating students, and measure the program efficacy and reach. And with such a specific goal, we could break it down further, measuring the cost to civically engage one student that would determine the Cost Per Result, or the price to achieve that particular desired social outcome. When Allstate invested funds to scale WE Schools across America, the company could predict that it costs US$34 per student per year to successfully increase civic engagement. And this, in turn, is one key motivating factor to vote.

Why is this relevant to a business or individual donor? Because when you develop your action plan, you should consider multiple solutions, strategies, and potential charitable partners. It makes fiscal sense for a company to look at unit costs and returns when they are considering CSR budgets. Similar to

WE Schools students are rock stars

In the 2016–2017 academic year alone, they:

7K+
Charities

Supported 7,211 charities

2.5
Million

Donated 2,555,483 pounds of food to shelters

Raised $24,210,167 for local and global causes

8.8
Million Hours

Volunteered 8,837,826 hours

comparing the costs of any service, it's worth calculating your best charitable ROI, determining how to achieve the greatest impact in the most cost-effective manner. We acknowledge that this is a more rigorous process than many individual donors want to undertake. But you work hard for your money, and you should understand how it's impacting lives. The formula below still works, if you're really keen.

Here's how you can calculate cost per outcome, or return on investment, for any corporate sponsorship funding or charitable donation.

Charitable Returns: Cost per Social Outcome

Calculating the cost of results is one way to measure effectiveness of an action plan in terms of it producing a desired social outcome for your cause.

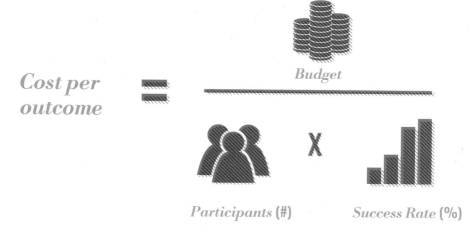

- **Budget:** Cost of your program (e.g., total cost of a six-week seminar)
- **Participants:** The total number of people who experienced the program (e.g., the number of seminar students)
- **Success Rate:** The percentage of participants who achieve the chosen result, outcome, or KPI (e.g., the rate at which seminar students move on to the next grade)

"You don't need to be a corporate giant
with hundreds of thousands of contacts
and clients. From SMEs to individuals,
we all have networks we can tap into
to help us amplify the good."

WECONOMY IMPACT ENGINEERING, STEP THREE: ENGAGE YOUR NETWORKS

By Craig Kielburger

Power to the people: Leverage your networks for big impacts

From C-suite to mud hut, it was a serious skills swap: a lesson in small business management delivered by one of the world's top accountants, in exchange for a demonstration on cooking chapati from a woman who wanted to sell her snacks.

Inside a small dwelling in the village of Udawad in northern India, Bill Thomas, now chairman of KPMG International, watched Ganeshi Bai, a shy amateur cook, expertly shape dough into a ball before flattening it on a round pan that rested over an open fire. She motioned to him to try. As Thomas leaned in, so did those around him, including junior accountants, middle managers, their accompanying family members, and several curious goats. As Thomas pancaked the dough, his would-be chapati crumbled. Bai whispered to the translator that he would never get married with those culinary skills. When she learned Thomas's wife was actually there, she turned to her and empathetically quipped, "How unfortunate for you."

The cooking lesson over, they got down to business. Or more precisely, to questions about business and how to scale. Bai had many questions. How do you get the best price for flour? If other women also sell chapatis, will it saturate the market and drive down prices? Should she diversify, embrace technology, invest in a cellphone, and charge others who want to use it?

For Thomas, who at the time was CEO of KPMG Canada and typically worked on multi-million- or multi-billion-dollar government audits and the acquisition of large corporations, this was small potatoes, er, chapatis. Cross-legged on the floor, he kindly gave his best advice.

Community engagement is considered a core competency at KPMG, alongside team leadership and building client relationships. Thomas went above and beyond to exemplify those values to his team during a ME to WE trip to northern India, the farthest leg on the company's long journey with us to boost team values and satisfaction.

KPMG, one of the "Big Four" professional services networks in the world, performs scrupulous audits for major corporations, organizations, and governments (the firm certified the election of Nelson Mandela in South Africa in 1994).[1] It measures complex data and scrutinizes the tiniest of details in financial deals. So, several years ago when they asked us to a meeting to discuss a partnership, we arrived equipped with piles of metrics and third-party studies to show the impact of our domestic and international programming. "Quantifiable data only" had been our mantra.

When I finished, the executives in the room exchanged knowing glances.

"We're in. But for more than the reasons you just mentioned."

To my pleasant surprise, they had brought us in, in part, to help with staff engagement. Of course, social change was the primary goal of the charity partnership. Toward that outcome, KPMG had already researched and approved of our impact model and organizational efficiency—those requirements were table-stakes, and passing that muster got us through the door to deliver our pitch. They were seeking more from a full

90%
of Partners

90 percent of partners reported that the purpose plan increased their sense of pride for KPMG.[2]

charity partnership, a way to meaningfully engage KPMG partners, staff, clients, and loved ones. KPMG wanted to create volunteer experiences for their employees and their families. In this case, the cause and action plan fulfilled an HR objective.

The firm wanted a plan that would speak to its 180,000 people worldwide—executives, midlevel management, and junior associates. Like any big organization, KPMG has distinct layers: a one-size-fits-all approach would not work for the team, let alone its massive network of contacts, clients, suppliers, and families. In such a large company, there were so many diverse talents and interests, a virtual army of caring people ready and eager to help a good cause. So together we tailored a strategy to fit each tier. Every large company has an existing HR system for amplification, engagement, and recognition. A good purpose plan or partnership leverages all of those resources to amplify the good, giving employees the chance to find more meaning at work.

Now that you have your cause and an action plan, it's time to look at the third phase of WEconomy Impact Engineering: Engage Your Networks. Whether you are the CEO rallying the company, or a team member approaching coworkers and stakeholders with your action plan, we'll help you recruit. Use our engagement blueprint to come up with a plan to amplify your internal cause, or give it to your partner charity to execute.

With KPMG serving as our corporate model, we'll start with a plan for employees or colleagues, then we'll move on to customers, suppliers, business partners, and the wider community. We'll consider case studies and examples that offer lessons for any situation.

Let's first consider how to customize engagement for team members based on their position at the office. You don't need to be a corporate giant with hundreds of thousands of contacts and clients. From SMEs to individuals, we all have networks we can tap into to help us amplify the good. If you have a small workplace with flat management, you can pick and choose which level of involvement you seek. You could cut your pyramid into different layers, but for the sake of ease, these are the most common structures for medium and large businesses and how to best engage each team in a corporate social mission.

Catering to each group with unique volunteer or campaign opportunities ensures that everyone participates to help the cause, which lends human capital, but also staying power. An action plan executed at every level is much more effective than one managed from the top down. Get your whole team invested in purpose; consider what suits them best and what will encourage them to be most involved.

Employee Engagement by the Tier: A Pyramid
C-suite

Wants and needs

CEOs have control over capital, internal influence, and wide networks, but they have very little time. Executives are not going to read through fundraising campaign kits and offer detailed instructions to staff. They want high-touch: customized delivery options that leverage their unique ability to shine a spotlight within the company. Executives are role models for the entire team and ambassadors for the brand.

KPMG cause commitment

Lynne Doughtie, U.S. Chairman and Chief Executive Officer of KPMG, joined us as co-chair for WE Day UN in 2017. One of Doughtie's passions is women's empowerment; she joined Liberian President and Nobel Peace Prize winner Ellen Johnson-Sirleaf to address 6,000 student

C-SUITE

Low time, high customization

MID-LEVEL MANAGEMENT

Moderate time, moderate customization

STARTING STAFF AND ASSOCIATES

More time, low customization

leaders attending WE Day UN at New York City's iconic Madison Square Garden Theater. Throughout the year, Doughtie leveraged her scarce free time to provide WE Charity with advice and guidance on growing its presence in New York City. She also hosted information sessions for prospective supporters to achieve the same goal. Doughtie shared messages among her fellow partners and staff to rally volunteers from KPMG to join in the year-long WE Schools service programs and WE Day stadium celebration.

Mid-level management

Wants and needs

Mid-level executives manage and motivate teams. They have a bit more time, but not loads of it, and it's more difficult for them to leave the office for a purpose project, having more direct reports than top management. They want moderate touch: customized offerings and tools to incentivize that they can easily distribute to teams within the office. This group is also keen for more one-on-one time with clients. And every group, from the top down, wants to spend more time with their families.

KPMG cause commitment

KPMG hosted WE Family workshops at offices throughout North America to enable participants to create a customized family action plan. These sessions are held in the office, on lunch or after hours to ease planning and lesson time commitments. KPMG staff and their families join clients along with their own families for a unique bonding opportunity unrelated to work. Experienced facilitators help each family design a personalized action plan to make change on an issue they care about most. Staff often stay involved outside the office when they find and help a personal cause. The chance to leave a legacy as a family motivates more actions on weekends and evenings, getting more people working for good on their own time.

Starting staff and associates

Wants and needs

This team has more time to volunteer on an ongoing basis. Resources can involve less customization but must have a tangible and profound connection to the cause. Every employee is seeking more meaning at work, hoping to clock in for a company that cares to engage their values. This group has a bit more time to read a pamphlet or fundraising kit, especially if it is tied to career-building incentives. The expectation is that the steps are still simple, though not hand-delivered as with the executives.

KPMG cause commitment

Many KPMG employees are involved with our service campaigns, including WE Read Together. Staff read to students and run other literacy workshops in at-risk schools, where much of the student population comes from low-income families. This partnership was a natural extension of KPMG's Family for Literacy program, a larger initiative that involves regular book drives and donations. Since the program's launch, KPMG has donated three million books to kids across America.

WE helped KPMG develop an action plan that got employees even more revved up about the company leadership in the cause of literacy. That passion helped generate more social impact. With KPMG's support, more than 3,800 U.S. schools received free resources with the service campaign WE Read Together, which encourages older students and volunteers to read to younger peers. At one WE Day event, KPMG donated 20,000 books to Los Angeles–area schools—one book in honor of every student in attendance. Donations were linked to a hashtag #TheBookThat,

"With great purpose and passion, we apply our collective skills to improve our communities, drive inclusion and diversity, develop next-generation leaders, and advance environmental sustainability."

—Lynne Doughtie, U.S. Chairman and Chief Executive Officer of KPMG

which garnered 11.3 million social media impressions, in large part because engaged staff used their own social platforms to discuss the importance of literacy, tweet about their favorite books, and get their own personal networks involved. As is evident at KPMG, workers on every tier will appreciate more meaningful time to connect to a cause, facilitated by the office.

For managers, there is an additional opportunity to use purpose as an incentive tool.

Frontline Worker Incentives: Purpose Can Increase Productivity

Klick Health is a digital marketing agency with big pharma clients. Headquartered in Toronto, the company offers custom web development, e-learning modules, and other training resources with a team of 450 across North America. Rather than bill by the hour, Klick tracks projects. The idea is to avoid low-performers meandering, taking frequent trips to the water cooler or to Facebook, and generally running out the clock. With these potential distractions, one hour is not an equal amount of work for everyone. Instead, the agency calculated the average number of hours it would take a mid-level performer to complete any given task. Let's say that it takes 100 hours to build a website (this is my estimate; I don't know how to code). That is the amount of time allotted to the team to complete the project. Of course, managers and client representatives ensure efficiencies and keep everyone on task.

That left a problem. High performers can wind up doing more projects at a faster rate of completion, all for the same pay per project as average performers. There's no financial incentive to work at peak performance and finish early. Like many offices, Klick offers opportunities for annual bonuses and the occasional promotion. These larger incentive tools are more expensive, and delivered less frequently. Klick needed a daily motivator that was relatively less expensive, but still meaningful recognition for top staff. The company devised a solution for those who finished a 100-hour project in 80 hours, or anything under the benchmark time. Employees bank the difference—in this case, 20 hours—to save up "Klick dollars,"

Bake purpose into your staff experience

Include your cause in:

 Onboarding materials and training

 Mentorship systems that use your team's skills for good

 Mission statements

 Public materials, including websites and annual reports

 Internal surveys to seek ideas for improvement

 Incentives and awards that offer public recognition for purpose-engaged staff

 Quarterly reviews to assess the intervention then pivot, if necessary

which are redeemed as donations to a charity of their choice, including ours. In short: Employees can purchase social impact with their banked time. Efficiency is directly linked to the incentive of helping a good cause.

You don't have to implement a complex, specific, or long-term system to reward positive actions with a charitable connection. You might offer top performers the chance to make a donation to their favorite charity, or offer them an additional paid day off to volunteer.

For Klick, what started as a solution to an efficiency problem also led to increased employee engagement as staff became more involved with various charities. The program increased the team's connection to the local community, and to service. It also helps with recruitment and keeps staff morale high. And, the company told us that top performers have increased productivity even further.

External Networks: Customer Engagement

Doing good is made better when everybody knows how to get involved. You already have a marketing budget; make sure some of it is earmarked as a platform for your cause. Standard cause-marketing is a company trying to flaunt that it's doing good. Even better, now companies are starting to treat ads like an engagement plan to involve customers in their mission, inviting customers to take specific actions to create change.

Many big businesses use awareness campaigns to promote better health and safety practices, or green habits to protect the environment. At H&M, shoppers can offload outdated fashions—no matter what brand or condition—in exchange for a discount on future purchases. Old material is upcycled into new creations or donated to charity. The retail giant connects with customers over the message to recycle and reclaim. Of course, the next time they do buy new, they'll probably do so with their discount code at H&M. Similarly, many electronics retailers offer cell phone upgrades when you return old hardware.

Perhaps the most drastic example of an about-face from product- to values-based marketing is beer commercials. Once known to flaunt bad decisions and debauchery on TV, brewers now send out pleas: "Moderate Drinkers Wanted," says one ad for Heineken. Industries from beverage makers to comms companies are now acting as agents for self-regulation, asking consumers to be more responsible.

In the age of digital distractions, texting and driving is a huge threat to public safety. Every day in the U.S., eight people die in crashes reported to involve distracted drivers.[3] Dallas-based communications giant AT&T started the It Can Wait campaign in 2010 to discourage people from driving while otherwise occupied. Part of the campaign is an online pledge, signed by users who promise not to text and drive.

Internal research shows the program is building momentum, with more than half of AT&T survey respondents saying they honor the pledge and no longer use their smartphones while driving.[4] A telecommunications company helped to thwart dangerous behavior. And it used more aspects of the business to support this change. A free, downloadable app developed by AT&T, called DriveMode, will silence cell phone alerts and send automatic replies that the user is on the road. These are big commitments involving ad budgets and mobile app development, all for an issue that isn't directly related to increasing subscriber rates. Instead, these efforts influence the choices people make that relate to a cause. Marketing functions are huge machines meant to drive certain actions. Use those powers to reach a wider audience for good.

In many cases, inviting customers to join you in positive actions can also serve a business goal. Wise companies know it's important to be recognized as good corporate citizens. They also know how to identify and dodge potential threats. Texting while driving is already banned in most U.S. states, but can you imagine the implications for telecom providers if, say, the law banned cell phones in cars altogether? Instead of silencing phones on car trips, people would have to store them in trunks or stop traveling with them altogether, and usage would drop drastically. For a telecommunications conglomerate, it makes more sense to get ahead of this issue than to be regulated. Awareness and positive behavior are in the company's best interest.

Supplier Relations

We've said it before: no company is an island. Every business feeds on a complex network of environmental and social factors to keep running. Part of that ecosystem extends to other companies in the food chain. An organization might work with hundreds, if not thousands of other companies, sourcing and selling, depending on its size. Why not tap into that sphere of influence for a good cause? Any company can engage its network of suppliers, from small companies sourcing fair-trade coffee beans for the break room to large retailers moving the needle in an entire industry. Business-to-business purchases that are socially responsible can exponentially amplify that positive impact.

Individual consumers can also encourage positive corporate actions through daily purchases.

In terms of influencing an entire industry, at the front of the pack is Unilever, with purpose-driven CEO Paul Polman at the helm. The venerable Polman once considered priesthood, and now the *New York Times* calls him a "sustainability evangelist" for preaching stricter industry regulations and condemning a short-term profit mentality.[5] In the midst of the financial crisis, Polman put shareholders on notice that quarterly reports would be scrapped. It was his first day as CEO; Polman dropped this bomb early because he reasoned he couldn't be fired on his first day.[6] Under his leadership, the company is thinking long term about its footprint, with a rigorous goal to source 100 percent of its agricultural raw materials sustainably by 2020. That's no small feat for the world's third-largest consumer goods company and its long roster of brands, which are used by 2.5 billion consumers every single day. Among the big names are Ben & Jerry's ice cream, Lipton tea, Lifebuoy soap, and Hellmann's mayonnaise.

A key ingredient in mayonnaise is soybean oil, which in Hellmann's case comes from soybeans grown in the U.S. Despite regulations elsewhere in the world, the U.S. had no existing standard for certified soy production. Unilever created its own metrics for sustainability, working closely with American farmers on a plan to reduce water consumption and increase nutrient density near the soil surface. Unilever brought on soy industry associations and the World Wildlife Fund agreed to act as scientific consultants to form the standards. Farmers changed daily habits, decreasing tractor fuel usage and storing harvests in silos closer to fields to prevent unnecessary transport. They also shared data about their crops and submitted to testing. In return, farmers were offered 10 cents more per bushel of soybeans and increased access to state subsidies—in addition to the capacity-building support network that launched the program.[7]

For context, this is one ingredient in one product—a small star in the Unilever universe. The company's ambitious 100 percent sustainable sourcing goal works with 70,000 suppliers and 1.5 million farmers, with a transport network that travels more than one billion miles each year. In the case of a huge parent company (Unilever is worth just over

US$140 billion[8]), other brands will inevitably be swayed by its gravitational pull. When Unilever certified tea leaves for Lipton with the Rainforest Alliance, competitors Twinings and Tata followed.[9] "Hopefully [our brands] will drive transformational change in the industry," Polman says. "For example, Lipton has a wonderful story about working with small-hold tea farmers, but we also need to look at how to convert the whole tea industry to sustainable farming. If Unilever achieves all of these wonderful things and nobody else does, it still doesn't solve the problem."

This was a complex process for a conglomerate that sources an overwhelming number of ingredients. Still, the principles can be applied elsewhere, especially in terms of thinking beyond natural resources. Environmental preservation is a huge consideration in the supply chain— perhaps the biggest for manufacturers. Of course, Holly devoted a whole chapter to sustainable sourcing at Virgin Atlantic Airlines, so I won't belabor the point. Like Virgin and Unilever, don't forget social factors when looking at your own (or your organization's own) suppliers.

It's not just multinationals that are able to sway networks. Small and medium businesses often have a lot of influence over regional suppliers. If your organization issues Requests for Proposals (RFPs) prior to purchasing products or services, why not make sustainability or fair treatment of animals mandatory elements for all bids? You might also look for suppliers that have equal opportunity hiring practices.

You can hire sustainable food vendors in the cafeteria or order team lunches from caterers who use local ingredients. You can work with companies that offer training for marginalized groups such as at-risk youth, or encourage their own employees to volunteer in the community.

Even if you're not in charge of buying, you can do your own research on suppliers and vouch for the ones that act with a conscience. And, postpurchase, think about the lifecycle of the things your workplace does decide to buy: you could start a recycling program, or coordinate the donation of old office equipment to a charity when your organization upgrades.

From individuals to corporate teams, we all have the ability to support companies that care.

"We basically ask a lot of questions of a lot
of people who are a lot smarter than we are."

IT'S TIME TO GET YOUR PITCH ON...

By Holly Branson

Many Sunday evenings, while sitting on my sofa watching budding business moguls pitch their idea or product to a room full of dragons (or a tank full of sharks in the United States), I'd thank my lucky stars that I wasn't one of them. If you've ever had to pitch to a room full of strangers, you know what I mean.

That first day of school, the first moments of a blind date, a dream job interview you've been praying for all pale to insignificance compared to the trepidation and anticipation of putting your dream in the hands of people who could make it a reality. It's the 10 minutes that could change your life forever—just as long as you don't mess it up!

Whether you are part of a business being pitched to—or an individual hoping to slay a few dragons—I hope that by sharing our learnings from Big Change and introducing you to an incredible young woman named Esther, you'll discover some tips to make your purpose proposal stand out from the crowd the next time you get your pitch on.

Finding Your Ideal Purpose Partner the Big Change Way

Go external

Every year, at Big Change, we go on a search to find, fund, and partner with the best and brightest new ideas and projects capable of driving positive system change for young people in the UK, to set them up to thrive in life, not just exams.

To aid us on our quest to find the innovative purpose projects that will deliver this change, over the past five years we have built relationships with incredible organizations, networks, and individuals who have their ear to the ground within the sector. They help connect us with those projects that have the potential to realize the change we want to see—they understand us and know what we are looking for. Essentially they are our Big Change Purpose scouts.

I strongly suggest you do the same—as a business GO EXTERNAL and find the missing links that (to paraphrase Tom Cruise in *Jerry Maguire*) "complete you." Leverage the people who already have knowledge and networks in the field and can help identify the opportunities or gaps in our society to help young people thrive.

We basically ask a lot of questions of a lot of people who are a lot smarter than we are.

Through them, and the incredible people who share their ideas with us, I have come to realize that as a business (or funding organization in this case) we have just as much responsibility not to mess it up as the individual who is pitching.

Do your research

To get the most out of any purpose-pitch process and to determine what individual, charity, project, or organization will best serve the system change you wish to see, you need to do your research. At Big Change this has been one of our greatest learnings. As we shared earlier, when we launched, we worked with some great grassroots organizations, but it was more about incremental rather than system change. We realized if we wanted to create big change, we needed to know more about the root causes rather than the symptoms of the broken system—the things that would make a real difference, long term.

We knew we had the capability to use positive disruption, within the system surrounding young people in the UK, as a catalyst to bring about real change. But we simply hadn't done enough research.

I don't want to take away from what was achieved in the early days with our amazing project partners. We did good work. But we knew we could to do great work; we just had to put in the right amount of legwork first.

Put bluntly, the responsibility to create the greatest amount of impact lies with you and your team during the pitch process, not solely with the project or organization who are pitching you. You can't achieve that without knowledge.

At Big Change, to secure the most effective and impactful purpose partnerships, we learned that a lot of research and conversations are needed when choosing and inviting project pitches.

With an ultimate goal of backing big ideas that will support young people to thrive in life, not just exams, we realized that one of the areas where we needed to implement changes was in teacher well-being. Over a couple of years, we had received a number of proposals that looked to address the question of the well-being of teachers. At the time, we didn't feel that we understood the dynamics of the sector well enough to commit meaningfully to it. So we spent six months speaking with a wide range of people and organizations—teachers, teacher unions, and sector experts—to help us develop a clearer picture of what was happening, what needed to change, and how we as an organization could help effect that change. We captured the learnings and formed an emergent narrative on the whole sector. We then shared it with everyone we had spoken to—so that each expert was able to gain knowledge from all the others. A win-win for everyone involved.

Spending the time doing this research allowed us to reach out to the best possible projects, individuals, and organizations working in the field of teacher well-being (at Big Change we call it Teacher Thriving). This gave us a deeper understanding of the terminology they used (a small but important point!). Most important, we could judge, from a position of knowledge, whether the idea we were being pitched would bring about the system change we wanted to see. It was clear early on that there was a real crisis going on with brilliant teachers burning out and leaving the profession. While many schools had started to offer Well-Being programs and perks, it wasn't really scratching the surface. The issue went deeper into how teachers were valued and supported in the daily realities of the role. We ended up supporting projects that were innovating on teacher training, support, and leadership that could lead to long-term change.

So do your homework.

Gain the knowledge you need to be the most positive disruptors for change that you can be.

The brief

A tip from experience: you get out what you put in. The fuller and more informative the brief, the more rewarding the pitches you receive will be. As a suggestion, your brief should include an introduction to your company or organization, the pitch process with full timeline, key selection criteria and a note explaining them, what you want to see from the proposal, and it is also good to add your focus and detailed next steps. As mentioned, we spend months researching the social issue we want to address. As this isn't research for the sake of research, we include the emergent narrative from the research in our brief to prospective projects. This narrative helps to inform the projects about where they fit and how their idea is driving the big change we want to see. It also helps them focus their pitch and clearly outline how they fit into the bigger picture.

Doing the research and pulling together a strong brief has really improved the quality and alignment of the projects we receive. We no longer have to go through thousands of ideas that are simply not relevant. Our call for ideas breaks down into two parts—a short two-pager that outlines the idea, the team, and the change they wish to facilitate. We then measure them against the brief and only progress with those projects that answer the specific change sought. This saves already overworked charities a lot of time and effort. We respect that they don't have the time to waste filling in the dozens of pages of a grant pitch, especially if it's clear that they would not meet the parameters we set out in the brief.

Please start with a brief overview of your understanding of the sector as a whole.

1. **What is the Big Change you want to see?**
   - *What are your goals and objectives?*
   - *What are some of the key metrics/KPIs that will demonstrate success?*

2. **Why is this important?**
   - *Any evidence and case for change*
   - *Insight behind this particular focus or opportunity versus other approaches*

3. **How will you drive change?**
   - *Strategy and plan*
   - *Key phases and timescale with milestones*
   - *Key activities*
   - *Key people*

4. **What do you need to make it happen?**
   - *Resourcing plan and budget*
   - *Detail on what the specific elements for which you are requesting funding (and any other funders/income streams)*

5. **Plan for sustainability/exit after Big Change funding**

6. **Learning and system-wide impact**
   - *What do you hope to know at the end of the grant that you don't know at the start?*
   - *How will this learning be shared?*

7. **What would happen if we funded you at a lower amount?**

   For example, what if we funded you for 50 percent of the amount you are requesting? Would this mean the work could not go ahead, that you would need to change the model, that you would need to fundraise elsewhere, or that it would all still be possible, but perhaps have fewer resources to make it work?

8. **Accelerator support**
   - *How do you think Big Change could add value as a partner beyond the financing stage?*

9. **Please add anything else you think is important or relevant.**

For those ideas that get through to the next stage, we then very clearly lay out what we would like to see from the proposals. Hopefully the questions we pose in the box on the previous page will help inform your next proposal on your journey to embedding purpose firmly in your business by finding the right partner (feel free to plagiarize!).

Diversity of perspectives

A great turn of phrase coined by our wonderful M.D. of Big Change, Essie North—diversity of perspectives—sums up our approach when we pull together the panel we assemble to hear project pitches. We want to hear opinions from experts in different roles and industries, who might offer a perspective that we would never even think of. We like to call it our Impact Council, and you may want to set up your own version.

Here's why we changed our approach. In the early days of Big Change our "pitch panel" consisted solely of the team at Big Change. We quickly realized we were all too similar. Having worked for years on distilling the values on which Big Change is built and our core purpose, we were so aligned in our thinking and our experience (in some areas very limited) that we were not getting the most from the pitch process. We weren't always asking the right questions.

We needed to call in the cavalry. Using our usual premise—if you don't ask, you don't get—we targeted some brilliant people in our network and were amazed at how honored they were to be asked. From a former gang leader to business leader, at first glance they seemed to have little in common. But they all had different experiences and insights to bring to the table. All are positive, forward-thinking pioneers who believe in challenging the status quo, constantly learning, and looking to the future.

I've listed below some of the types of experts we call on—we have found that between 6 and 12 is a good number—you may need to get even more specific expertise involved. These are just our suggestions from our experience. Forming our Impact Council vastly improved the outcome of our project pitches due to the fact that it is made up not only of a range of internal stakeholders, but external experts, as well.

Who should make it onto a great Impact Council?

- *Business leadership team/CEO*
- *Sector expert: He/she will have a deep understanding of what a good project looks like within the sector*
- *Researcher or thought leader within the sector: She/he will know the players within the sector, including all stakeholders*
- *Expert within your organization: Depending on the area you wish to invest in, pull individuals with the most knowledge and experience from your own organization*
- *Previous project partner: If possible, involve a partner you have worked with successfully in the past. They will have a good understanding from the other side*
- *Venture capital/investors: Investors are accustomed to investing in early stage ideas and know what to look for*
- *Potential donors/funders/partners: Engage them in the process (they often have great experience to add as well!)*

It's decision time.

So you've assembled the most informed, effective Impact Council the world has ever seen—what next?

The Scorecard

I love the whole pitch process, from the research and learning about the sector and talking to experts in the field to drawing up the brief, with the team to deciding who should make up the Impact Council to best inform the final decision. We've also worked hard to make the selection process as enjoyable as possible. The advantage of bringing together a diverse group of people to help us make the selection is that we can call on their networks to help place a purpose project with a good partner, if it was not quite right for Big Change. The vast majority of projects are so worthwhile, with every team passionate and driven to make change—but we can't support them all, and you won't be able to, either. Take the time to think of how you can best serve those projects that may not be quite right for you. Again, if you have built a group of people around you to help steer and advise you, it is likely that they will also be willing to help vet the projects to find the best fit for them. This will not only leave you with the warm and fuzzies, but means you can keep in touch with those projects, invite them to staff conferences to raise awareness for them, feature them on your blogs and internal communications challenges, and so forth. In a way, they can become additions to your Purpose Portfolio.

At Big Change, to help us make that final decision, we pulled together a Scorecard that not only speaks to the passion of the team pitching but also the bigger picture and the operational structure. Again I hope our Scorecard helps you to make those difficult decisions. As always it is just a guide—feel free to add/delete/tweak as appropriate.

I feel like a teacher writing these WEconomy "How to . . ." sections. I hope a teacher you actually like—rather than the one with the horrible nickname! All of the tips, tools, and pointers are based on our experiences and learnings when deciding on what projects we invest in at Big Change. You may already be doing lots of the things I detail here—hopefully by breaking this section up into boxouts and takeaways—you can easily ignore the ones that aren't relevant to your business. Ideas like the Impact Council may be new to you, and I hope you find it inspiring—it certainly made a massive difference to us.

As an individual you, too, can make your purpose dreams come true

Now let me introduce you to the ultimate DRAGON SLAYER . . .

What if you are an individual with an idea that you believe will make a significant difference to people's lives, but need the support of your workplace to make that dream a reality? How do you even begin to get in front of the people who can make that happen? Just as it takes bravery as an organization to change the way their business operates by embedding a sense of purpose at the very core of what it does—it

The Scorecard

Criteria	Ranking Notes
Is this a big idea that can create systemic change?	1. Nice idea but only local impact 2. Smart idea with potential for impact in multiple locations 3. Insight-led idea for addressing a system-wide problem, with narrow impact 4. Insight-led idea for addressing a system-wide problem, with broad impact 5. Insight-led idea with ability to effect or inspire change in the wider sector
Is there a clear business case for why this is needed and that it will be taken up by the market?	1. Anecdotal evidence of need from one or two people 2. Some evidence of the need from multiple sources 3. Solid evidence that there is a pressing need 4. Lots of people discussing the need within and outside the sector 5. Solid cross-sector (or discipline) evidence of a critical need and desire for change
Do we feel confident around the operational plan?	1. Operational plan is patchy—serious questions around delivery 2. Outline of a plan but with some question marks on delivery 3. Solid theory of change and plan 4. Clearly articulated operational model, with resources and support to match 5. Solid operational model with a clear plan (and evidence) for sustainability
Is it led by a Big Changer?	1. Not feeling the leader's potential 2. Led by someone with the potential to be a strategic, system-level thinker 3. Led by strategic, system-level thinker 4. Led by strategic, system-level thinker with great experience on other initiatives 5. A true Big Changer—a visionary leader who will lead the way on this project and the sector more broadly
Is Big Change excited about it?	1. Meh 2. It has value, but not much Big Change potential 3. Big Change team wants it to happen and feel we could add value 4. Big Change team is excited about it and there is lots of positive energy behind it 5. Can't wait to get started—we feel it could be a seminal Big Change project

also takes incredible bravery to send that email, pick up the phone, or knock on the door of your boss and ask them to believe in your dream. I have had the privilege of meeting one such individual. Her name is Esther Marshall. I learned a lot from her, and I hope you do, too.

In 2017, my cousin Noah invited this incredible young woman to join the Big Change team at WE DAY UK. Before Esther tells you her story in her own words, here's a little background: she graduated from the University of Leeds with a degree in Geography in 2011. One of the lucky (and bright) ones, she then successfully gained a place on the Unilever Graduate Scheme, initially working and training with the HR Department. No easy feat in the current job market in the UK.

But Esther's story did not start off as a happy one. As you'll see, her tale is ultimately one of bravery. Not only did she conquer paralyzing fear in her personal life but she went on to slay one of the most famous dragons around—Paul Polman, CEO of Unilever. (Only joking, Paul; we know you're more of a kitten than a dragon, but "dragon" better suited our theme!)

Throughout Esther's story, we'll pick out her key learnings, tips, suggestions, and advice on how to use the position you are in right now—whether that be as a 26-year-old member of a graduate scheme, an entry-level employee, a middle manager, or simply someone with a passion for purpose who desperately needs help making a dream into a reality.

I could never do justice to Esther's story, so I'm not even going to attempt to—instead, let me introduce you to one of the bravest young women I have ever met: Esther Marshall.

Esther: *Eight years ago I thought I had found someone who loved me. Sometimes he did seem to love me. But at other times, after the drug taking and the drinking, he became a different person. He would hurt me to the point that I was scared of him. What happened shook me and shattered my self-confidence to rock bottom. I would sit in the bathroom crying and in pain. But I never told anyone any specific details—because I was afraid. I was afraid of people thinking I was weak.*

In 2014, I went to the One Young World Conference as a UK Ambassador for Unilever. I heard the North Korean defector and human rights activist Yeomi Park speak about the abuse she had encountered in her life. It had a deep effect on me. I couldn't stop thinking about how other people's journeys can be an inspiration to others. I felt that all I had done was hide from my issues. I had written down my feelings, but kept them to myself. Inspired by Yeomi, I felt a strong desire to do something, to share my story in an attempt to help others.

I went back to my room each night and started to dream of possibilities of how I could share my story with the world. I knew I wanted to make a change, but had no idea how to start. I decided to reach out to the founders of One Young World, David Jones and Kate Robertson, two people who had empowered a generation of change-makers. Their support and encouragement motivated me to keep going. I wanted to help every other girl out there in the same position that I was. This was my calling, but I didn't know where to start.

I needed to get my story out. David and Kate advised me that in order to be bold, you have to go big. And it doesn't go any bigger than the CEO of Unilever and Counsellor for One Young World, Paul Polman. It was hard enough to tell my story to my closest friends and family, let alone to one of the most famous global business leaders. David Jones kindly offered to let Paul know to expect my email. Writing down my story for the first time in years, I struggled on every word. I scrutinized every sentence and imagined what his response would be. Eventually I gained the courage to just press send.

Unsurprisingly, Esther had never presented to anyone as senior as Paul—so she reached out to friends, family, and colleagues rather than falling into a blind panic in isolation. If you are facing a similar challenge, hopefully the following tips will help with that first crucial presentation.

You Aren't the First and You Won't Be the Last

Learn from the triumphs of others and even from their "epic" pitch fails. The people around you (whether at work or in your personal life) will have experience that is invaluable to you. Ask for their advice and talk through what you hope to achieve and what your end goal is. This often focuses your mind and helps hone your pitch.

Know Your Dragon

I realize this is easier said than done when you are several rungs on the career ladder below the person you are presenting to, but in an office environment you have the opportunity to pick the brains of colleagues who work with that person. Take her/his executive assistant, or other directors who work with them, out for a coffee, explain that you are nervous and would be very grateful for a couple of pointers when presenting to the CEO. The vast majority of people are willing to help if you are honest and upfront about your fears and concerns. In fact many are flattered that you chose them as a sounding board.

Keep It High Level

Once you've gleaned the inside track on whether your Dragon loves or hates PowerPoint, prefers pie charts to bar graphs, is colorblind or not (yes, Paul, your secret is out!), or has an attention span that lasts no more than five minutes, then it's time to get your pitch on. First, take emotion off the table (not easy when it's your dream) and distill your pitch down to 10 key points. Esther was advised that five minutes is about the maximum time people can concentrate on a presentation without itching to interrupt and ask questions. Below are the key points she followed to structure her pitch—all within that important small window of time she'd been allotted.

 Introduce yourself and the name of your venture/charity.

 Identify the problem you are hoping to solve.

 Explain how what you are proposing will solve that problem (keep it short!).

 What difference (for the better) will your idea make to the people affected by the problem?

Growth: How do you see your impact growing over three years? Be honest and don't be tempted to exaggerate growth—it is always better to overdeliver. Try to link it to the business as this will capture their attention.

The playing field: Why is your idea/ new organization needed? Is there a lack of organizations working within the area you wish to operate in?

The team: Is it just you and your dream or a group you have pulled together? Again, be honest about what you have and, even more important, what you'll require. It is likely that you will still have a day job to perform—so don't overextend yourself from the outset—failure is almost certain if your idea is not resourced effectively.

Funds: What is it you need to make your dream a reality? Are money, personnel expertise, office space, and overheads accounted for? Don't just think cold hard cash—it may be that a small amount of initial funding is required alongside less costly support. Marc touches on this in the chapter "Change without Cash."

Why now? This is your call to action—emotion can come back on the table, so let your passion shine through.

End by encouraging questions—which leads neatly to my next piece of advice.

Know the Details

It may seem obvious but sometimes you can be too close to your dream. Practice is crucial—ask your friends and colleagues to grill you, to ask as many questions as possible. If you have no choice but to go it alone—anticipate as many questions as you can and get ready to overcome any objections you may encounter along the way. Most of the time overcoming objections is the absolute key to a successful pitch. You can never be too prepared.

Be Yourself

I have always believed in investing in people. Yes, the idea can be great and the need obvious but it's the passion of the individual that makes something amazing and remarkable happen. So show yourself—be yourself—ultimately it is YOU they will want to invest in . . .

So, back to Esther and her journey to sTandTall:

When I walked into Paul's office, sweaty palms and racing heart, I didn't know what to expect. I had planned a 5-minute presentation and prepared myself for the inevitable questions. It didn't go exactly as I imagined. I went through the painfully personal nature of recounting those years of questioning my self-worth at the hands of an abusive partner. Paul listened, and desperately wanted to understand the realities of the trauma I'd experienced. I revealed more to Paul than I had ever shared with my own husband. The hour that followed changed my life. I left Paul's office with a promise to support other girls to stand tall after abuse.

I remember writing: One day I will sTandTall. I couldn't have imagined it would evolve into a fully fledged project, supported by the CEO of Unilever. sTandTall aims to help women access help anonymously and safely, educate young girls on abuse, and establish holistic centers for restorative care for victims of abuse.

A year later, I was standing behind the microphone, terrified to tell my story to 1,500 young leaders gathered at One Young World 2015. I was blinded by the lights and frozen on the stage. As soon as the first words came out, I felt a new strength rush through my body. I stood tall for the first time in 9 years. I walked off the stage to a standing ovation that was the most surreal moment of my life. This was the day I launched sTandTall and pledged to help half a million women achieve their full potential.

The response I received was overwhelming. I hear countless stories of women and girls in similar positions, and I've received unprecedented media attention and heartfelt offers of support from my colleagues at Unilever. I had no idea how I would take this passion to establish sTandTall while juggling my career at Unilever. Over the next few months, I was promoted to a role where I could make a positive change in the world through business in the Sustainability team. The personal response from Paul Polman and all my Unilever colleagues has been astounding. The support I have gained from their social media outreach, to the initial investment I've received, has allowed me to launch sTandTall while having a meaningful career at Unilever.

It took 9 years to build the confidence to get to where I am today. I'm grateful to work at a company like Unilever, which acknowledges the importance of employees fulfilling their potential and having purpose at work. I'll always remember Paul's encouraging words after that first meeting: "Esther, don't let me down." Those five words motivate me every day to go above and beyond with sTandTall.

I've used the words Be Brave and Be Bold throughout this book, but it is at the very start of your journey when these words are most apt. I have been extremely fortunate to meet the incredible author Dr. Brené Brown (her books *Rising Strong* and *Daring Greatly* are definitely worth checking out if you haven't). Brené tells of a quote she found (while Googling the time period *Downton Abbey* was set in) that changed her life. I'd like to share it with you here, in this section, in the hope that it inspires company bosses and graduate trainees alike to Be Brave and Be Bold when it comes to embracing Purpose in the day to day working of your company.

Theodore Roosevelt (26th President of the United States): *It is not the critic who counts; not the man who points out how the strong man stumbles, or where the doer of deeds could have done them better. The credit belongs to the man who is actually in the arena, whose face is marred by dust and sweat and blood; who strives valiantly; who errs, who comes short again and again, because there is no effort without error and shortcoming; but who does actually strive to do the deeds; who knows great enthusiasms, the great devotions;*

who spends himself in a worthy cause; who at the best knows in the end the triumph of high achievement, and who at the worst, if he fails, at least fails while daring greatly."

sTandTall

sTandTall brings together girls and women from all over the world to build their self-esteem and help them achieve their full potential and sTandTall.

STANDTALL

The ultimate ambition of sTandTall is to build centers around the world that provide holistic restorative care to victims of abuse, ensuring they are able to overcome their trauma and achieve their incredible potential.

The sTandTall platform—www.standtall.org—aims to:

1. Provide relevant NGOs and charities with a single platform to publicize their services and tools, helping victims to find them and broadening their positive impact.

2. Provide a cathartic opportunity with anonymous people who have been through abuse or have seen others go through abuse to share their story, helping both themselves and others.

"You don't have to write a check
to change the world."

CHANGE WITHOUT CASH

By Marc Kielburger

Think pro bono...
and we don't mean U2

When the Great Recession hit in the late 2000s and early 2010s, giving back became secondary to keeping businesses afloat. Among the hardest hit corporate sectors was the North American auto industry. With people losing jobs and homes at unprecedented rates, buying a new car was the last thing many consumers considered as they weathered the financial storm.

Ford Motors, like its competitors, struggled for survival. Automakers were understandably very careful with their resources, especially when it came to "extras," like donations to charity. Ford knew it had to be more inventive with its giving, so it looked at existing assets.

In addition to manufacturing cars and trucks, Ford also operates a national network of local dealers, which have body shops and huge warehouses to store cars. While that might not seem like an asset beyond the obvious land value, it was a gold mine for us, because we were a charity with a storage problem.

One of our most popular campaigns is WE Scare Hunger, a Halloween food drive that has participating kids collect canned goods along with candy while trick-or-treating. Neighbors are warned in advance with posters. Kids bring parents in tow to carry nonperishables in red wagons or wheelbarrows—a fine transportation solution for one or two families.

This isn't a scalable solution for the hundreds of thousands of kids across North America who participate, many as part of schoolwide efforts. Cavernous spaces are necessary to store the millions of pounds of packaged goods collected. The campaign was taking over school gyms for weeks on end, disrupting classes and assemblies. It's hard to play basketball in between stacked boxes of canned goods. And, once stored, some bulk items needed to be unpacked, sorted based on need, and reboxed for distribution to food banks, taking up additional space. It is a massive undertaking, and though the kids do most of the hard work, raiding pantries dressed as superheroes, we couldn't solve the space constraints across hundreds of communities.

Ford saw an opportunity. They made car lots available to campaigning kids and offered empty warehouses as drop-off points. Ford flatbeds picked up and dropped off supplies at local food banks, taking over for the red wagons. It became a team effort, as employees joined in to help load, sort, and unload boxes and cans. Many were inspired by the kids and brought in their own donations.

Today, more than 250 Ford dealerships participate across North America.[1] The partnership didn't cost Ford a dime, beyond standard operations and perhaps some work hours—and was repaid with boosted staff morale. Dollars do matter. Still, this was an investment of time and space that was much more reasonable for the company's financial circumstances at that moment. Ford donates cars often; this was the first time the company had used its dealer network of warehouses for a social cause. When a cash donation was off the table, the company didn't give up on finding a cause. They prioritized Purpose enough to get creative, and it paid off.

You may be thinking, "That's great for a billion-dollar enterprise like Ford, but how can this be applied to my small business or organization that doesn't have millions in assets to pick and choose from?" The lesson of rethinking your assets can apply to organizations of all sizes, and even to individuals.

> *"The only true test of values, either of men or of things, is that of their ability to make the world a better place in which to live."*
>
> —Henry Ford, founder of the Ford Motor Company

Most companies think only about products as in-kind donations to charity, overlooking the wider definition of "product." I don't just mean the things you sell. Think of a product as whatever you have to offer that a charity is lacking, be it time, space, use of your technology, or corporate discounts. Engage in more creative purpose partnerships by assessing a charity's needs, then matching those needs to your assets. Offer mentorship to groups looking for guidance, or infrastructure to groups needing capacity. Think about supply chains and distribution systems, mailing and transport solutions, staff volunteer potential, a donation of office space—the list goes on! A well-aligned partnership can take some of the work out of drumming up a purpose plan from scratch if you're not quite ready for that yet. And, by giving much-needed resources to charity, you or your company is still helping to scale social impact by leveraging core competencies. In fact, you may be able to offer more than you first realize when you expand thinking into partnership opportunities that draw on resources outside of CSR departments or traditional donation budgets. When purpose is ingrained into the whole business, the entire system is working for good.

What's pro bono, anyway?

The term pro bono is derived from the Latin "pro bono publica," which means "for the public good." Historically, it's referred to legal work provided for free to those who couldn't afford it. But it's taken on a broader usage over time and encompasses all sorts of "in-kind" donations—like free services from companies or people with specific skills or assets.

I was once offered pro bono "integrated media planning" and immediately accepted. When asked if I understood the full meaning of this specialized planning approach, I admitted I did not. But I did understand that "pro bono" meant "free," so I was all in. Latin or English, "free" is a universal language for charities.

On this note, pay close attention to requests. If you're not able to make a cash donation, reconsider the charity's pitch to determine other needs. And if you are a charity, rethink your pitch to include more than cash. (Holly talked about tips for the pitch in her previous chapter.)

No matter who you are or what your role, you can do good at your workplace.

Trust me, WE has asked for free stuff from everyone. It is thanks in part to our corporate partners that WE maintains an administration rate under 10 percent. On average, more than 90 cents of every dollar donated goes directly to youth-serving programs.

I give a lot of speeches to corporate teams about infusing purpose into the workplace. Every time, someone approaches me with the desire to do something positive at the company. This is usually followed by, but . . . I can't right now. Pick a reason—they had a bad quarter, tough margins, not enough cash on hand to make a difference (for individuals, substitute I'm too busy, I still have a mortgage, I'm not the CEO and don't have the authority to write a check). I always reply that no matter who you are or what your role, you can do good at your workplace. This can range from the obvious—getting your team together to race for a cause, an internal recycling program—to maximizing your resources by lending them out. Think more carefully about what you and your company have to offer. Chances are, it's more than cash, and not everything requires the CEO's sign-off.

You don't have to write a check to change the world.

Become a Professional at Pro Bono: A Snapshot of WE's In-Kind Offers

 Twitter designed a WE emoji

 GoodLife Fitness offers staff free memberships to help WE add an HR incentive

The Keg restaurant hosts our charity events

 Freshii caters staff lunches during team retreats

 WestJet provides free flights for kids and staff to attend WE Day events

 Cinemark & Cineplex run WE videos during the previews before movie screenings in their theaters

 Facebook donates ad credits

 Tether and Leo Burnett offer pro bono creative design services

 Microsoft gives us free hardware and software

 TELUS provides free phones and telecommunications services

 Kinetic Worldwide and PATTISON Onestop offer free billboard space

 Accenture offers pro bono consulting services

NELSON Nelson Education lends warehouse space to store our WE Schools educational material

Want to Give Back? Head to the Mall

When you think about charity, a shiny shopping mall is not the first thing that comes to mind. Malls are consumer magnets where handbags are encased in glass, multiplex theaters screen blockbusters, food courts fry up funnel cakes, and public restrooms display ads. But in fact, your disposable spending at the mall can go a long way toward doing good, and I don't just mean retail therapy.

A Partnership on the Move

International courier DHL Express offers free shipping for our Artisans products—from Africa and Ecuador, no less! Since the partnership began in 2012, DHL has shipped more than 5 million Artisans products, helping to connect Maasai mamas in Kenya to a greater market for their traditional beadwork. And the company moves more than just product. DHL employees travel on service trips to Kenya and Ecuador to meet with the mamas empowered by new employment opportunities.

For our part, the mall offers evidence of charity partnerships helping companies give back and helping customers buy the change they want to see in the world.

Let's take a hypothetical tour of the big mall on Main Street, in Anytown. On one floor, you'll find teenagers checking out the display windows at Boathouse and PacSun, popular retailers featuring ME to WE's co-branded clothing options. Over at the Cineplex and Cinemark movie theaters, a couple on their third Tinder date—let's call them Chris and Ella—are taking in WE promos on the big screen, which the chains run in their commercial reels before the main feature. Both theater companies also host Community Days, where audiences watch free films with proceeds from concession sales going to support WE Charity. Just as the opening credits are set to roll, Chris decides to run out for popcorn. As he's checking out topping options, he notices they also sell artisan Rafikis and picks one up for Ella.

In the food court, cubicle workers on lunch break are enjoying the Warrior Bowl from Freshii, with partial proceeds from the quinoa, corn, and black-bean dish going to fund school lunch programs in Kenya. Jack from accounting pops over to the restroom to freshen up, and while standing at the urinal takes in an ad about WE's latest service campaign, courtesy of Kinetic Worldwide or PATTISON Onestop, who each loan us billboard space, including in public urinals. You're standing there anyway; may as well have something to read.

While in the mall, swing by the WE Store. Cadillac Fairview is one of the largest owners of office and retail space in Canada and its crown jewel, the Eaton Centre, a Toronto shopping mall, welcomes 50 million visitors a year.[2] Cadillac Fairview understands the tremendous value of its storefronts in the CF Toronto Eaton Centre, and it knows an organization like WE could never afford to operate there. You guessed it: the company gave us a free space for WE's flagship outlet, lending us its biggest asset to make the most impact. Visitors can learn more about our programs, sign up for service campaigns, and pick up a WE Schools or WE Family action kit.

Big brands get kind with in-kind giving

$10K

Google Ad Grants awards registered charities up to $10,000 per month in free online ads.

Home Depot's "Framing Hope" program diverts excess merchandise from its stores away from landfills and into local homes in need of rebuilding or refurbishment.

$180K

IKEA Canada donated $180,000 in furniture and housewares when the country resettled 25,000 Syrian refugees into new homes in 2016.

Virtually every tap of a credit card at the mall is an opportunity to give something back because the companies mentioned got creative with philanthropy. These corporate–charity partnerships delved into the entire business, drawing more of the company's networks and resources into the cause and affecting greater social change. They did more than cut a check for charity, investing in original solutions that leveraged assets. This, in turn, gives consumers the opportunity to increase the value of their purchases. You were going to spend the money anyway, so why not infuse purpose into those purchases by buying from companies that care? Why just write a check to charity once a year at tax time when you can also support a cause through your daily shopping choices? (Side note: Charities still like checks. Keep writing them, but also consider the multitude of additional options.)

Don't Show Me the Money

Just like speed dating for singles, there is speed dating for companies looking to match with charities. The process is considerably less romantic, but the time-bound conversation that leaves a permanent first impression is the same. One of those sessions is run by the Skoll World Forum for Social Entrepreneurship and held at Oxford University. There, WE had five-minute dates with a rotating roster of companies, including the up-market watchmaker and accessories retailer Fossil. WE's "date" with Janiece Evans-Page, Global Head of the Fossil Foundation, was an instant love connection. She was impressed with our sustainable development model overseas and was ready to make a donation. Our team loved her enthusiasm and commitment to efficient philanthropy, and saw incredible potential in the company's long-term intentions for social impact.

Before we walked down the aisle of partnership, we realized we could have more than a hasty Las Vegas wedding. Evans-Page knew that Fossil could offer something much more valuable than a one-time donation. She saw that our artisan program needed a retailer with a designer's eye, a marketing strategy, and distribution channels—a true partner. This took some finessing. Fossil sold products and its corporate foundation funded causes, but one had no direct business with the other. This is a common philosophy for many companies who want to keep purpose projects out of the spotlight. With skeptical consumers wary of the kind of cause washing we talked about earlier—those less altruistic companies looking to fake it—I don't blame them.

Together we realized that Fossil's greatest asset isn't money; it's people. In fact, this is true of most every company. Fossil offered us its marketing, design, and e-commerce experts to consult with our artisan teams in Kenya and Ecuador. They hosted workshops for our teams at Fossil headquarters in Dallas to show us how artisans could add leatherwork to their handbags. Glass beads from the Maasai Mara could adorn Fossil's watch straps. Artisans design collaborations now sit in Fossil's storefront windows, another asset leveraged. Thanks to this partnership and the prime marketing real estate of a front display, our co-branded products are a top seller. ME to WE styles are consistently among Fossil's weekly top 10 performers in the jewelry category. What does this all mean for change without cash? At the end of 2016, just one year into the partnership, Fossil had provided more than 97,000 social impacts in the form of clean water and food delivered to communities overseas. Each product sale provided a unique and specific social impact, like a baby chick for a woman in Ecuador that will lay eggs for her family to eat and to sell. Furthermore, a more robust, capacity-building partnership employed more artisans around the world, lifting the participants and their families out of poverty.

Change without cash can pay off: in-kind donations are often tax-deductible

In the end, Fossil did make a monetary donation to WE Charity, and we're very grateful. By also providing human capital, Fossil grew its social impact exponentially—creating change on an even bigger scale by using every arm of the company for the cause. Fossil helped the women employed by Artisans and their families, as well as the local economy in our partner countries. The team helped to empower the women economically in a sustainable way that will offer benefits beyond a single corporate donation.

Good Housekeeping: Our Deal with a Seal

Print publishers are still navigating the new digital world, in which ad revenue has fallen off a cliff since classifieds went online. Adjusting to new advertising models and reader habits, publications like Hearst

Magazines' Good Housekeeping are forced to get creative with charitable giving. The magazine looked inward and realized its biggest asset beyond cash was a sterling reputation.

Good Housekeeping, in print since 1885, is best known for its Good Housekeeping Seal, created in 1909. More than a gimmick, the seal is branded on products that pass rigorous testing standards carried out by its renowned Good Housekeeping Institute (GHI). Earning the label from the GHI is no small feat and no small promise. Good Housekeeping stands by its Seal with a two-year product guarantee. The magazine will refund or replace a product carrying its seal if the item is found to be defective within two years of purchase.[3]

What does this have to do with WE?

After working with the magazine as our title sponsor at the first WE Day in New York City in 2017, Good Housekeeping saw an opportunity to expand the partnership. Not with money, but by scrutinizing our charity just like they would a new flat screen TV or shampoo. They studied our financials, legal background, organizational structure, workforce, and our state and federal filings in the U.S. Once they completed their due diligence, the deal was, well, . . . sealed.

Good Housekeeping granted WE Charity its first-ever Good Housekeeping Humanitarian Seal, developed to give people a sense of confidence when choosing to support a charitable organization.

For a brand to lend us its reputation is a very big deal, especially one that has such a profound resonance with consumers. The original Good Housekeeping Seal boasts a legacy that is over 100 years old and is among America's most trusted shopping standards; 90 percent of consumers say the seal would influence their purchasing decision.[4] The launch of the Humanitarian Seal received by WE Charity helps build that same trust in the organization, giving donors the knowledge that it holds up to business standards. It's not a cash transaction, it's a priceless testimonial.

So you're not the CEO: How middle managers can do good at work

If you don't control the checkbook, don't worry.

Here are some creative ideas for managers or even entry-level staff to make change without cash. Some ideas still need to be pitched to the boss, but all are low-commitment options for the company.

- Donate company travel reward points
- Give away surplus office supplies (like the letterhead you ordered before the rebrand)
- Host a charity's website or store their data on your server
- Offer discounts on your product or service to your charity partner's staff
- When you buy supplies in bulk, let the charity in on your sale price
- Donate excess or out-of-date inventory—get a tax deduction on stuff that likely won't sell
- Lend office space or large auditoriums for a charity event
- Offer use of equipment—photocopiers, printers, video cameras
- Give your team time off to volunteer
- Donate your old laptops or cellphones when you upgrade
- Offer expertise with charity training sessions from accounting, sales, or other departments
- Give them a ride—your delivery trucks would be great for transporting cans during food drives
- Set up a display for your charity in the lobby
- Include a charity's message in your own advertising
- Invite charity partners to attend your HR capacity-building opportunities
- Donate leftover food from meetings. Groups like Second Harvest will come collect it

The takeaway here is simple: you, your workplace, or your small business have more to offer charities than a check. Each of your unique assets can be leveraged to help make an impact in the world.

How can you make change without cash?

"We spent a whole lot of time as a family coming up with experiences, ways of working together, identifying a wise circle of advisors, rituals, and other ideas that will support us every day in living our plan—and having the impact we dream about in this world."

YOUR WECONOMY ASSIGNMENT: BUILD A 100-YEAR PURPOSE PLAN

By Holly Branson

I started my WEconomy journey by telling you how Craig caught me unaware (and left me red-faced) by asking me what I wanted my legacy to be. The years since have been a massive learning curve for me in my new career at Virgin, as the Chair of Virgin Unite and a Founder and Trustee of Big Change.

At times the lessons were challenging, but they were, and are, always rewarding. I hope that by sharing my learnings and experiences, through the lens of the business and foundations I work for, you have a clearer understanding of some of the ways you can find meaning and make a living.

At Virgin, the desire to "Change Business for Good" started almost 50 years ago and it continues to be our focus. For my brother Sam and me, this means we are spending a lot of our time looking to the future. We believe our legacy is to build on the innovative work of people like Jean Oelwang, the team at Virgin Unite, and, of course, our father.

It's difficult to give a WEconomy how-to guide on building a century-long purpose plan. In many ways it is personal to you as an individual or so specific to the sector that your business/social enterprise operates in that only you will be in a position to pinpoint that legacy. I hope my experiences—first, through our business and foundation, and second, by sharing the journey we are currently on as a family—will give you some hints and tips to help you on your way to building a better future for generations to come.

> Your journey through WEconomy has brought you to this point—no matter what stage you are at in your quest to define and embed your purpose, never lose sight of the future. It is there that your greatest positive impacts will be realized.

To talk about the future and building your purpose legacy as a company, charity, or social enterprise, I first need to take you to the past.

Thirteen years ago I was still knee-deep in my medical training when Virgin Unite was launched. I attended their Unite events with what precious little free time I had between rounds at the hospital and my studies. I was fascinated by Virgin Unite's innovative approach to business and charity and how they should work together. Believe me when I say that Unite's approach, now with over a decade of success, was truly revolutionary. This was all thanks to one passionate, inspiring, and driven woman, the wonderful Jean Oelwang, now the President of Virgin Unite.

Jean took me through all of Virgin Unite's plans around the time of launch, but to me, back then, they were so unique and my brain was so full of medical jargon that I couldn't quite grasp some of the concepts. Jean and the team at Unite planned to move beyond traditional charity to tackle social and environmental problems with an entrepreneurial lens and a business-based approach. I cannot stress how innovative this was back in 2004.

But then again pretty much anything is possible when two visionaries unite . . .

It all started with a car journey . . . and the planets aligning, of course.

As Virgin's success grew globally, and dad was no longer hiding from the company's bank manager who camped out on our doorstep on quite a few occasions, his attention started to shift. Instead of worrying about how to keep the brand afloat and pay the wages, he wanted to focus on what sustainable difference the brand could make in the world.

I've talked previously about some of the great initiatives that the group launched to address pressing social crises—some of these initiatives were rapid response answers to immediate needs. They raised crucial awareness and funds at critical times but then, as is always the case, the world would move on. Dad got to a place where he wanted to build a legacy, through business, that would result in positive, long-term change on a global scale.

Simultaneously, a young marketing director named Jean Oelwang, working for mobile phone company MTN in South Africa, had an epiphany. MTN had just launched a prepaid phone service against the advice of experts who said there was no mass market for mobile phones in the townships. One month into its launch, however, MTN blew past its annual sales target and Jean and the team were dispatched to understand why. What they found in the townships was a beehive of entrepreneurial activity: people selling phone calls out of suitcases and trailers; vendors using mobile phones to buy and sell food and services. "That was a huge turning point in my life," Jean later told me. "I realized that you didn't have to work for a nonprofit to do good. You could cook it into an existing business." MTN had introduced an affordable tool that

> *"Of course an individual can make a huge difference, but it's when those individuals come together with like-minded souls that they can change the world forever and, importantly, for the better."*
>
> —Richard Branson

allowed the country's poorest citizens to improve their lives and raise their family incomes.

Now, let's get back to the planets aligning, this time over Australia. That same marketing director was now joint CEO of Virgin Mobile Australia and just happened to find herself sharing a car with the big boss—a.k.a., my dad. During the ride Jean was amazed to discover that the Virgin Group supported around 2,000 charities, but each was supported on an individual basis. It was yet another lightbulb moment— Jean was buzzing with excitement—surely there was a way to combine the efforts of all the Group companies to make a far greater impact, this time together.

Easy, right?!

They set about the task of redefining how a diverse, global brand viewed charity. First, the fledgling Virgin Unite team developed and presented a compelling business case for change. Remember that 13 years ago this was a very unusual approach for a charity to take. They encouraged the businesses to think longer term. Instead of forming short-term partnerships with charities, they asked them to think about a social issue the business could really stand for, and have real and lasting impact on. They pitched the idea that the businesses could achieve much more by mapping and leveraging all their assets rather than by simply writing charity checks.

Over the past decade the team have used Dad's entrepreneurial spirit and the best of Virgin to grow and develop organizations and partnerships such as The Elders, Ocean Unite, Carbon War Room, and The B Team (you're familiar with The B Team from the chapter "People Are Your Purpose"), to name just a few. I am unashamedly proud to say that Virgin Unite broke the charity mold by bringing together business, charity, governments, civil society, and entrepreneurs to find solutions to the greatest challenges we face today.

But what does the future hold? Or, more importantly, who will be responsible for holding and protecting it?

As we look into the next 10 years and beyond at Virgin Unite we are working on our next disruptive collaboration—this time with young people from all over the world. Just as we turned to The Elders for their wisdom and advice in tackling many of the world's most pressing

Virgin Unite

Virgin Unite is the entrepreneurial foundation of the Virgin Group and the Branson family. Virgin Unite was started with the aim of bringing people together to encourage them never to accept the unacceptable, to turn challenges into opportunities, and to always push boundaries that make both businesses and the world better.

Overhead costs are covered by the Branson family and the Virgin Group, meaning that 100 percent of all donations received go directly to initiatives that Virgin Unite creates or supports.

Virgin Unite's goal is to unite people and entrepreneurial ideas to create opportunities for a better world. There are so many challenges facing the world today, but Virgin Unite believes that by bringing the right people together and taking an entrepreneurial approach, they can create positive change.

Virgin Unite works in several ways

Uniting Leaders: *Virgin Unite's convening power and entrepreneurial spirit has enabled them to build new alliances and work with some great partners to incubate and launch new leadership initiatives such as The Elders, Carbon War Room, The B Team, and Ocean Unite.*

Uniting Entrepreneurs: *Virgin Unite supports entrepreneurs to put people and planet at the heart of their businesses and, in turn, impact the communities around them.*

Uniting Voices: *Virgin Unite speaks up and uses the strength of their voice to shine a spotlight on unacceptable issues, raising awareness and driving action on important issues ranging from conservation to human rights.*

At the heart of Virgin Unite is collaboration; in everything they do they bring together like-minded people, organizations, entrepreneurs, philanthropists, and inspirational leaders to collaborate for good, creating a powerful global community that is able to drive positive change.

issues, we believe that now is the time to harness the power, energy, and ideas of a younger generation in a similar way—a group we call: The New Now.

While young people feel accountable for these global challenges, their voices often go unheeded when the powers that be make decisions that will affect generations to come. This generation must have a say in what happens in the world. After all, these are the people who will shape the future: for us, for them, and for those who will come after.

Our ambition is to bring together a group of future-focused leaders who will collectively inspire a rising generation to shape decisions for tomorrow's world. We hope that by supporting this group, we will play our part in lifting up new leaders in their communities and the wider world and ensure that the voices of this generation are influential and transformational.

The New Now is just one approach—we are mindful of the shoulders we stand on and those we stand beside. We intend to work with and support other individuals, organizations, and movements to ensure we always act in the most effective and positive way possible. By working together for humanity and the planet, we will hopefully build a better future for everyone.

I see this organization as the next step in shaping tomorrow's world. Working with the team at Virgin Unite (and with Sam) to convene, develop, grow, and launch an organization run by the young men and women who are the guardians of our future gives me a profound sense of hope for what is yet to come.

Over half of the world's population is under 30 years of age; this is a generation who have an unprecedented opportunity and capacity to innovate new solutions and scale new movements to drive positive change. As we have touched on elsewhere in the book, it is also a generation that has inherited a raft of global challenges—from climate change to increasing inequality and rising intolerance.

As an individual, a community, or a family, how do you want to shape tomorrow's world?

As a family, when we started to look to the future we asked ourselves two questions:

What do we want the world to be like in 100 years' time?

How do we want to leave the world for our grandchildren?

By making these questions personal to you they really help focus your efforts to invest in a long-term purpose plan that will shore up the future for generations to come.

Finally I believe I am in a position to answer Craig's tricky question: "What do you want your legacy to the world to be, Holly?" Simply put, I want to build one that will last, with my family.

We have just started to lay the foundations of what we are calling our Seven Generations Plan, based on the beautiful Iroquois philosophy:

"In our every deliberation, we must consider the impact of our decisions on the next seven generations. As we begin our sacred work of tribal decision making, let us hope that our decisions today as well as the care, deliberation, and wisdom we use in making those decisions will be honored by and truly beneficial to the members of our tribe seven generations from today, as we today honor the decisions made by our ancestors seven generations ago."

—Iroquois Maxim (circa 1700–1800)

So why not choose today to get started on your WEconomy assignment: Build Your 100-Year Purpose Plan. You'll be amazed at what you'll discover along the way and how much you will grow. It'll be emotional at times (and not just in a good way!), but rewarding and powerful always.

I am lucky to live a life where I am constantly being challenged, one in which I continue to learn and am surrounded by inspirational and innovative people. The day-to-day demands of business, Virgin Unite and Big Change, and motherhood gives me a reason to wake up and embrace the day, every day, with a smile.

I'd like to take you through some of the steps we have taken so far. It is still early in the development of our Seven Generations Plan but I hope you'll find the steps below easy to follow whether you are a business, an organization, or an individual.

Tips to kick-start your WEconomy 100-Year Purpose Plan:

Individual life-planning: This was the first important step for us, making sure we each individually put in the work before we came together as a family. Going through the exercise of individual life planning really helped us to figure out how we should focus our energy and get crystal clear on what's important and what's not. This process helped me further clarify who I am—defining my values and purpose—then helped me better understand the values of my husband, Freddie. This foundational step was incredibly important before we started the wider family work. It's not as difficult as it sounds, either—if you can't access an organization to help you get started, then you can find guidance in books, websites, blogs, and other sources. Even sitting with colleagues and friends and discussing what you would like to achieve and the steps you can take to achieve them can be very useful.

Listening and learning: We were in The Rockefeller Foundation office and I noticed that they had over 100 years of plans lining the wall. We didn't want to reinvent anything, so we took lots of time (and continue to take time) listening to others to see what's worked and what hasn't across the generations.

Purpose: What positive impact does each member of the family (or team!) want to have both on their own and collectively? What is your why AND our why together as a family? Define your collective purpose. Many of the principles outlined in this book have shown you exactly how to do this as a company, charity, or social enterprise and as an individual.

Identify: Define your individual or company or family virtues and values to create a moral compass for future generations. This is a bit like building a great trunk for your family tree that will help ensure all the branches have support in future decision making.

A vision of the world we want: What is the world you want to leave to the next seven generations? How can you bring this to life as something that can evolve and be shared with future generations? A truly inspiring part of the process was seeing what emerged from the collective family vision. It was loads of fun to visualize it to remind us of what we are hoping to achieve in the future. Why not make this a team away-day, an all-company brainstorming; make it as creative and fun as possible so your people feel free to be open about the future they would like to realize for the world. Remember, we are thinking BIG here!

Structure: None of this is worthwhile unless you have a plan for how you are going to make it happen. This step is about creating an ongoing framework for implementation that evolves with your family, business, or organization and provides lifelong learning, joy, and, most important, lasting impact.

Capturing and living your plan: We spent a whole lot of time as a family coming up with experiences and ways of working together, identifying a wise circle of advisors, rituals, and other ideas that will support us every day in living our plan—and having the impact we dream about in this world.

The Elders: The Elders are an independent group of global leaders working together for peace and human rights. The Elders represent an independent voice, not bound by the interests of humanity, and the universal human rights we all share. **Meet the Elders:** Nelson Mandela (1918–2013) Founder, Martti Ahtisaari, Kofi Annan (Chair), Ban Ki-moon, Ela Bhatt (Elder Emeritus), Lakhdar Brahimi, Gro Harlem Brundtland, Fernando H Cardosa (Elder Emeritus), Jimmy Carter (Elder Emeritus), Hina Jilani, Ricardo Lagos, Graca Machel, Mary Robinson, Desmond Tutu, and Ernesto Zedillo.

Ocean Unite: Definitive science and clear policy options point the way to what must be done to restore and protect marine life. But like many global challenges, the intelligence, science, policy knowledge, and expertise are often fragmented and frequently do not reach the right ears at critical moments. Ocean Unite has been set up to assist with this unique challenge: to unite and amplify impactful voices to secure a healthy and vital ocean.

Carbon War Room: This group was founded in 2009 by Richard Branson and a team of like-minded entrepreneurs wanting to speed up the adoption of market-based solutions to climate change. In December 2014, Carbon War Room (CWR) merged with the Rocky Mountain Institute (RMI), a U.S.-based NGO dedicated to transforming global energy use to create a clean, prosperous, and secure low-carbon future. Together, they work across all energy sectors to accelerate the energy transition and reduce carbon emissions.

The B Team: See the chapter "People Are Your Purpose" for more information.

THE
WECONOMY
NEEDS
YOU!

CONCLUSION

THE WECONOMY NEEDS YOU

By Craig Kielburger, Holly Branson, and Marc Kielburger

We'll finish where we started, with this promise: In the WEconomy, you can make money and change the world—you can make money by changing the world. It's that simple. We believe this even more so today, as our writing comes to a close, than we did at the start. By sharing our exploration of the WEconomy, we hope we've made a true believer out of you, too.

All of us want to live for something greater than ourselves. We want to see our priorities and our values reflected in our daily actions, responsibilities, and decisions. And since the average person spends 90,000 hours on the job over a lifetime, work has become a significant part of that desire for daily meaning. Is it too much to ask that all those office hours amount to something more?

We don't think it is.

Coming into this book with varying perspectives from the worlds of business, charity, and social enterprise, we have learned much from each other, and from the wonderful companies and individuals we have met along the way. We discovered that cross-sector partnerships between business and charity are increasing in number and magnitude, and that the rapid growth of social enterprise and impact investing funds are changing the face of business. Ultimately, the lines between business, charity, and social enterprise are blurring—a change fueled by the individual and collective desire for purpose.

Our research cemented our belief that purposeful business *will* be the next seismic shift that helps to lift people out of poverty and protect our planet.

The Challenges of Our Time

Before the United Nations announced its Sustainable Development Goals in 2015, a set of 17 objectives to protect the planet, foster peace, and ensure prosperity for all, experts calculated how much money they'd need to achieve it all by the target date of 2030. Essentially, analysts measured the cost of this economic and social progress, and it has a price tag of $2.5 trillion dollars—per year.[1] Frightening, right?

Suffice to say, there will be a funding gap if you leave it all up to charity and government. The world needs investment from the private sector. To let companies off the hook when they account for most of the global GDP and the largest percentage of job creation is, at the very least, a huge oversight. Early success stories in the WEconomy reveal what can be achieved when you blend the power of capitalism with the heart of altruism. It is critical that we follow these trailblazers. Purpose pays, and if government policy, consumer spending, and new talent set Purpose as their North Star, companies that are doing it right will be rewarded, causing a ripple effect among competitors.

In the past, business was linear: the making and selling of products, a production output that is used and discarded, and a short-term profit. What does the future of the WEconomy look like? Every company will be responsible for the full circle: what they sell and what happens to it afterward. Companies will track their results from resource to the conveyor belt on the assembly line and throughout a product's life cycle, to upcycling and repurposing—so-called cradle-to-cradle production. Short-term thinking will be outdated. Corporate goals won't be quarter-to-quarter, but decade-to-decade, considered in balance with the reality of day-to-day operations. Every product will have a purpose. If it doesn't benefit the world, why should it take up space?

If brands can't finish the sentence: *I am making the world better because* _____, they can't and won't compete. In a matter of decades, companies that disregard the health of the people and planet will be obsolete.

We hope we've shown you that in the WEconomy, you don't have to be a clone of Gandhi or Mother Teresa to succeed. In fact, we need *ordinary* people to fuel this movement. When we say ordinary, it is a call to action for every worker, consumer, entrepreneur, and CEO looking to infuse more meaning into their daily lives, at home and at work, and to use those hours to positively impact both local and global communities. The coming together of millions of people who embrace simple positive actions will achieve greater impact than a single extreme altruist.

Ultimately, the fate of this movement falls to you. Massive companies will only change from within because you push them to embed purpose into their very DNA. Using the tips you have gleaned throughout this book, we hope you'll convince your senior team that a purpose-driven business is in the best interest of the bottom line—no matter what position you hold in your organization. The WEconomy will be built on the purpose-driven power of millions of people around the world.

Early success stories in the WEconomy reveal what can be achieved when you blend the power of capitalism with the heart of altruism.

We hope every reader is also looking inward, asking themselves: What is my purpose as an individual? Maybe your passion is rooted in faith, family, or the fact that there is now more plastic in parts of the ocean than there are fish. Maybe you're furious at social injustice or famine or discrimination or a warming planet. Maybe your cause is youth unemployment or girls' education and economic empowerment for women. In the WEconomy, there's nothing stopping you from introducing your personal purpose into your nine-to-five. In fact, it is actively encouraged. It is imperative that everyone adds value. This is an economic system based on the power of the purpose-driven collective, not the self-interested desires of the individual. Everyone has a part to play in changing business, charity, and social enterprise for the greater good.

It's down to the community, the collective, the WE, to take the best of business, with its incredible ability to scale and its power to innovate, and to combine it with the lifeblood of charity and social enterprise: purpose. We need you to encourage charities to develop more effective cross-sector partnerships and enforce long-term funding structures, to adopt the rigor of a business. And we need you to push social enterprise to continue to marry purpose and profit into the very structure of a single organization, to spur innovation using an inherent social mission.

The WEconomy is about finding something greater than yourself and making it work for you, for the planet, and for your business.

In this economic movement there is a role for everyone. To truly change the world the WEconomy needs you. All of you.

EPILOGUE

Sir Richard Branson

October 2017

Make no mistake; this is one of my proudest moments as a father. No point denying it. My daughter has written a book; what father wouldn't be proud!

It was humbling to be asked by Holly, Craig, and Marc to play a role in promoting an emerging economic movement that has purpose at its very core. In the WEconomy, these three young authors from the worlds of business, charity, and social enterprise have unearthed a growing economic movement, one fueled by purpose—individual, collective, and corporate. That is *the* best way to find meaning, make a living, and change the world.

And change it must.

It's sad but true that the world we live in can, at times, be frightening. Our smart device, that constant companion with its immediacy, often paints a picture of human nature at its most base. Images of the horrors of indiscriminate global terrorism, violent and xenophobic rhetoric from all sides, and our failure to address climate change can make us forget that people are inherently good. To truly see the beauty in human nature you need to be present. We all need to communicate face to face, to share stories, to be active participants at home, at work, and in our local and global communities.

The WEconomy shows what can be achieved if we put self-interest and fear behind us and strive for the change that embracing purpose can bring to all aspects of our lives. Positive change is already happening all around us. The role you play, within the businesses you work for or run, is driving that change.

You may not read much about the WEconomy yet in HuffPost or on TMZ. But talk to your friends, your neighbors, check out TED Talks online, discuss the themes in this book with everyone you know, and you'll see that the lines between business and charity are blurring more and more each day.

Agitate the companies you work for and with, from without and within, to embed purpose into their very DNA. You will be the generation to nurture and grow the WEconomy for generations to come.

Holly, Craig, and Marc kindly named Oprah Winfrey, Jeff Skoll, and me as their mentors. I'm sure my co-mentors would agree that we learn more valuable lessons every day from passionate and purpose-driven young people than we could ever wish to impart. Mentoring goes both ways.

It's been almost a decade since Holly made one of the hardest decisions of her life and decided to take some time away from her chosen field of medicine to explore what good could also be achieved by the world of business. Working alongside Holly (and my son Sam) is invigorating, inspiring, educational, and enlightening. Over the past few years Holly, Craig, and Marc have been driven by the desire to learn all they can about the individual, yet blurring, sectors that they work in. It's been a real eye-opener and a rush to support them on their journey of discovery.

I've discovered that I am surrounded by WEconomists. Every day, in my tiny corner of the world, I work with 70,000 challengers of the status quo at the Virgin Group. As part of this emerging WEconomy movement, these are women and men who refuse to accept business as usual and demand to see business as a force for good.

But we're just one brand. To truly get a sense of the momentum behind this movement, you need to get your calculators out. Add our 70,000 to the many, many organizations and companies cited in this book. Add those to the thousands of others—from individual community entrepreneurs in Africa, to the socially conscious cottage industries popping up all over the world, to the massive businesses currently embedding purpose at their very core. Very quickly you get a sense of the scale of the change that is happening right now. The WEconomy, driven by millions of *you*, has the ability to change the world we live in, for the benefit of all.

I've even had the great privilege to witness firsthand the kind of wonderful world that the next generation of WEconomists will create.

Recently, Holly and the team at Virgin Unite invited me to join them and some of the most awe-inspiring people I have ever met—a group called The New Now—for breakfast. Several 20-somethings—among them a nuclear physicist, a peace activist, an entrepreneur, and a climate change expert—had come together from all over the globe to meet in New York. What drew them? The belief that together they could make a positive difference in the world.

I learned about their hopes and desires, and listened to the creative and innovative plans they had, both individually and collectively, to tackle some of the world's most pressing problems. As one young man so eloquently put it: "The world we want to live in is a world that we will have to construct for ourselves."

Surrounded by the business, political (a future president or two, no doubt), scientific, and environmental leaders, I was struck that they saw no boundaries to their collaboration. Gender diversity, politics, race, geographical regions, and sector expertise were not viewed as negatives but as positives to the effectiveness and potential of the group as a whole. I watched them struggle to understand the economic and charitable sector silos of the past. Simply put—they just didn't get it. To quote another young leader: "I'd rather work with a group that wakes up every morning and wants to try."

Thanks to Holly, the driving force behind The New Now, I was able to witness the leaders of the WEconomy in action, and have my belief that our world is in safe hands confirmed over breakfast!

Cooperation and collective responsibility for the well-being of people and the planet by business, government, NGOs, and social enterprise is the bedrock of the WEconomy. To give us the greatest chance of prosperity for all and to protect the beautiful, complicated ecosystems we all rely on to survive it's the *only* way of doing business in the future.

I truly believe that if every company in the world adopted this philosophy, all of the world's problems could be solved.

Craig and Marc, thank you for inviting me along on your exploration of the WEconomy.

Holly, you make me so proud every day. I love you.

—Richard Branson

APPENDIX

Since 1995, WE has built programs to enable people to create community and do good.

WE infuses social impact into our daily lives—to fundamentally alter the way people give, shop, travel, live, work and use technology. What makes a WE entity or program different? Impact is baked into the DNA: our team painstakingly rebuilds a regular experience into one that changes lives. WE takes daily actions and turns them into extraordinary opportunities to do good.

These are a few of our programs that help unlock the good—every day.

WE Schools provides 15,000 partner schools with free service-learning programs rooted in our **WE Learn Curriculum** resources and service campaigns such as **WE Are Love, WE Won't Rest, WE Are One, WE Give Where WE Live, WE Give Health, WE Read Together,** and **WE Rise Above.**

WE Families engages millions of parents, extended family, and children to teach the next generation to care and contribute through their daily choices and service campaigns such as **WE Create Change, WE Stand Together** and **WE Volunteer Now.**

WE Companies partners with Fortune 500 companies, startups and mom-and-pop shops, offering turn-key programs that connect partners' employees and customers to causes.

WE Living empowers consumers at 12,000 partner retail stores with socially conscious products and experiences to better the world. It allows individuals to make daily choices to change the world. It also educates the next generation on how to make a difference through initiatives such as the "We Give Where WE Live" speaking tour and resources.

WE Campus provides social entrepreneurs and purpose-driven businesses the accelerator of space, mentorship, technology, venture capital, and other resources to scale their vision. It includes the **WE Global Learning Center** as our movement's global headquarters, and the **WE Incubation Hub** that assists the next generation of change-makers to scale their best ideas to tackle the foremost social challenges of our time.

WE Day fills stadiums celebrating change-makers. *WE Day Community* brings the same energy to local groups, theaters, and schools. Finally, the *WE Awards*, presented on the WE Day stage and educational celebrations, celebrates outstanding innovation and impact.

WE Villages is our international development model providing holistic and sustainable empowerment through the 5 five pillars of *WE Education, WE Water, WE Health, WE Food, WE Opportunity.*

WE Give is high-impact philanthropy programming, transparently delivered to villages around the world and to at-risk communities domestically.

WE Shop is our online and brick-and-mortar curation of socially responsible products and services, including **WE Eat** socially-conscious chocolates and foods, **WE Drink** coffee and beverages empowering small-hold farmers, **WE Play** with toys and products that teach children and families about community as global citizens.

WE Trips gives everyone a chance to connect with other cultures and serve global communities through a bursary program in partnership with ME to WE Trips.

WE 365 is our "WE Operating System." Namely, it is how we live WE 365 days a year. Launched in 2013, it underpins all of our programs, including the *WE Day* app which tracks volunteer hours and connects with a wider community of change-makers. *WE Impact Rewards* and *Track Your Impact* technology enables you to make socially conscious choices to live WE and better the world.

These programs are part of a larger offering created over the past two decades, and even more daily actions are ready to be transformed. WE can't wait to see what the future holds.

ACKNOWLEDGMENTS

This book has been a journey. We are grateful to many who guided us along the way.

First, our gratitude to the wonderful Holly Branson. What started with a partnership through Big Change and WE Day became a deep friendship that took us through the mountains of India, the grasslands of Kenya, and beyond. We were honored to partner with you on your first book and loved every minute of our collaborative writing experience. And to Jackie McQuillan, for your sharp wit, insightful input and edits, and your distinct outlook that truly challenged us to think differently.

A special thank-you to Katie Hewitt, who poured herself into this book for several years alongside us, dedicating countless hours, clever writing, research, insightful edits, and critical analysis. Your sense of humor and stubborn perseverance helped bring this book to completion.

With thanks to the incredibly talented Andrew Duffy, our first collaborator, who helped us brainstorm initial concepts and provided us with the foundational draft on which everything was built.

Shelley Page, our dear friend and confidante, will always be our editor-in-residence, a voice of reason, guidance, and an invaluable perspective. No project would be complete without your input.

To Sheryl Sandberg and Sir Richard Branson, thank you for the inspiring words. We couldn't think of two better people to open and close this book; each of you embodies the principles of the WEconomy, putting purpose at the forefront of business.

We are grateful to Brian McGregor, Sue Allan, Rick Groves, Kieran Green, and Lee-Anne Goodman for their writing contributions, insights, and research. Thank you to Stanley Hainsworth, Renee Perry, Paul Huggett, Gillian Gerrard, and Ivana Manzon for the striking design and your enduring patience.

We are always thankful for our parents, Theresa and Fred Kielburger, our earliest champions and strongest role models who taught us about compassion and service. And for the unwavering support and unfathomable patience of our loving partners, Leysa Cerswell Kielburger and Roxanne Joyal. We love you more than words can ever express.

Our entire WE family—our staff, board of directors, and supporters—is our daily reminder that a movement is made up of caring individuals.

Finally, we remain inspired by the passionate change-makers at the forefront of the WEconomy, and by everyone who believes that a better world is possible.

We could not have completed this book without the help, guidance, and generous sharing of knowledge by so many inspiring individuals.

Marc and Craig, thank you for being my "WE" on the incredible road to discovery we've taken—together—in writing this book. Your energy, passion, and absolute belief in the power of young people to bring about the change we need in this world are a constant inspiration. For that, and your unwavering friendship, I thank you both.

To my "WEconomy" partner in crime, Jackie McQuillan, a 25-year veteran with the Virgin brand and someone who has watched my personal story unfold in real time, thank you for being by my side throughout and helping me pull this all together. I could not have done it without you.

Thank you to Katie Hewitt, for being our WE Charity/Canadian voice of reason, our Brit-to-U.S. translator during edits, and for making so many trips across the Pond. We know it wasn't just for the free lunches and snacks! And thanks go out to all at WE Charity, ME to WE, and Team Tether for your invaluable insights and design work.

As for my Virgin family, I have been blown away yet again by the power of all these incredible individuals.

Charlotte Goodman, you are our North Star of Purpose. Thank you for not only helping all the Virgin companies stay true to their values but also for your time and effort in bringing this book to fruition. To Josh Bayliss and Peter Norris, thank you for all you do for Virgin. You are invaluable to the company and you are both amazing mentors to me. I'm so impressed, given your hectic schedules, that you found time to read this book! Jean Oelwang and all of the team at Virgin Unite—I am